Four Critical Years

Effects of College
on Beliefs, Attitudes,
and Knowledge

Alexander W. Astin

Four
Critical
Years

Jossey-Bass Publishers

San Francisco · Washington · London · 1977

FOUR CRITICAL YEARS
Effects of College on Beliefs, Attitudes, and Knowledge
by Alexander W. Astin

Copyright © 1977 by: Jossey-Bass, Inc., Publishers
615 Montgomery Street
San Francisco, California 94111
&
Jossey-Bass Limited
28 Banner Street
London EC1Y 8QE

Library of Congress Catalogue Card Number LC 76-57308

International Standard Book Number ISBN 0-87589-346-5

Manufactured in the United States of America

JACKET DESIGN BY WILLI BAUM

FIRST EDITION

Code 7745

The Jossey-Bass Series
in Higher Education

A Publication of the
Higher Education Research Institute

Preface

Four Critical Years really began some seventeen years ago, when I joined the staff of the National Merit Scholarship Corporation to conduct studies of environmental factors that influence highly able students to pursue doctoral degrees. Early results highlighted the importance of longitudinal data in studying college impact, since a college's "output" of graduates who attained doctorates depended heavily on its "input," as reflected in the abilities and aspirations of its entering students. These results led to a decision, in the fall of 1961, to conduct the first national survey of entering freshmen, in which students at 248 four-year colleges and universities provided data on their family backgrounds, secondary school achievements, and educational aspirations.

This survey served as the prototype for the Cooperative Institutional Research Program (CIRP), launched in 1966 at the

American Council on Education in Washington, D.C., and since 1973 conducted jointly by the council and the University of California, Los Angeles. Data from CIRP provided an opportunity not previously available to enhance our understanding of college impact. Over the past decade, its sample of institutions has grown to more than 300 of all kinds, and it has accumulated longitudinal data on over 200,000 students. This book presents major findings from the first ten years of this major longitudinal research program.

The first chapter describes the rationale and design of CIRP and its longitudinal analyses. Chapters Two through Six present the principal empirical findings. Primarily through a review of the literature on long-term impact, Chapter Seven discusses the possibility that college effects reported in Chapters Two through Six persist over long periods. And Chapters Eight and Nine summarize findings in terms of their policy implications for educators and public policymakers. Results of this summary are not particularly encouraging, for they suggest that policy in American higher education is now being shaped more by economic considerations than by concern for enhancing student progress. Indeed, if favorable impact on students is the principal raison d'être for American higher education, many recent institutional and governmental policies seem to be directly contradicted by the findings of this study. Chapter Nine focuses on these policies and suggests some alternatives to them.

Certain highly technical tabular material is not presented here because of its limited interest to most readers. This material, referred to as "supplementary tables," is available at cost from the Higher Education Research Institute, Inc., 924 Westwood Boulevard, Los Angeles, California, 90024.

A project of this magnitude and complexity requires the collaboration of many people. Data preparation and analysis were conducted by a number of colleagues: C. E. Christian and Marsha D. Brown not only carried out the bulk of the analysis of affective and behavioral outcomes for Chapters Two, Three, Four, Five, and Seven, but they also provided good sounding boards for my thoughts and contributed a number of important ideas of their own. James W. Henson helped design and also conducted the complicated analysis of career outcomes for Chapter Six. David Webster provided several helpful suggestions that have been incorporated in Chapter Eight. Gerald T. Richardson and Paul Hemond provided valuable assistance in programming.

The manuscript's readability was significantly improved by Beverly T. Watkins' fine editorial hand. The major responsibility for typing the manuscript and keeping track of bibliographical material was carried by Mary Ruth Swint, who willingly worked many nights and weekends to accommodate my disorganized life-style. Some of the final typing and loose ends were ably handled by Julie Locke. To them, as well as to the students whose responses to the Cooperative Institutional Research Program form the basis of this book, my thanks.

Los Angeles, California   Alexander W. Astin
August 1977

Contents

Contents

The Author

Alexander W. Astin is professor of higher education at the University of California, Los Angeles, and president of the Higher Education Research Institute, where he is directing the Cooperative Institutional Research Program. Currently he is also directing a five-year study of institutional planning and management and a two-year national assessment of federal and state student financial aid policies. Previously he served as director of research for both the American Council on Education (1965-1973) and the National Merit Scholarship Corporation (1960-1964).

Among Astin's previous books in the field of higher education are *Academic Gamesmanship* (1976), *The Power of Protest: A National Study of Student and Faculty Disruptions with Implications for the Future* (with H. S. Astin, A. E. Bayer, and A. S. Bisconti, 1975), *Preventing Students from Dropping Out:*

(1975), and *The Invisible Colleges* (with C. B. T. Lee, 1971).

Astin has received awards for outstanding research from the American Personnel and Guidance Association (1965) and the National Association of Student Personnel Administrators (1976). Astin has also been a fellow at the Center for Advanced Study in the Behavioral Sciences (1967-1968).

Astin received his doctor's and master's degrees in psychology from the University of Maryland and his bachelor's degree in music from Gettysburg College.

A jazz pianist by avocation and an amateur photographer, Astin is also interested in art and politics. He is married to a prominent psychologist and author, Helen S. Astin, and has two sons, John and Paul.

To John and Paul,
who are about to begin college

Four
Critical
Years

Effects of College
on Beliefs, Attitudes,
and Knowledge

I

Studying College Impact

Few people will argue with the premise that attending college can have a profound effect on one's life. With the possible exception of getting married and having children, few choices have more far-reaching implications than the decision about college. For most prospective college students, this decision involves three issues: (1) whether or not to go, (2) where to go, and (3) how to go. The matter of "whether" is particularly critical for that substantial minority of young people whose academic interests and achievements are minimal or whose financial situation is tenuous. Is it likely to be a worthwhile investment of their time and money? Among those for whom college attendance is a foregone conclusion—the college-bound students

1

—the issues of "where" and "how" are paramount. The "where" of college choice involves which kind of institution to attend: large or small, public or private, religious or nonsectarian, and single sex or coeducational. The "how" of college attendance—a critical set of issues often poorly understood by counselors and parents—concerns such matters as financing (whether to borrow money or get a job); where to live (at home, in a dormitory, or in a private room); what to study (choice of major and electives); and which extracurricular activities to pursue.

But what is the impact of college attendance on students' personal, social, and vocational development? Are some students affected differently from others? Do different types of colleges produce different outcomes? And how important is it to attend college away from home, to work, or to participate in extracurricular activities? Until recently, few research-based answers could be offered.

At the same time, public policymakers have questions of their own about the value of higher education. While during the 1950s and early 1960s a substantial national investment in higher education was regarded as an insurance policy in the Cold War and as a way to enhance our technological and scientific position in world trade, many public officials now are asking whether the soaring costs of higher education are draining off resources that could be better used for more important public purposes. Economic pressures have forced legislators to look for programs where public spending can be cut; and federal and state investments in higher education underscore the need for better information on how colleges affect students. Does higher education influence students' career opportunities and aspirations? Does it have significant impact on their values, personality, behavior, and life-styles? Do they become more competent and knowledgeable? And are certain colleges better for some students than for others?

Why Study College Impact?

The sheer volume of publications on college impact (see Feldman and Newcomb, 1969, for a synthesis of the literature to that date) might tempt one to conclude that a great deal is already known about the answers to these questions. However, since much research is limited in scope and inadequate in design, there is surprisingly little one can say with confidence about the impact of college. Much early research failed to meet the two minimal requirements for adequately designed studies of college impact: (1) multiinstitutional data, that is, data collected simultaneously from students at contrasting types of institutions and, ideally, from young people who do not attend college as well; and (2) longitudinal data, that is, information on the ways in which students change between admission and some subsequent point in time. Other features missing from that research include large and diverse samples of students and institutions; multiple measures of entering student characteristics; multiple follow-up measures of student development, including both cognitive and affective outcomes; multivariate designs for controlling differences among students entering different types of institutions; and methodological provisions for separating college effects from maturational effects or the simple process of growing up. (For a detailed description of requirements for data and methods of analysis, see Astin, 1970a, 1970b.)

The purpose of this book is to answer questions about the effects of college that have been raised by students, parents, public officials, and educators themselves—and to answer them on the basis of the first ten years of an ongoing research program that was designed to overcome the limitations of earlier studies and to produce data for definitive studies of college impact: the Cooperative Institutional Research Program (CIRP). CIRP was initiated at the American Council on Education in 1966 and is now conducted jointly by the council and the University of California, Los Angeles. It is the largest ongoing study of the American higher educational system. Its longitudinal data now cover some 200,000 students and a national sample of more than 300 postsecondary institutions of all types. Its follow-up surveys of several different entering classes during the 1960s and 1970s provide an opportunity to replicate findings from one sample to another. Its data cover a wide range of cognitive and affective student outcomes, allowing this book to examine how the college experience affects more than eighty different measures of attitudes, values, behavior, achievement, career development, and satisfaction. And its size and scope make it possible to employ highly sophisticated multivariate controls over a large number of potentially biasing variables—in particular several means to differentiate purely maturational changes from those directly attributable to the college experience.

The task of assessing how students are affected by their college is composed of three major undertakings: (1) understanding the meaning of student change; (2) developing student outcome measures; and (3) designing the analyses of college impact. As an introduction to the findings from CIRP discussed in later chapters, the following pages of this chapter describe how CIRP deals with each of these three requirements.

Understanding the Meaning of Student Change

In response to the question, "How does college affect students?" one can legitimately ask, "In relation to what?" While this response may seem flippant, it captures a fundamental truth regarding research on college impact: If students are not attending college, they are doing something else. Thus the concept of college impact has meaning only in relation to what would happen if students did not attend college.

In other words, potential students are in a continuous state of growth and change. These developmental processes go on whether or not students attend college. If researchers could somehow put young people who do not attend college in cold storage or in a state of suspended animation, they might be able to obtain a "pure" measure of the effects of college attendance by comparing them after four years with students who went to college. But such a measure would make little sense. In the real world, those who do not attend may get married, join the armed forces or find other work, go on welfare, join communes, raise families, travel abroad, or just loaf—but they continue to develop and learn. The real issue in research on college impact is to determine what *difference* college attendance makes in the development of the individual.

Unfortunately, most of the literature on "college impact" involves *change* or *growth* in students rather than impact as such. Typically, students complete a personality inventory or attitudinal questionnaire when they first enter college (in the jargon of educational research, a *pretest*) and again after one year, four years, or—in a few cases—many years following graduation (*posttests*); and change or growth is assessed by comparing the two measures. Most investigators, by equating measured change with college impact, have assumed that any observed changes result from the students' college experience. The major weakness of this approach is that it fails to consider whether the same changes would have occurred if the students had attended different kinds of colleges or had not gone to college at all.

For adequate research on college effects, it is essential that observed changes in students over time be seen as having two major components: The first is change resulting from the impact of the college; the second is change resulting from other influences, such as maturation and the environment outside of college. Note that the first component may (1) bring about changes that would not occur under other conditions; (2) exaggerate or accelerate changes originating in other sources; or (3) impede or counteract changes originating elsewhere. A major goal of CIRP and this report is to isolate changes that result from the college experience from those attributable to other sources.

Some investigators have concluded that the ideal solution to these inferential problems is a control group of young people who do not attend college. Such a "college-noncollege" research design has some advantages over the traditional single-institution designs that are discussed later in the section of this chapter entitled "Assessing the Impact of College Experiences," but the difficulty with the college-noncollege design is that it grossly oversimplifies the issue of college impact. As the proportion of high school graduates who go to college increases and as the number and variety of postsecondary opportunities and institutions proliferate, the distinction between "college" and "noncollege" experiences grows increasingly blurred. Indeed, for many thousands of students these days, the college experience consists of little more than driving to campus for a few hours of class each day and then driving home again. It is not unreasonable to suppose, for example, that the total environmental experiences and life-styles of those community college students who work at off-campus jobs are much more similar to those of their nonstudent coworkers than to those of students attending, say, four-year residential liberal arts colleges. Thus the variety of experiences possible within the collegiate sphere is so great that it renders any simple comparison of college attendance with nonattendance virtually meaningless. The real issue is not the "impact of college" but the "impact of college characteristics" or, more precisely, the "comparative impact of different collegiate experiences." More information is needed on the relative impact of various *types* of collegiate experiences. The current study seeks to meet this need not only by focusing on differences among different types of institutions but also on differences among students' experiences at these institutions.

Developing Outcome Measures of College Experiences

Recent controversy over the "value" of higher education (Freeman and Hollomon, 1975; O'Toole, 1975; Solmon, 1975) implies that the most important outcome of college attendance is economic: Having a college degree is supposed to help students develop cognitive skills, get better jobs, and make more money. But colleges potentially have much more pervasive influence than this. An eighteen-year-old who is leaving home for the first time to attend college is subject to wide-ranging influences from faculty, staff, and fellow students. The possible influence of parents is reduced proportionately, simply because they are no longer present. Many freshmen experience their first intensive encounter with peers who have markedly different beliefs, backgrounds, and attitudes. For some, enrolling in college may also provide the students' first direct experience with drugs, sex, alcohol, and political activism. For others, college presents the first real challenge to their academic motivation and skills. The fact that many students spend four or more years attending college under these circumstances highlights the great potential of the college experience for producing both short- and long-range changes in values, attitudes, aspirations, beliefs, and behavior.

In short, a thorough examination of the impact of college must take into account a wide range of possible outcomes. There is no easy way to capture the impact of college adequately in one or two simple measures such as credits and degrees or job placement. The need for a variety of outcome measures thus was anticipated in the design of CIRP. Rather than simply generating a list of miscellaneous measures, we developed a conceptual scheme to guide the selection of various measures. This "taxonomy of student outcomes" involves three major dimensions: (1) type of outcome; (2) type of data; and (3) time.

Type of Outcome. Behavioral scientists have traditionally classified human performance into two broad domains: cognitive (sometimes called *intellective*) and noncognitive (sometimes called *affective*). Since cognitive outcomes involve the use of higher-order mental processes such as reasoning and logic, they are clearly relevant to the educational objectives of most students, faculty, administrators, trustees, parents, and others concerned with higher education. Noncognitive, or affective, outcomes concern the student's attitudes, values, self-concept, aspirations, and everyday behavior, and are important to many educators. Information on affective outcomes is relatively easy to obtain through self-administered questionnaires, whereas measurements of cognitive outcomes often require more controlled conditions of administration and larger amounts of the student's time. But both deserve attention in studying the impact of college.

Type of Data. The second dimension of the taxonomy, type of data, refers to the types of information gathered to assess the cognitive or affective outcomes. Again, two broad classes can be identified: *psychological* data, relating to the internal states or "traits" of the individual; and *behavioral* data, relating to directly observable activities. The measurement of the psychological phenomena is usually indirect, in the sense that the investigator, from responses to questions, infers some underlying state within the individual. Behavioral measures, which might also be called *sociological,* reflect transactions between the person and the environment and are usually of intrinsic interest.

Any student outcome measure can be classified simultaneously by the type of outcome involved and the type of data used (see Table 1). Each cell provides examples of different

Table 1. Classification of Student Outcomes by Type of Outcome and Type of Data

Data	Outcome	
	Affective	Cognitive
Psychological	Self-concept	Knowledge
	Values	Critical Thinking Ability
	Attitudes	Basic Skills
	Beliefs	Special Aptitudes
	Drive for Achievement	Academic Achievement
	Satisfaction with College	
Behavioral	Personal Habits	Career Development
	Avocations	Level of Educational Attainment
	Mental Health	Vocational Achievements:
	Citizenship	Level of Responsibility
	Interpersonal Relations	Income
		Awards or Special Recognition

Source: Astin, Panos, and Creager (1967, p. 16).

types of outcome measures obtained using different types of data. The cell on the upper left, for example, includes psychological measures of noncognitive or affective states: the student's ambition, motivation, and self-concept, as well as subjective feelings of satisfaction and well-being. The cell on the upper right includes cognitive measures such as the student's grade-point average or performance on multiple-choice tests of ability and achievement. The lower left cell includes sociological or behavioral features of the individual's development that reflect primarily affective states. Under personal habits, for example, one might include such behaviors as reading, eating, use of drugs, tobacco, and alcohol. Citizenship would include such outcomes as voting behavior, participating in community activities, and earning special awards for community service or, on the negative side, welfare or arrest records. The lower right cell gives examples of behavioral or sociological measures of cognitive outcomes. Basically, this category contains outcomes that reflect the behavior of the student (or former student) in society and that usually require cognitive skills. Presumably, real-life achievements represent the behavioral manifestations of the cognitive traits listed in the cell immediately above it.

The two dimensions that make up Table 1 are really more continua than true dichotomies. For example, a person's earned income probably depends in part on cognitive abilities, but it may also be affected by noncognitive or personality traits.

Time Dimension. Since attending college can have both short- and long-term effects, the four cells in Table 1 could be extended into a third dimension representing temporal differences in student outcomes. Table 2 shows examples of related measures taken at two points in time.

Table 2. Examples of Measures Representing Different Types of Data and Outcomes

Types of Outcome	Type of Data	Time 1 (During College)	Time 2 (After College)
Affective	Psychological	Satisfaction with college	Job satisfaction
Affective	Behavioral	Participation in student government	Participation in local or national politics
Cognitive	Psychological	Law School Aptitude Test (LSAT) score	Score on law boards
Cognitive	Behavioral	Persistence in college (staying in versus dropping out)	Income

Although timing is seldom considered in discussions of educational outcomes, it is of fundamental importance. Most colleges hope to produce long-term rather than short-term changes. The goals stated in college catalogues, for example, imply that the institution is primarily concerned with making an impact that will last throughout a lifetime. The college, it would seem, tries to provide experiences that will help the student make the fullest possible use of his or her talents and become an effective, responsible member of society. Presumably such effects will, in turn, result in a more satisfying and rewarding life.

For many prospective college students, however, such long-term effects may be too remote and too difficult to comprehend. These students are primarily interested in more immediate goals— their actual experiences during the undergraduate college years— rather than in how these experiences will affect their later development. Educators frequently overlook the fact that the two, four, or eight years of college represent a sizable portion of the student's total life span. For students, then, college experiences are important in themselves, not merely for what they will mean later.

Organization of Subsequent Chapters. This three-way taxonomy, which provided the major frame for selection of student outcome measures in the Cooperative Institutional Research Program, has been used to organize the major findings from Chapters Two through Seven of this book. Affective-psychological outcomes are reported in Chapter Two ("Attitudes, Beliefs, and Self-Concept") and Chapter Six ("Satisfaction with the College Environment"). Affective-behavioral outcomes are included in Chapter Three ("Patterns of Behavior"). Cognitive-psychological outcomes are reported in Chapter Four ("Competency and Achievement") and cognitive-behavioral outcomes are noted in Chapter Five ("Career Development"). The time dimension is considered in Chapter Seven ("Permanence of College Effects"). Because most new evidence in this book concerns relatively short-term outcomes of college attendance (up to five years after matriculation), Chapter Seven also summarizes evidence from several earlier studies of longer-range impacts. Chapter Eight ("Summary of Effects") summarizes the major findings, and Chapter Nine ("Implications for Policy and Practice") outlines certain policy implications for prospective college students, faculty, administrators, and policymakers.

Assessing the Impact of College Experiences

Assessing the impact of college experiences on students involves two basic problems. The first, as discussed earlier, is to identify the relevant outcome variables. The second and more complex task is to determine how these outcomes are affected by college attendance. The widespread confusion about how to handle this second task is reflected in the variety of methods and procedures that has been used in research on college impact. Investigators often forget, however, that each methodology implies a somewhat different conception of the purposes of higher education and the nature of the college experience. For this reason, it is important at the outset to describe the particular conception of higher education that underlies this study and to sketch in some detail the methodology employed to assess the impact of higher education on student development.

Two models from outside education are most commonly used in describing the functioning of colleges and universities: those of industry and of medicine.

The Industrial Model of Higher Education. Economic problems in the early 1970s forced many college administrators to come to grips with such issues as "accountability" and "efficiency" of institutional management. Many administrators responded to these pressures by experimenting with computerized management information systems, by hiring management consultants, and by instituting such procedures as program budgeting and management by objectives. One consequence of this business orientation is that it portrays students and their degrees as "produced" by the institution, in much the same way an automobile is produced at the factory.

Manufacturing is a physical process where raw materials are fabricated into parts that are put together on an assembly line. The finished product is a result of the manufacturing process. But graduates of college are clearly not "produced" by the institution in this way. Their personal characteristics at the time of graduation may, to be sure, have been influenced by their college experience, but their physical and psychological makeup depends heavily on background and environmental factors largely independent of the institution. Students, in other words, are fully functioning organisms before they get to college; the purpose of college is presumably to enhance the student's functioning.

Hence a major assumption of the current study is that industrial analogies are simply not applicable to higher educational institutions. Although it is possible to assess the output of a plant in terms of the number and quality of its products, the impact of a college is not necessarily reflected in the number of graduates or even in the quality of their achievements.

The Medical Model. A better institutional analogy for the college is the hospital, clinic, or doctor's office. The main function of both medicine and education is to improve the condition of their clients. Patients (students) are admitted to treatment facilities (colleges) because they need or want medical assistance (education). Medical facilities administer treatment programs based on a diagnosis of the patient's illness; colleges administer educational programs that presumably are relevant to the student's educational needs. Just as some patients do not benefit from medical treatment, so some students do not benefit from college education. At the same time, some patients improve and some students learn, even if their programs are ineffectual.

Although the medical model is clearly inappropriate in one respect—in that students are not ill—students and patients are both seeking some sort of personal service. Most important, both colleges and medical treatment facilities attempt to bring about desirable *changes* in the condition of their clients. For this reason, a critical ingredient in the assessment of college impact is to measure *change* in the characteristics of students over time.

It has already been suggested that student change should not be equated with institutional impact. Does the same hold true for patient change? Can the hospital always take credit when the patient gets better? Should the hospital always take the blame if the patient's condition shows no change? Can one assume that the hospital has had no impact? In medicine, there is a convenient means for dealing with such conceptual issues: the *prognosis*. When the newly admitted patient has a poor prognosis, the treatment program may be judged highly successful if the condition of the patient simply stabilizes. By the same token, a treatment program could be judged a failure if a patient with a highly favorable prognosis fails to improve after admission. In other words, neither the patient's status at discharge nor changes in the patient's condition between admission and discharge provides an adequate indication of the success or failure of a treatment program. Such information has meaning only in the context of the initial prognosis.

The concept of change from admission to discharge is simpler than the relationship between outcome and prognosis. For example, a patient with a high fever caused by a bad cold will generally have a favorable prognosis, regardless of treatment. Fevers caused by bad colds usually disappear without any treatment. Thus, the positive *change* from high to low fever is not remarkable, given that the *prognosis* was favorable. Fevers caused by other causes (for example, pneumonia) may not present such a favorable prognosis in the absence of treatment.

Clinical medicine thus utilizes two types of prognosis: those that assume no treatment and those that assume particular treatment. Diseases for which no effective treatment exists have the same prognosis, regardless of treatment. Under these conditions, the essential aspect of effective treatment is that it *changes the prognosis*.

In many ways, assessing the impact of an educational program is analogous. People will continue to grow and to develop regardless of whether or where they attend college, and, because human behavior tends to be consistent over time, it is possible to predict (prognosticate) from current information what a person will be like at some later time. High achievers in secondary school, for example, tend to be high achievers in college. The basic issue, then, is whether attending a given college *changes the prediction* of how the student will develop.

Medical prognosticating relies on the fact that the illnesses of patients who show particular patterns of entry information (medical history, symptoms, laboratory findings, and so forth) frequently follow predictable courses. This is basically a statistical matter—particular illnesses under specified conditions frequently produce similar outcomes. In many ways, studying the development of college students is analogous: Particular outcomes (for example, high grades) tend to be associated with particular characteristics at entry (high grades in high school, high test scores, and so forth). The precise weight assigned

to each entering freshman characteristic depends on the outcome predicted.

Modern statistical procedures can be used to combine
much information into a prediction about how the entering student will perform later on. Just as the physician arrives at a
prognosis using data from a patient's history, physical examination, and laboratory tests, the educational researcher can combine information on the entering freshman's past achievements
and behavior to predict that student's subsequent performance.
Separate predictions can be developed for each student outcome. In predicting whether the student will complete a baccalaureate degree, for example, considerable weight should be
given to past academic record, degree aspirations, and social
background (Astin, 1975b). In predicting such affective outcomes as political beliefs at graduation, considerable weight
should be given to the student's *initial* beliefs at college entry
(see Chapter Two). Put more simply, an entering student who
supports conservative beliefs is much more likely to hold similar
beliefs at graduation than is an entering student who supports
liberal beliefs.

Whether such predictions are changed by particular college experiences is analogous to the medical question of
whether particular treatments change the prognosis. One major
difference, however, is that the *causal* connections between certain treatments and certain medical outcomes are much better
understood than the connections between educational programs
and student outcomes. This difference underscores the need for
better studies in education where many student characteristics,
such as sex, ability, and socioeconomic status are measured at
entry and then statistically controlled in an effort to identify
causal connections between educational experiences and outcomes.

Data for Assessing College Impact. The need for multiple
indicators of the entering student's propensity for change and
also the need for multiple-outcome measures were a major consideration in designing the Cooperative Institutional Research
Program. Each fall, the entering freshmen at institutions participating in CIRP complete an extensive questionnaire composed

of two types of items: (1) pretests on possible outcome measures and (2) personal characteristics (age, race, educational background, and so forth) that might affect the propensity to change or to attain certain outcomes. Because of time constraints during freshman orientation and registration, it is not possible to include pretests on all relevant outcomes in any one questionnaire. Thus, different freshman surveys have pretested somewhat different outcomes. In the fall 1966 freshman survey, for example, the student's self-concept at college entry was pretested with a lengthy list of self-ratings; these same ratings were posttested four years later in 1970 (see Chapter Two). In the 1967 survey of entering freshmen, however, these self-ratings were replaced by a list of "competencies" that were posttested one year later, in 1968 (see Chapter Four).

Although it is possible to assess change in some outcomes with freshman pretests and posttests, certain other outcomes do not lend themselves to a pre- and posttest design. Whether a student drops out, for example, is an event for which no pretest is available. (One might argue that dropping out of high school is an analogous pretest, but its occurrence would simply preclude any measurement of college performance.) Similar outcomes for which pretests are either unavailable or inappropriate are getting married, winning special honors or awards, and being admitted to graduate school. To deal with this problem, CIRP freshman questionnaires incorporate two types of items: (1) personal background data that might relate to the student's chances of attaining such outcomes, and (2) the *student's own predictions* about the likelihood of each outcome. Thus, the entering freshman questionnaires ask the student to estimate his or her chances of getting married, dropping out, participating in extracurricular activities, and so on.

Not all CIRP follow-ups include posttests of items from the freshman questionnaires, primarily because of constraints imposed by the agencies that fund the follow-ups. In the 1974 follow-up of 1969 entering freshmen, for example, the data are of limited value, because posttesting of most freshman questions was not possible. Major longitudinal surveys used for assessing college impact are as follows:

Entering Freshman Year	Follow-up Years	Number of Students
1961	1965-1971	16,674
1966	1969-1970	19,422
1966	1970	25,399
1967	1968	5,351
1967	1969-1970	20,958
1967	1971	34,346
1968	1969-1970	21,458
1968	1972	41,356
1969	1969-1970	17,771
1969	1974	24,395

Results of analyses reported in subsequent chapters are based on these numbers of students. With the exception of the 1969 follow-ups, all follow-up surveys have been conducted in the late summer or early fall of the year indicated. The 1969 "ACE-Carnegie" follow-up of four freshman classes, which was conducted jointly by the American Council on Education (ACE) and the Carnegie Commission on Higher Education, was carried out between late December 1969 and February 1970.

Follow-ups of each entering freshman class are conducted by sampling approximately 300 students from each participating institution. (Students from institutions enrolling more than 300 freshmen are selected at random.) Follow-up questionnaires are mailed to students' homes. With postcard reminders and second questionnaires sent to nonrespondents, response rates varied from 40 to 65 percent, depending on the complexity of the questionnaire. Because extensive freshman input information is available on both respondents and nonrespondents, it is possible to develop a sophisticated weighting procedure to adjust for nonrespondent bias. In essence, the procedure gives greatest weight to those respondents who most resemble nonrespondents. (For details, see Astin and Molm, 1972; Cartter and Brown, 1976.) Unless otherwise stated, all tabulations reported in subsequent chapters utilize weights that are designed to approximate the results that would have been obtained if all first-time, full-time entering freshmen had participated in the freshman and follow-up surveys. The results, in other words, are generalizable to the national population of entering freshmen.

Statistical Methodology. The analyses in Chapters Two through Seven involve two stages. First, information on each entering freshman is combined statistically through multiple-regression techniques to obtain a predicted or expected score (prognosis) on each outcome measure under investigation. Those freshman characteristics most closely associated with the particular outcome receive the largest weights, while freshman characteristics unrelated to the outcome are given no weight. Freshman pretests, when available, usually receive the largest weight in predicting the corresponding posttest outcome measure.

The second stage of the analysis determines the effects of college experiences by comparing predicted outcomes based on entering freshman characteristics with actual outcome measures separately for students in different college environments. If an outcome is positively affected by attending a particular type of college, the actual outcome scores should be consistently higher than the expected scores among students enrolling at that type of college and consistently lower than expected for students enrolling at other types of colleges. An important characteristic of multiple-regression analysis is that, for the *total group* of students used to derive weights for entering freshman characteristics (in this instance, students across all colleges), the discrepancies between expected and actual outcome measures will sum to zero. In other words, students whose actual outcomes exceed their expected outcomes are balanced by an equal number whose expected outcomes exceed their actual outcomes. If a particular type of college has no effect on a given outcome, students entering colleges of that type should perform like the total group: The positive and negative discrepancies between expected and actual outcomes should balance out (that is, sum to zero). However, if a particular environment positively affects an outcome, the actual outcome measures for students in that environment will tend to exceed their expected measures. In other words, the *mean* actual outcome for those students will be higher than the mean expected outcome based on entering characteristics. The reverse will be true, of course, when an environment has a negative effect on an outcome: The mean expected outcome will exceed the mean actual outcome for students in that environment. The strength of the effect of a particular environment will be reflected in the magnitude of the difference between mean expected and mean actual outcomes for students in that environment. This difference can be expressed in terms of a partial correlation between the environment and the outcome (that is, the correlation, if any, that remains after the effects of entering characteristics have been "partialed out").

The logic of this type of research design can be illustrated with an example from the data in Chapter Three. In a follow-up questionnaire completed three and a half years after entering college, students were asked whether they smoked cigarettes frequently (score 3), occasionally (score 2), or not at all (score 1). Responses to this follow-up question could be predicted with moderate accuracy from the students' entering freshman data, as indicated by a multiple-correlation coefficient of .57. It is not surprising that freshman pretest responses to the same smoking question carried by far the largest weight; but a number of other freshman items, such as being black and being female, also carried significant positive weights. In other words, blacks and women were more likely than nonblacks and men to have increased their smoking during the three-and-a-half-year interval.

Because some students ended up smoking less and others more than predicted, the correlation between entering freshman data and posttest smoking behavior was not perfect (R was less than 1.0). However, the nature of regression is such that, for the *total* sample used to develop the regression weights, the mean predicted and mean actual posttest scores were equated. The question then became: Does the equivalence occur when expected and actual scores are examined *separately for students attending different colleges*? If the students' inclination to smoke is not affected by the type of college, the mean actual and mean predicted scores would tend to average out for students in each college, and the partial correlations between posttest smoking behavior and the various college types would be zero. However, if attending a particular type of college encourages smoking, the actual scores of students attending those colleges would tend to be higher than their expected scores and the partial correlation between that type of college and posttest smoking would be positive. As it turned out, attending a two-year private college appears to decrease tendencies to smoke, since expected smoking behavior exceeded actual behavior for students attending two-year private colleges, whereas the reverse was true for students attending four-year colleges and universities (see Chapter Three).

Control Groups. Many scholars in higher education believe that a definitive study of college impact should include a "control group" of persons who never attended college. By comparing such a group with college attenders, the investigator would presumably be able to differentiate purely maturational changes from changes specifically attributable to the effects of college.

The current study takes a somewhat different approach to the task of separating college effects from maturational effects. Rather than comparing college attenders with nonattenders, students have been sorted into groups according to their *degree of exposure* to the college experience. The underlying rationale for this approach is quite simple: If certain outcomes are facilitated by the experience of attending college, the likelihood of such outcomes should be greatest for those students who have the greatest exposure to the college environment. However, if an outcome is a normal part of maturation and is not affected by going to college, its occurrence should not depend on *how much* exposure to college the student has had.

Because of the great diversity of institutional types and the substantial variations in college attendance, students differ widely in their exposure to the college experience. The current study approaches the issue of exposure from two perspectives: *time* of exposure and *intensity* of exposure.

Time of Exposure. Time of exposure can be handled quite simply: How long was the student enrolled in college? Some students register for college and never show up for their first classes. Others drop out before completing the first term. Still others persist for the entire four undergraduate years. In subsequent chapters, the relative importance of college effects and maturational effects is assessed by determining answers to two questions: (1) Are changes in people who stay in college for a short time comparable to changes in people who stay longer? and (2) Are the effects of particular college characteristics stronger for people who stay longer?

The lowest point on the time continuum lacks the extreme case of a group that had *no* exposure to college. Nevertheless, this continuum-of-exposure approach has certain advantages over the college-noncollege design. In laboratory experiments, the control group is supposed to be comparable to the experimental group in all respects except the "treatment" variable—in this case, degree of exposure to the college environment. It may be that a group of students with little exposure to college is a less biased control group than one that has never attended college. The latter group would differ from college attenders in certain critical respects: Most would not have gone through the process of applying to college and presumably many were never motivated to attend college in the first place. Although it is true that college dropouts differ from nondropouts in such characteristics as ability and achievement (Astin, 1971, 1975b), similar differences between those who do and do not attend college may be even greater (Sewell and Shah, 1968; Trent and Medsker, 1967; Cooley and Flanagan, 1966). Furthermore, since much is known about factors that predispose students to drop out of college (Astin, 1975b), this knowledge can be utilized to control for preexisting differences between early dropouts and college completers.

One problem with using time of exposure to the college environment is that student dropout rates differ widely among different types of institutions. Students entering private universities, for example, are much more likely to complete four years of undergraduate work than are students initially entering other types of institutions. Ignoring such institutional differences would confound *time of exposure* with *type of institution attended*. To deal with this problem, analyses involving time of exposure to the college environment were limited in two ways.

First, all students who attended more than one institution were excluded. Next, within any given institution, equal numbers of students were selected from each time-of-attendance category (for example, less than one year, one and a half years, and so forth). One effect of this latter procedure was to limit the students selected from each time category at any institution to the number in the category containing the fewest students—usually, but not always, the shortest time interval. Although these selection criteria necessitated excluding some institutions (notably the two-year colleges, because few have any students attending more than two years), they remove any correlation between time of attendance and type of college attended.

Intensity of Exposure. The quality or *intensity* of the student's college experience can be measured in terms of student *involvement* in the college environment. The construct of involvement, first proposed in a recent study of dropouts (Astin, 1975b) is the time and effort expended by the student in activities that relate directly to the institution and its program. Students at the low end of the involvement continuum are those who live off campus, who come only to attend classes, who devote minimum effort to their academic activities, and whose lives are concerned primarily with persons and events outside the institution. At the high end of the continuum are students who spend most of their time on campus, are committed to their studies, are actively involved in campus organizations, and interact frequently with faculty and other students.

These stereotypic descriptions of persons at two extremes on the involvement continuum suggest that the construct of involvement may be multidimensional. That is, a person can manifest involvement in different aspects of the college experience: academic, social, political, and so forth. For this reason, a number of preliminary analyses were performed to determine if there were identifiable *patterns* of student involvement in the undergraduate college experience. The results of these analyses are described briefly here. (For details, see supplementary Tables A1-A3, available at cost from the Higher Education Research Institute, 924 Westwood Boulevard, Los Angeles, California 90024.)

The search for different patterns of involvement first

meant identifying items from the follow-up questionnaires that reflected student involvement in the institutional environment. These items included the student's residence, extracurricular activities, membership in academic honor societies, and patterns of interaction with fellow students and faculty.

Involvement items were identified in three follow-up surveys: the 1970 follow-up of 1966 freshmen, the 1972 follow-up of 1968 freshmen, and the winter of 1969-1970 American Council on Education-Carnegie follow-up of 1966 freshmen. Involvement items from each follow-up were intercorrelated and factor analyzed to identify possible patterns of involvement.

These analyses did not reveal a single general involvement factor. Instead, the involvement items formed a number of relatively independent clusters, or "factors" in statistical parlance, as noted in the supplementary Tables A1-A3. Several patterns appeared in all three analyses. Other patterns were unique to only one analysis, primarily because comparable items were not included in the other two. Results are summarized in the following sections for eight major areas: place of residence, involvement with faculty, familiarity with professors in major field, verbal aggressiveness, academic involvement, involvement in research, student government, and athletics.

Place of Residence. Where the student lives is a potentially important index of student involvement. First, on purely intuitive grounds, one may assume that students who live on campus in a dormitory have many more opportunities and incentives to become involved in campus life than students who live at home. Second, a growing body of literature (Astin, 1973, 1975b; Chickering, 1974a) indicates that students who live in residence halls have more contact with faculty, interact more with student peers, do better academically, and are more satisfied with their undergraduate experience than are commuters. Although residential factors appeared in all three longitudinal samples, the most detailed data were available from the 1968-1972 sample. The principal analysis of these data involved only those students who were in continuous attendance at the same institution for all four undergraduate years ($N = 9,682$). Results showed considerable consistency in the students' residential patterns during the first two years. Over half (58 percent) lived in a dormitory both years. About 8 percent moved from dormitories to fraternity or sorority houses between the first and second years, and about 5 percent moved from dormitories to private rooms or apartments. Only 2 percent moved out of dormitories to live with parents. Thus, of the nearly three in four students (72 percent of all freshmen) who lived in dormitories as freshmen, most (eight in ten) continued to live in dormitories as sophomores.

A comparable pattern was observed for students who spent their freshman year living with parents. One student in five (20 percent of the total group) lived with parents during the first year and moved into a dormitory during the second year, and only 1 percent left parents to live in private rooms or apartments during the second year. Again, of the nearly one freshman in four (24 percent) who lived with parents, the large majority (eight in ten) continued to live with parents during the sophomore year. Only 2.5 percent of the students who stayed in the same college for four years initially lived in a private room or apartment as freshmen, and most of these (1.9 percent of the total sample) lived in this fashion during the first two years. Virtually no freshmen who lived either with parents or in private rooms or apartments moved into fraternity or sorority houses during their sophomore years. In summary, among students who attend the same college for four years, most who live in private rooms or apartments during the sophomore year and nearly all who live in fraternity or sorority houses as sophomores initially begin college living in dormitories.

Analyses involving the 1966-1970 sample yielded several additional patterns of residence involving the third and fourth undergraduate years. Basically, students who lived in dormitories during the first two years split into two groups of about equal size: those who continued to live in dormitories and those who moved into private rooms or apartments. The latter group was about equally divided between rooms and apartments.

These analyses suggest three distinct patterns of student residence: (1) living continuously at home; (2) living continuously on campus in dormitories or fraternity or sorority houses;

and (3) mixed patterns. One would expect the students living on campus to be most involved in the institutional environment, students living at home to be least involved, and students with mixed patterns, or living in private, off-campus housing, to fall somewhere in between. Thus, if a particular student outcome is not merely maturational but is affected by the college experience, that outcome should be most likely for students living on campus and least likely for those living at home.

Involvement with Faculty. The factor analysis of the 1966-1969-1970 ACE-Carnegie data revealed a clear-cut pattern of student involvement with faculty. The thirteen items with the highest loading on this factor were:

Factor Loading	Item
.62	Sometimes engage in social conversations with a professor in my major field (2 = yes, 1 = no)
.57	Talk about personal matters with a professor in my major field (2 = yes, 1 = no)
−.56	Don't discuss personal matters with professors (2 = true, 1 = false)
.55	Often discuss topics in my field with a professor in my major (2 = yes, 1 = no)
.52	Often discuss other topics of intellectual interest with a professor in my major field (2 = yes, 1 = no)
.46	Sometimes engage in social conversations with professors in other fields (2 = yes, 1 = no)
.43	Talk about personal matters with professors in major field (2 = yes, 1 = no)
.41	Talk about topics of intellectual interest with professors in other fields (2 = yes, 1 = no)
.39	Have personal contacts with faculty (3 = too much, 2 = about the right amount, 1 = not enough)
.38	Often discuss topics in my field with professors (2 = yes, 1 = no)

Factor Loading	*Item*
.33	Asked an instructor for advice after class (3 = frequently, 2 = occasionally, 1 = not at all)
.31	Most faculty at my college are strongly interested in the academic problems of undergraduates (4 = strongly agree, 3 = agree with reservations, 2 = disagree with reservations, 1 = strongly disagree)
.30	In a recent lecture course in my primary field of interest, I sometimes argued openly with the instructor (2 = yes, 1 = no)

To obtain an involvement score for each student, responses to these items were summed (with the scoring reversed on all items with negative loadings). A similar procedure was used in scoring the other involvement factors, as follows.

Familiarity with Professors in Major Field. This factor was identical to one reported in an earlier study of the college environment (Astin, 1968a). Students were asked to rate one of their major instructors as follows: "Think about the course you took during your most recent college term that was most closely related to your primary field of interest. Please mark 'yes' for all the following statements that apply to this course. (If the course had a lab portion, mark 'yes' only for those items that apply to the lecture portion.)" Four items making up the factor were as follows:

Factor Loading	*Item*
a. .53	The instructor knew me by name (2 = yes, 1 = no)
b. .51	I was in the instructor's office one or more times (2 = yes, 1 = no)
c. .50	I knew the instructor's first name (2 = yes, 1 = no)
d. .27	I was a guest in the instructor's home one or more times (2 = yes, 1 = no)

Not surprisingly, scores on this factor correlate substantially (r = .47) with scores on faculty-student interaction. The fact that the relationship is far from perfect, however, indicates that there may be important information contained in one factor but not in the other. For this reason, it was decided to retain both factors in the analyses of involvement variables.

Verbal Aggressiveness. This factor from the 1969-1970 ACE-Carnegie follow-up replicates another factor from the earlier environmental study. It involves two items:

Factor Loading	Item
.91	I sometimes argued openly with the instructor (2 = yes, 1 = no)
.70	Argued with an instructor in class (2 = yes, 1 = no)

Academic Involvement. This factor was also obtained from the analysis of the 1966-1969-1970 ACE-Carnegie data. The following thirteen items were used to derive each student's score on academic involvement:

Factor Loading	Item
.57	Work hard at my studies (4 = almost always true, 3 = usually true, 2 = usually false, 1 = almost always false)
−.51	Studied less than 5 hours in any given week (3 = frequently, 2 = occasionally, 1 = not at all)
−.49	Not interested in most of my courses (2 = true, 1 = false)
−.47	Find myself bored in class (4 = almost always true, 3 = usually true, 2 = usually false, 1 = almost always false)
−.42	Am not really learning anything important (2 = true, 1 = false)
−.41	Really don't care what grades I get (4 = almost always true, 3 = usually true, 2 = usually false, 1 = almost always false)

Factor Loading	Item
—.41	Overslept and missed a class or appointment (3 = frequently, 2 = occasionally, 1 = not at all)
—.38	Am not really learning anything new (2 = true, 1 = false)
.33	Would rather be going to college now than anything else (4 = strongly agree, 3 = agree with reservations, 2 = disagree with reservations, 1 = strongly disagree)
—.33	Failed to complete an assignment on time (3 = frequently, 2 = occasionally, 1 = not at all)
—.33	Came late to class (3 = frequently, 2 = occasionally, 1 = not at all)
.30	Studied more than thirty hours in any given week (3 = frequently, 2 = occasionally, 1 = not at all)
.27	Studied in the library (3 = frequently, 2 = occasionally, 1 = not at all)

Involvement in Research. This is the only involvement factor that was unique to the 1970 follow-up of 1966 freshmen. (The other follow-ups did not include items of this type.) The three items used to score the factor were:

Factor Loading	Item
.60	Assisted on a professor's research project (2 = yes, 1 = no)
.40	Served as a laboratory assistant (2 = yes, 1 = no)
.36	Worked on an independent research project (2 = yes, 1 = no)

Involvement in Student Government. The analysis of the 1969-1970 follow-up survey revealed a clear-cut pattern of student involvement in student government that yielded moderate loadings on four items:

Factor Loading   *Item*
.62   Participate in student government (5 = nearly
                        every day, 4 = once or twice a week, 3 = a few
                        times a month, 2 = a few times a year, 1 =
                        never)
.59   Attend a meeting of some college organization
                        (5 = nearly every day, 4 = once or twice a
                        week, 3 = a few times a month, 2 = a few
                        times a year, 1 = never)
.47   Elected to a student office (2 = yes, 1 = no)
.43   Worked in a college political campaign (2 =
                        yes, 1 = no)

Athletic Involvement. The final involvement factor, also identified in the analysis of the 1969-1970 follow-up survey, included three items pertaining directly to athletic activities:

Factor Loading   *Item*
.70   Play a nonvarsity sport (5 = nearly every day, 4
                        = once or twice a week, 3 = a few times a
                        month, 2 = a few times a year, 1 = never)
.61   Attend an athletic event (5 = nearly every day,
                        4 = once or twice a week, 3 = a few times a
                        month, 2 = a few times a year, 1 = never)
.48   Played on a varsity athletic team (2 = yes, 1 =
                        no)

Still another way to estimate the effects of maturation is in terms of the age of the entering student. If a particular change is in part the result of maturation, the older the student the less likely that student would be to exhibit the change. That is, if a particular change occurs in most young people during the interval from, say, eighteen to twenty, regardless of whether the person attends college, then it is reasonable to expect that students who are already twenty when they first enter college would be less likely to exhibit these changes than students who are seventeen or eighteen. In short, a negative relationship be-

tween any given change and age at college entry would consti-
tute evidence that the change is in part maturational.

Summary

This chapter has considered a number of conceptual and
methodological problems associated with studying college impact, presenting in some detail the general design of the impact
analysis used in Chapters Two through Seven.

First, the fact that students change in certain demonstra-
ble ways while attending college is not sufficient evidence to
conclude that college attendance per se had produced the
change. One also needs some basis for judging whether the same
change would have occurred if the student had attended a different college, or no college at all.

Second, because the college experience has the potential
to affect many aspects of students' lives, the impact of college
cannot be adequately assessed in terms of one or two simple
outcomes, such as attaining a degree or earning a certain income. An adequate assessment requires a variety of cognitive
and affective outcome measures.

Third, the factory or production model of higher education, in which credits, degrees, and graduates are "produced" by
the institution, has been rejected as a conceptually inadequate
representation of the process of higher education. To assess college impacts, a medical or treatment model is a more appropriate analogy, primarily because both medical and educational
institutions provide services designed to enhance the development of the individual. The effectiveness of these services
cannot be assessed solely in terms of the status of the individual
at some end point; rather, the person's final status must be eval-
uated in terms of initial status at the point of entry into the
institution. Initial status (the person's educational potential) is
analogous to a medical prognosis.

Fourth, much early research on college impact has produced inconclusive findings, primarily because of limitations in
the data and methods of analysis. The Cooperative Institutional

Research Program, which provides the principal empirical basis for the findings reported in Chapters Two through Seven, has a number of advantages in studying college impact. Its data are collected from students attending a wide variety of collegiate institutions representing all major types. Several independent student samples are included, making replication possible. A variety of outcome measures, covering both cognitive and affective as well as psychological and behavioral outcomes, are included. And CIRP data are longitudinal, with both freshman pretests and posttests available for most outcome measures. Freshman data also cover a wide range of personal and background information, which makes possible control of numerous potentially biasing variables.

Fifth, and finally, many investigators have assumed that the "ideal" study of college impact requires comparing college attenders with a "control" group of nonattenders, but that design oversimplifies the college impact problem. Given the great variety of institutions and programs, it is necessary to assess the impact of college *characteristics* and collegiate *experiences* rather than "college" as such. In addition, the matter of attendance versus nonattendance is more a continuum than a dichotomy. Thus, the current study has been designed so students can be compared in terms of their *degree of exposure* (minimal time in attendance versus full-time attendance for four years) and *intensity of exposure* (degree of actual involvement in the collegiate experience). Through such comparisons, the following chapters separate purely maturational changes from those changes attributable to college experiences.

II

Attitudes, Beliefs, and Self-Concept

Studies of student values and attitudes account for much of the voluminous literature on college impact. A wide range of variables can be included in this category of affective-psychological outcomes: personality characteristics, values, attitudes, beliefs, and self-concept. Because of the diversity of the domain, freshman and follow-up questionnaires in the Cooperative Institutional Research Program (CIRP) over the years have incorporated fifty-seven different affective-psychological items. (Still another category of affective-psychological outcomes, student satisfaction with the college environment, is discussed in Chapter Six.)

The fifty-seven items cover four general categories: (1) self-ratings, twenty items; (2) values, seventeen; (3) religious affiliations, four; and (4) attitudes, sixteen. Since a separate analysis of each outcome would have been prohibitively expensive and the results difficult to interpret, a series of factor analyses was undertaken to reduce the fifty-seven items to a more manageable number of general outcome measures. Results of the factor analyses and college impact analyses are thus presented separately for the four general groups just described.

The presentation of results for each group begins with a description of changes from pretest to posttest. It includes entering student characteristics and college characteristics that relate to change (as revealed in the stepwise multiple-regression analyses). Finally, results of the analyses of the involvement variables are presented, with a discussion of the relative importance of maturational and college effects.

Self-Concept

Since only the 1966-1970 sample contained pretests and posttests of student self-ratings, analyses of college impact on self-concept are based largely on the data from this group of some 25,000 students. Students compared themselves with students their own age and responded to each item on a five-point scale: top 10 percent (five), above average (four), average (three), below average (two), bottom 10 percent (one). The factor analyses of scores on the twenty self-ratings produced four identifiable self-concept factors: liberalism versus conservatism, interpersonal self-esteem, intellectual self-esteem, and self-criticism.

Table 3 shows the change in students' self-concepts during the four years. Items listed under each factor were used to compute the factor score. (Factor scores are the sum of individual items scores.) The seven items under "other self-ratings" were not used to compute factor scores, because they did not produce high loadings on any single factor.

Table 3. Changes in Self-Concept Four Years After Entering College

Self-Concept Factor / Item	Loading on Factor	Percentage of 1966 Freshmen Rating Selves		Percentage of Change Between 1966 and 1970	
		Above Average	Below Average	Above Average	Below Average
Political Liberalism					
Liberalism	.38	18.0	30.6	+17.0	− 4.5
Conservatism[a]	−.30	14.2	14.5	+ .3	+10.5
Interpersonal Self-Esteem					
Leadership ability	.61	35.5	14.3	+11.3	− .6
Popularity with the opposite sex	.66	26.6	11.6	+ 9.6	− 3.0
Public speaking ability	.51	20.0	37.3	+ 6.3	− 7.9
Self-confidence (social)	.70	28.9	18.9	+ 5.4	− .2
Popularity	.65	30.8	5.8	+ 4.1	− .5
Intellectual Self-Esteem					
Self-confidence (intellectual)	.46	35.4	11.5	+14.0	− 1.1
Academic ability	.70	58.3	3.5	+ 3.9	− 1.8
Mathematical ability	.63	36.2	28.6	− 2.2	− 1.3
Self-Criticism					
Sensitivity to criticism	.34	26.5	13.9	+ 8.0	+ 2.1
Stubbornness	.43	35.1	13.6	+ 4.3	+ 2.9
Defensiveness	.31	28.2	9.3	+ 2.2	+ 5.5
Other Self-Ratings					
Understanding of others		60.6	1.8	+ 7.8	+ .3
Writing ability		23.9	22.1	+ 6.7	+ 1.3
Artistic ability		18.9	48.4	+ 6.5	− 6.0
Originality		37.0	9.4	+ 3.9	+ 1.9
Mechanical ability		26.6	35.9	+ 3.3	− 2.2
Cheerfulness		51.9	3.5	+ 1.0	+ 2.8
Drive to achieve		58.6	4.8	− 2.6	+ 4.7

Note: Students were asked to "Rate yourself on each of the following traits as *you really think you are* when compared to the average person of your own age."

[a]Direction of scoring was reversed when item was combined into factor score.

Changes in self-concept over the four years appear in the last two columns. Most items show an increase in the number of students who consider themselves above average. The percentages of those who rate themselves below average tend to decline, but these declines are frequently smaller than the increases in above-average ratings. Indeed, for one third of the items *both* above- and below-average ratings increased. Students tend to become more *variable* in their self-concepts during the four years following matriculation. Apparently, students' conceptions of themselves become more sharply differentiated after they enter college.

The positive changes in both measures of self-esteem suggest that college attendance may increase the individual's sense of competence and self-worth. Similar changes have been reported by other investigators (Chickering, 1969, 1974b; Constantinople, 1969; Madison, 1971; McConnell, 1972; Schmidt, 1970). The shifts toward political liberalism are consistent with most earlier studies of changes in student political attitudes during the college years (for example, Feldman and Newcomb, 1969) and with a number of more recent studies (Bayer, Royer, and Webb, 1973; Burchard, 1969; Finney, 1974; Nelson and Uhl, 1974; Nosow and Robertson, 1973).

The general design of the college impact analyses requires that differences in students when they first enter college be controlled statistically. Fifty-two different freshman characteristics from the 1966-1970 sample were used: age, sex, race (white, black, Oriental, American Indian), ethnicity (Mexican, German, Italian, Polish), religion of parents (Protestant, Roman Catholic, Jewish, none), student's religious preference (same categories as parents' religion), mother's and father's educational level, parents' income, type of high school (public or private), average high school grade, academic ability (American College Testing and Scholastic Aptitude Testing program scores converted to a common scale), four measures of degree aspirations (overall level, Ph.D., professional, and graduate), four measures of freshman major field plans (mathematics, physical science, engineering, and social science), three measures of career choice (physician, lawyer, scientific researcher), and seventeen pretests of student outcome factors covering self-concept (four factors plus two special measures of political orientation), six value measures, and five behavioral factors (drinking, hedonism, religiousness, smoking, and use of the library). (Major and career categories were selected from a larger list by preliminary analyses involving various outcome measures.)

For each follow-up self-concept factor, these fifty-two freshman characteristics were entered one at a time into a stepwise multiple-regression analysis until no additional freshman characteristic could add significantly ($p < .05$) to the prediction of the outcome measures. To conserve costs, a one-fourth sample of the 1966-1970 students ($N = 6,321$) was used. For most outcomes, the corresponding freshman pretest entered the regression first. Freshman measures that entered subsequently were, in essence, those characteristics associated with change (from pretest to posttest). In general, freshman characteristics that entered the regression after the pretest tended also to be correlated with the pretest measure. For example, if men as a group scored higher than women on the pretest, individual men were more likely to increase their scores than were women with identical pretests.

To determine if the results applied equally to different types of students, most analyses were repeated for students separately by sex and by academic ability. This repetition involved five subgroups: men ($N = 3,271$), women ($N = 3,050$), low-ability students ($N = 881$), middle-ability students ($N = 3,228$), and high-ability students ($N = 2,212$). Low-ability students included those with SAT composite (verbal plus mathematical) scores below 925 or ACT composites below 20; high-ability students included those with SAT composite scores above 1,075 or ACT composites above 23.

After the fifty-two entering freshman variables had been controlled, a set of six "college-experience" variables were allowed to enter the regression analysis. These variables included three measures of financial support (scholarship, loan, parental support) and three dichotomous measures of the student's residence for most of the freshman year (dormitory, private room or apartment, or with parents).

Characteristics of the students' colleges were allowed to enter the regression last (that is, after the fifty-two freshman characteristics and the six college-experience measures had been controlled). Twenty-four different measures of college characteristics were employed. They included three quantitative measures of enrollment, selectivity (average test scores of entering freshmen; see Astin and Henson, in press), and prestige (based on a nonlinear combination of size and selectivity; see Astin and Lee, 1971), four qualitative or dichotomous measures of geographic region (Northeast, Midwest, South, West and Southwest), two dichotomous measures for single-sex colleges (men only, women only), and fifteen dichotomous type-control measures formed by dividing the institutions into the following groups:

Selective public institutions
Nonselective public institutions
Selective private institutions
Nonselective private institutions
Public four-year colleges
Selective Protestant four-year colleges
Nonselective Protestant four-year colleges
Selective Roman Catholic four-year colleges
Nonselective Roman Catholic four-year colleges
Very selective private, nonsectarian four-year colleges
Selective private, nonsectarian four-year colleges
Nonselective private, nonsectarian four-year colleges
Public two-year colleges
Private two-year colleges
Predominantly black colleges

The final stage in the regression analyses determined the relationship between each student outcome and involvement variable (that is, after entering freshman characteristics, college experiences, and college characteristics had been controlled).*

Liberalism versus Conservatism. The freshman pretest measure on the political orientation factor correlated modestly ($r = .42$) with the posttest outcome four years later. After the pretest measure had been controlled, the freshman characteristic most closely associated with change in political liberalism

---

*Multiple-correlation coefficients (R) at each stage in each regression analysis are shown in the Appendix. A summary of the multiple-regression analyses for all outcome variables is provided in Tables A, B, and C in A Note on Measurement Error.

was having Jewish parents. Children of Jewish parents were substantially more liberal on the freshman pretest than children of
non-Jews, and they also became liberal more often during the
four years. Other student characteristics associated with greater-
than-average increases in political liberalism are being black and
male; having Roman Catholic or no religious preference; and
having high academic ability and high scores on artistic interests, altruism, hedonism, and drinking. Freshman characteristics
negatively associated with increasing liberalism are being female,
being older than average, scoring high in religiousness, and having strong business interests. In general, these findings support
the stereotype of the political liberal as either Jewish or nonreligious, open to experience (that is, drinking and hedonism),
young, altruistic, interested in art, and uninterested in business.

One potential problem with the liberalism-conservatism
measure is that a substantial minority of students gave inconsistent responses: For example, among those who rated themselves in the lowest 10 percent on political conservatism on the
follow-up, 16 percent also rated themselves among the lower 10
percent on liberalism. Similarly, 4 percent of those who rated
themselves in the highest 10 percent on conservatism also rated
themselves in the highest 10 percent on liberalism. Even higher
percentages rated themselves above average or below average on
both traits. To explore the possible bias associated with these
discrepancies, two additional dichotomous posttest measures of
political orientation were developed. The first measure defined
"pure liberals" as those who rated themselves in the top 10 percent on liberalism *and* in the bottom 10 percent on conservatism (5.9 percent of all students on the posttest). The "pure
conservatives" included those whose posttest responses were in
the top 10 percent on conservatism and the bottom 10 percent
on liberalism (1.8 percent of the total sample). Comparable pretest measures for both these outcomes were also computed
from the freshman data. The stepwise regression using the pure
liberal outcome produced results almost identical to those obtained with the liberal-conservative continuum. Regressions
with the pure conservative measure produced somewhat different findings, with the following characteristics predicting con-

servatism: aspirations for a political degree (Doctor of Medicine, Doctor of Dental Science, Bachelor of Laws), father's education, and being Oriental or Polish. These findings suggest that students' political orientations do not necessarily fall along a continuum, particularly when it comes to conservative beliefs.

Majoring in the social sciences was associated with greater-than-average increases in liberalism and majoring in either engineering, mathematics, or physical sciences was associated with less-than-average increases. Because faculty in the social sciences tend to be highly liberal and those in engineering tend to be among the least liberal, it is tempting to conclude that the political attitudes of faculty may rub off on their students (see Ladd and Lipset, 1975). However, results of the analyses of involvement factors (which follow) suggest that peer-group effects may be more important: Students in the social sciences, like faculty, tend to be more liberal than students and faculty in engineering.

Political liberalism is positively associated with receiving support from parents and from scholarships. Living at home is negatively associated with liberalism, but living in a dormitory is associated with larger-than-expected increases in liberalism. This finding supports the notion that the increasing trend toward liberalism that occurs after college entry is due at least in part to the effects of the college experience.

Increases in political liberalism are larger than expected among students who attended prestigious and highly selective institutions.* Highly selective private four-year colleges, in particular, foster the largest increases in liberalism. Smaller-than-expected increases are associated with attending nonselective public universities and four-year colleges, men's colleges, Protestant colleges, and institutions in the South.

Because political beliefs have been included so frequently in studies of college impact and because of the obvious rele-

---

*Technically oriented readers should note that conclusions about environmental effects can be affected by errors of measurement in the entering student characteristics (Astin, 1970a). For details on how measurement errors were handled, see A Note on Measurement Error.

vance of political preferences for national policy, a second independent analysis of the effect of college on political views was
made with data from the ACE-Carnegie follow-up of 1966
freshmen carried out during the winter of 1969-1970. Although
the questionnaire for this follow-up did not contain the posttest
on the self-ratings of political orientation in the 1966 freshman
questionnaire, it did include a self-rating on political views:
strongly conservative, conservative, middle-of-the-road, liberal,
and left. That this item was comparable to the two freshman
self-ratings was suggested by a series of cross-tabulations. For
example, among students who were pure liberals as freshmen,
85 percent rated themselves as either liberal or left in the
follow-up, 4 percent rated themselves as conservative, and *none*
selected strongly conservative. Similarly, among the entering
freshmen who were pure conservatives, only 28 percent rated
themselves as either liberal or left on the follow-up questionnaire, 36 percent as conservative, and 13 percent as strongly
conservative. (See supplementary Table A4, available from the
Higher Education Research Institute.)

   Because these results indicated that the freshman self-
ratings could be used as pretests for the posttest question on
political beliefs in the 1969-1970 questionnaire, a new analysis
was carried out in which this political follow-up item was the
outcome measure and the same freshman variables used in the
initial analysis served as predictors in a stepwise regression. The
results were strikingly similar: Students attending selective,
prestigious, and private institutions show larger-than-expected
increases in liberalism. Students attending institutions in the
South and technological institutions (this variable was not included in the other analysis) show smaller-than-expected increases. Attending colleges for women and colleges in the Midwest is associated with increased liberalism.

   That highly selective and prestigious institutions should
foster the development of liberal political beliefs is consistent
with the oft-replicated finding that political unrest occurred frequently at such institutions during the late 1960s (Astin and
others, 1975). Although the precise causal agents for the development of such attitudes in elite institutions are not known, it

ćely that at least two factors are involved: the highly
political views of professors in the elite institutions
.nd Lipset, 1975) and the already highly liberal views of
s at matriculation (the entering student's self-rating on
political liberalism correlates .10 with the selectivity of the
institution).

Interpersonal Self-Esteem. The pretest score on interpersonal self-esteem had a moderately high correlation (r =
.57) with the posttest score. Increasing self-esteem is positively
associated with being black and with having strong athletic
interests at college entry and is negatively associated with academic ability.

Being supported by a scholarship has a positive effect on
interpersonal self-esteem, whereas being supported by a loan has
the opposite effect. Living in a dormitory during the freshman
year is associated with greater-than-expected increases in interpersonal self-esteem, a finding that once again supports the con-
tention that increases in this student outcome are associated in
part with attending college.

Positive effects on interpersonal self-esteem were observed at only one kind of institution: the private college or university. Conversely, smaller-than-expected changes in interpersonal self-esteem were observed among students attending
two-year public colleges, predominantly black colleges, and colleges located in the southern or midwestern states. Since virtually all students attending predominantly black colleges are
black, this negative effect appears to be limited to black students. Apparently, the experience of attending a predominantly
white rather than a predominantly black college facilitates the
development of interpersonal self-esteem among black students.
One possible interpretation of this effect is that black students'
feelings of self-esteem are related in part to their interactions
with white people and that the experience of attending a predominantly white institution enhances their ability to deal pro-
ductively with whites.

The positive effects of attending a private college, which
is similar to a finding reported earlier by Nichols (1967), may
result from the greater degree of intimacy and attention to the

individual student that characterizes the environment of many
such colleges (Astin and Lee, 1971). The relatively impersonal
environment of the public institution may be less facilitative of
the development of interpersonal competence.

Intellectual Self-Esteem. The pretest-posttest correlation
for intellectual self-esteem was substantial ($r = .66$). The freshman characteristic most strongly associated with increasing feelings of intellectual self-esteem is academic ability. Men increased their feelings of self-esteem more than women, and
students with high grades in high school and high degree aspirations increased their feelings more than students with low
grades and aspirations. The college environment appears to
strengthen feelings of intellectual competence most among
those students who display the abilities, academic records, and
aspirations that normally lead to academic achievement.

Majoring in one of three fields—mathematics, physical
science, or engineering—is positively associated with increased
intellectual self-esteem. Since engineering and physical science
majors are usually required to take a substantial amount of
mathematics, majoring in these fields may enhance the student's
concept of his or her own mathematical ability relative to that
of other students. (Table 3 shows that the student's self-concept
of mathematical ability is a component of the intellectual self-
esteem measure.)

As with liberalism and interpersonal self-esteem, intellectual self-esteem is positively associated with support by a scholarship and negatively associated with support by a loan—further
evidence that the financial aid a student receives is significantly
related to several self-concept outcomes.

Attendance at two types of institutions is associated with
greater-than-expected increases in intellectual self-esteem: colleges for women and Roman Catholic colleges. The student's
intellectual self-esteem may be enhanced by attending an institution where the academic standards are high and cheating low
(these attributes characterize the environments of women's colleges and Catholic colleges; see Astin, 1968a).

The analysis failed to confirm an earlier longitudinal
study (Skager, Holland, and Braskamp, 1966) in which a similar

outcome—"ability self-concept"—was negatively associated with institutional size and selectivity. The discrepancy is probably attributable in part to the greater number of entering student characteristics that were controlled and the more diverse sample of institutions used in this study. Although institutional selectively did not show any overall effect on intellectual self-esteem, a number of isolated effects did occur within particular types of institutions. For example, among middle-ability students, intellectual self-esteem was negatively associated with attending a selective Protestant college and also with attending a public university (selective or nonselective). However, among men, attending a selective (not highly selective) private college was *positively* associated with intellectual self-esteem.

Perhaps the most important result concerning environmental effects on intellectual self-esteem is the *failure* to support the commonly held view that attending a highly selective college has a negative effect on the student's—and in particular, the high-ability student's—ability self-concept. American higher education maintains that, for many students who have had outstanding academic records in secondary school, attending a highly selective institution where they are merely average in ability will have a depressing effect on their ability self-concept. This turns out not to be the case: Institutional selectivity has no effect on the able student's intellectual self-concept one way or the other.

Self-criticism. Table 3 suggests that increases in above-average self-ratings on the three self-criticism items are nearly balanced by increases in below-average ratings. Apparently, students become more heterogeneous after entering college in their tendencies to be self-critical. These three items present certain difficulties in interpretation. The factor might as well be labeled "abrasiveness" or "stubbornness." In any case, the pretest-posttest correlation was relatively low ($r = .33$). Women, much more than men, increase their tendencies to be self-critical. Greater-than-average increases in self-criticism are also associated with hedonism, a behavioral factor (see Chapter Three). Smaller-than-average increases are associated with being black and with being conservative at college entry.

Spending the freshman year in a college dormitory is associated with greater-than-expected increases in self-criticism. The student's tendency to be self-critical is also strengthened by attending a prestigious institution and weakened somewhat by attending a predominantly black college or an institution located in the South.

College Effects versus Maturation. To what extent can these increases in liberalism, self-esteem, and self-criticism be attributed to maturation rather than to the effects of the college experience per se? One strategy for detecting true college effects is to examine the impact of student *involvement* on the outcome in question (see Chapter One). If students who are more involved in the college experience show greater change than those who are less involved, the assumption of college impact is strengthened. If, however, changes are unrelated to the student's degree of involvement, the maturation hypothesis is strengthened.

Two simple measures of involvement are being a member of a social fraternity or sorority and participating in an honors program. Fraternity and sorority membership is associated with increased interpersonal self-esteem and with decreased liberalism. These findings support the stereotype of the college fraternal organization that emphasizes the development of social skills and conservative values. Even though the students in this study attended college during a period of campus unrest, when social fraternities and sororities were under attack and presumably changing (1966-1970), the impact of fraternal organizations is consistent with their popular image for the 1950s.

Another relevant finding concerns the relationship of interpersonal self-esteem to student persistence. Students who stayed in college showed much larger increases in interpersonal self-esteem than did dropouts even after entering student, college environmental, and involvement variables had been controlled. These results, which occurred for both men and women and for students in all three ability levels, strongly support the hypothesis that increases in interpersonal self-esteem are directly attributable to the college experience.

Participating in academic honors programs is associated

with positive changes on two self-concept measures: intellectual and interpersonal self-esteem. While these findings suggest that honors participation may have certain facilitative effects on student development, a certain question here makes these findings somewhat ambiguous (rather like the question about which came first, the chicken or the egg): For certain students, participation in honors programs depends first on getting high grades. For such students, the increased self-esteem may result from their superior academic achievement rather than from participation in honors programs per se. To test this assumption, the analysis was repeated, controlling for students' undergraduate grade-point average. This additional control had little effect on the relationship with interpersonal self-esteem. The control for grade-point average did, however, substantially reduce the relationship between intellectual self-esteem and honors participation but did not eliminate it completely.

Only one involvement measure was included in the 1966-1970 longitudinal file: student involvement in research activities. The possible impact of involvement on self-concept was examined after the fifty-two entering freshman characteristics, the six college-experience measures, and the twenty-four measures of college characteristics had been controlled. Research involvement has a highly significant positive relationship to three self-concept measures: intellectual self-esteem, interpersonal self-esteem, and liberalism. (The relationship with self-criticism is nonsignificant.) Since these relationships are consistent with the direction of change on these measures, the finding indicates that the positive changes in these three self-concept measures result at least in part from the college experience.

The data on the relationships between change in various self-concept measures and age at college entry provide further evidence of the presence of maturational effects. Because age did not carry a significant predictive weight in the analysis of any self-concept measure, the college-impact hypothesis is strengthened. Age did enter one stepwise regression (liberalism) with a significant negative weight, but the weight was later reduced to nonsignificance when student ability (college admission test scores) entered the regression. This result shows that older students change less in a liberal direction than younger students, not because of age per se, but because the older students have lower test scores (test scores are positively related to increased liberalism).

Because a measure of political beliefs was included in the ACE-Carnegie 1969-1970 follow-up of 1966 freshmen, it was possible to estimate the effects on political liberalism and conservatism of five other independent variables: involvement in student government, academic involvement, athletic participation, verbal aggressiveness, and student-faculty interaction. As with research involvement, the partial correlations of these five measures with political beliefs was computed after the entering freshman characteristics, college-experience variables, and college characteristics had been controlled.

It is not surprising that involvement in student government is positively related to changes toward greater liberalism. That is, students who are politically active while attending college show greater-than-expected shifts toward the political left during the four years. Similar results have been reported by Chickering and McCormick (1973) and Nelson and Johnson (1971). Two other factors—academic and athletic involvement —show significant *negative* relationships to change toward political liberalism. That is, students who are heavily involved with their academic work or with athletics move more toward political conservatism. These two types of involvement retard the expected change toward the political left that occurs in most college students. Academic involvement has by far the strongest association with political beliefs of any involvement factor (partial $r = -.14$).

These results suggest a somewhat ambiguous conclusion about maturation versus college impact. Results with one form of involvement (student government) support the college-impact hypothesis, whereas results with two other forms (academic and athletic) support the maturation hypothesis. One thing seems certain: The changes toward greater political liberalism observed in most college students are retarded, not facilitated, by becoming heavily involved in academic or athletic pursuits. Both academic and athletic activities can consume much time and energy. In a sense, one can regard different forms of student involvement as a kind of zero-sum situation where heavy involvement in one activity necessarily reduces the time and energy available for other activities. Is it possible that devoting a great deal of time to studies or athletics isolates students from their peers, reducing the impact that the peer group might have on values and attitudes? Studying is often a solitary activity; the stereotype "grind" spends a lot of time alone and does not participate in much social activity with peers. Although athletic involvement includes interaction with peers, the peer group of athletes is most likely politically conservative (the simple correlation between athletic interests and political liberalism is $-.08$). The nature of the interaction in athletics is highly disciplined and unlikely to involve discussion of political concepts or values. Also, because of the time typically spent practicing, athletes have less time to interact informally with nonathletic peers.

Involvement in student government is not the political activism characterized by protests and demonstrations. Rather, the measure reflects a more traditional involvement, such as holding a student office, participating in political campaigns, and belonging to student organizations. This involvement probably exposes the student to other wide-ranging student beliefs. That students who display high verbal aggressiveness show greater-than-expected changes toward political liberalism (partial $r = .10$) also supports this interpretation.

All forms of student involvement in the college experience may not be equally useful in assessing the relative importance of maturation versus college effects. On the contrary, involvement that tends to isolate the student from the peer group may retard changes that occur in most students as a result of their college experience.

What do these data say about college impact versus maturational effects on students' self-concept? All four self-concept measures tend to increase during the four years following matriculation. Age is not related to any of these changes, and in most cases the changes are smaller for students who live with their parents than for students who live in dormitories or private rooms. Changes in intellectual self-esteem are particularly large for students involved in honors programs or in research activities. Changes in interpersonal self-esteem are greatest for students who are active in social fraternities or sororities, and students who stay in college show much larger increases than do dropouts. Increases in political liberalism are strongest for students who attend elite colleges and are active in campus politics and organizations. Together, these findings strongly suggest that student changes in self-concept are not simply maturational but are also closely associated with the experience of attending college.

Values

Student values have been the object of many college-impact studies (Feldman and Newcomb, 1969). By far the most widely used instrument to measure these values has been the Allport-Vernon-Lindzey *Study of Values* (1960). This forced-choice instrument provides a profile of the student's values in six areas: theoretical, economic, social, esthetic, political, and religious. While constraints on the length of the freshman questionnaire in the CIRP precluded the use of such a complex instrument as the *Study of Values*, value items have been included in most freshman and follow-up questionnaires since the research program was initiated in fall 1966. These items have assessed areas similar to the Allport-Vernon-Lindzey instrument, as well as several other areas of student concern.

The CIRP questionnaires have asked the students to "indicate the importance to you personally of each of the following." The students, presented with value statements (also called "life goals"), provide one of four responses: "essential," "very important," "somewhat important," "and "not important." Unlike the Allport-Vernon-Lindzey instrument, in which the student is forced to choose between two competing values, the CIRP questionnaire permits the students to evaluate each statement independently.

Seventeen value statements were included in the 1966

and 1967 freshman pretest questionnaires and repeated in the four-year follow-ups of these two entering classes in 1970 and 1971. A number of these statements were also included in the ACE-Carnegie follow-up. To reduce computational costs and to simplify interpretation, these seventeen statements were included in the factor analyses to determine if a smaller number of general factor scales could be used to measure student change. Six identifiable value factors emerged: altruism; artistic, athletic, business, and musical interests; and status needs. Even though the factor analysis included self-ratings as well as behaviors, value items accounted for all but two of the highest loading items.

Table 4 shows the six factors with the highest loading items, used to compute the value factor score. Although the correlations between pretest and posttest measures for individual items are relatively low, the corresponding correlations for the factor scores are somewhat higher, a finding that once again demonstrates the greater reliability of factor scores based on several items.

Table 4 shows that, with few exceptions, the percentage of students who check each value as essential or very important declines during the four years after matriculation. One reason may be the unrealistic aspirations of many entering freshmen, who may endorse rather uncritically a wide range of life goals. In other words, the decline may represent an increasing realism in students' value patterns. The increased *variance* observed for many items supports this interpretation: That is, even though the overall importance of these values declines with time, there is a certain spreading effect where students' values move toward the extremes (essential and not important).

The major exception to the general decline in student values occurs in artistic interests, where both items defining this factor increased slightly during the four years. By far the largest decreases occur in business interests and status needs.

To what extent do these declines in commitment to certain values depend on student characteristics at college entry? How important are college experiences? Do these changes depend primarily on the college environment, or are they mainly maturational?

Table 4. Changes in Values Over Four Years of College Attendance

Value Factor / Item	Loading on Factor	Correlation Between Pre- and Posttest (1967-1971)	Percentage Checking Item as "Essential" or "Very Important"			
			Freshmen		4-year change	
			1966	1967	1966-1970	1967-1971
Altruism						
Helping others who are in difficulty	.45	.33	67.4	60.4	+ 1.5	+ 8.4
Participation in an organization like the Peace Corps or VISTA	.53	.31	20.7	17.8	−10.8	− 6.6
Artistic Interests						
Writing original works (poems, novels, short stories, and so on)	.60	.48	11.8	12.8	+ .1	+ 1.0
Creating artistic works (painting, sculpture, decorating, and so on)	.65	.53	14.0	15.0	+ 5.9	+ 5.1
Athletic Interests[a]						
Becoming an outstanding athlete	.67	.52	14.5	13.4	− 8.0	− 6.9
Business Interests						
Being very well off financially	.42	.32	42.2	44.3	−10.0	−14.5
Being successful in a business of my own	.50	.37	52.9	46.3	−19.7	−16.9
Becoming an expert in finance and commerce	.59	.38	11.7	11.5	− .4	− .9
Musical Interests[b]						
Becoming an accomplished musician	.67	.49	7.5	7.2	− 2.9	− 1.2
Becoming accomplished in one of the performing arts	.51	.39	11.2	10.1	− 5.3	− 1.6
Status Needs						
Becoming an authority on a special subject in my subject field	.51	.26	66.8	67.4	−13.8	−16.5
Obtaining recognition from my colleagues for contributions in my special field	.56	.24	44.2	41.0	− 9.4	− 8.9
Other Values						
Keeping up to date with political affairs		.36	56.7	50.0	+ 1.0	+ 3.0
Having administrative responsibility for the work of others		.29	27.8	24.7	+ 2.5	+ 1.6
Never being obligated to people		.26	26.6	25.4	− 1.3	+ .9
Making a theoretical contribution to science		.40	11.3	11.7	− 4.5	− 4.2
Becoming a community leader		.37	24.3	23.5	− 5.1	− 5.6

[a]Factor also includes self-rating, "athletic ability" (factor loading = .62).

[b]Factor also includes behavior, "played a musical instrument" (factor loading = .59).

Altruism. Although the general value of "helping others" showed a slight increase over the four years in both samples, the more concrete value of participating in the Peace Corps or Vista showed a marked decline. The regression analyses involving entering freshman characteristics revealed that both blacks and women showed smaller-than-expected declines in altruistic values during the four undergraduate years. Highly able students (as measured by college admissions tests) show somewhat larger-than-expected decreases in altruism. The only other freshman characteristic related to altruism was artistic interests, which tended to retard the degree of decline.

Majoring in social science and plans to become a physician were positively associated with altruism, whereas majoring in either engineering or physical science was negatively related.

A number of college characteristics were significantly related to changes in altruism after entering freshman characteristics had been controlled. By far the most pronounced relationships involve attendance at universities, which appears to have substantial negative impact (partial $r = -.13$) on altruism. Students attending universities show declines in altruistic values that substantially exceed the declines among students attending other types of institutions. Declines are also greater than expected among institutions located in the western and northeastern states.

Both Roman Catholic and Protestant colleges have significant positive impacts on altruistic values. Here is a clear case where the impact of a particular type of college on students' values is consistent with the educational objectives of those colleges: Christian teachings seem entirely consistent with the enhancement of altruistic motives.

Artistic Interests. Artistic interest is the only value area where the degree of student commitment increased during the four years. Women's interests show substantially greater increases than those of men. Greater-than-average increases are also observed among students with high aspirations, high interpersonal self-esteem, strong drinking habits, and no religious preference. Students with strong business interests at college entry and students planning to major in engineering show smaller-than-expected increases in artistic interest.

Increases in artistic interests are somewhat greater than expected among students attending private colleges, perhaps because the *relative* emphasis on artistic and literary pursuits is greater at private than at public institutions.

Athletic Interests. The freshman characteristic most strongly associated with changes in athletic interests is sex: Women showed greater-than-expected declines in athletic interests during the undergraduate years. Several other entering freshman characteristics also have negative relationships to athletic interests over time: being black, smoking, having strong artistic interests, and being Protestant or Jewish, or having no religious preference.

Only two college characteristics were significantly related to athletic interests after entering freshman characteristics and college experiences were controlled: Attending a selective institution was positively related, and attending a predominantly black institution is negatively associated with athletic interests. While this finding suggests no obvious interpretation, it is possible to regard it in a different light: for black students, attending a predominantly white (rather than black) institution strengthens athletic interests. Such a result might reflect the heavy involvement of blacks in athletics at predominantly white colleges.

Business Interests. Business interests declined sharply during the undergraduate years. Many entering freshman characteristics—in particular sex—are related to this decline: The decline of interests among women is much more pronounced than among men. Other entering characteristics associated with greater-than-average declines are academic ability, high school grades, aspirations for graduate study, altruism, and having parents with no religious preference. Smaller-than-average declines are associated with being black or Mexican-American, Jewish religious preference, interpersonal self-esteem, self-criticism, parental income, and attending a public high school.

Students majoring in social science show larger than expected declines in business interests, whereas students majoring in engineering show smaller increases than expected. These results may reflect the antibusiness bias of many social scientists and the heavy movement of engineering majors into business during the undergraduate years (Astin and Panos, 1969).

Of special interest is the finding that plans to become a physician appear to retard the decline in business interests. Here we have an interesting reflection of the mixed motives that may operate for many students in the field of medicine: It is both an altruistic profession as well as a business.

Attending a selective institution appears to accelerate the decline in business interest, as does attendance at private institutions and black colleges. The decline is retarded by attending large institutions and colleges for men. This pattern closely parallels the curricular emphases of these various institutions. That is, business as a field of study is deemphasized at the more selective institutions and substantially emphasized at larger institutions and institutions for men. This finding supports the theory of "progressive conformity" (Astin and Panos, 1969) or "accentuation of initial differences" (Feldman and Newcomb, 1969), wherein the interests and aspirations of the new students change in the direction of the dominant curricular emphases of the institution.

Musical Interests. Although the pretest-posttest correlation involving musical interests is relatively high ($r = .63$), only three other freshman characteristics entered the regression: Entering artistic interests had a positive weight, while business interests and being black had small negative weights.

Students who receive support from parents for their college expenses show smaller-than-predicted declines in musical interests after entering college, as do students who live with their parents as freshmen. Perhaps some students who leave home to attend college no longer have access to their musical instruments and are no longer subject to parental pressure to practice. Musical interests appear to be strengthened by attending a Protestant college or a college in the West.

Status Needs. With the possible exception of business interests, status needs showed a greater decline during the four years after college entrance than any other value factor. A number of entering freshman characteristics other than the pretest score are related to changes in status needs. Scores for women declined much more than scores for men (partial $r = -.19$). Other characteristics associated with greater-than-average declines are college admissions test scores and being reared as a Protestant. Smaller-than-average declines occur among blacks, Jews, Catholics, and students with strong interests in music or business. Belonging to a social fraternity is associated with smaller-than-expected declines in status needs among men of average or high ability.

The effects of different college characteristics seem to depend in part on the student's ability. Among low-ability students, college selectivity has a positive impact on status needs, particularly among those attending private nonsectarian colleges. However, among women and middle-ability students, attending a selective Roman Catholic college is associated with larger-than-expected decreases in status needs. Among high-ability students, attending a nonselective private university is associated with smaller-than-expected decreases in status needs.

Maturation versus College Impact. Evidence from college residence variables provides a mixed picture of the relative importance of maturation and college attendance. Living at home appears to retard changes on three value outcomes: Increases in artistic interests are attenuated, as are decreases in altruism and musical interests. These results suggest the possibility of a significant college effect, but it should be kept in mind that the relationships are quite small. Furthermore, residence variables have no effect one way or the other on other value outcomes.

Since the ACE-Carnegie follow-up included posttests on most value questions, it was possible to assess the impact of various involvement factors on all of the six value measures except athletic interests. Four measures—research involvement, student-faculty interaction, involvement in student government, and verbal aggressiveness—were *positively* associated with all posttest values except business interests. This finding suggests that the general tendency for students to endorse fewer value questions in the posttest than on the pretest is in part maturational and that interpersonal campus involvement tends to impede these declines. In one sense, college attendance may retard the general lowering of horizons that occurs during the years immediately following high school graduation.

The pattern of relationships for academic and athletic

involvement once again contrasted with that for other forms of involvement, particularly business interests, which showed smaller-than-expected declines among students who were heavily involved in academic or athletic pursuits. Apparently, the interpersonal isolation that results from these two forms of involvement insulates the student from the antibusiness sentiment that seems to exist on many campuses. The fact that being active in a fraternity or sorority is associated with smaller-than-expected declines in business interests suggests that such organizations may support values at variance with the larger campus community.

Involvement in academics and honors programs also appears to impede the decline in status needs that occurs among many students after they enter college. In fact, virtually every form of involvement except athletic participation is associated with lower-than-expected declines in status interests, which suggests that the direction of causation for this value factor may be reversed: Students who maintain their status needs over time may be more inclined to compete academically and to become involved with faculty, campus politics, and research activities. Perhaps the most compelling evidence that college serves to retard the decline in status needs is provided by the positive association between status needs and persistence in college that remains after entering student, college environmental, and involvement variables are controlled (status needs is the only value measure that retained a significant correlation with persistence after controlling these other variables).

Academic involvement is *negatively* associated with both artistic and musical interests and athletic involvement is also negatively associated with artistic interests.

The decline in the strength of student commitments to various life goals after college entry appears in part to be maturational. It can be impeded somewhat by college attendance, particularly when attendance is combined with active participation in campus life. This is especially true for status needs, which decline markedly after college entry but which decline substantially less among persisters and among students heavily involved in academic pursuits or in campus life. The finding for business interests is similar, except that involvement in campus activities and with faculty does not appear to impede the decline. Apparently, this result reflects the generally low esteem in which business is held among many campus communities. Involvement in campus life and with faculty impedes the decline in altruism and musical interests associated with college attendance and accelerates the slight increase in artistic interests that occurs during this same period. Heavy involvement in academic pursuits is negatively associated with the development of artistic and musical interests.

Religious Beliefs

The inclusion of pretest questions on religious affiliation in every freshman survey since 1966 and of posttest questions in both the 1970 CIRP follow-up and the 1969-1970 ACE-Carnegie follow-up provided an unusual opportunity to examine changes in religious affiliation at several points after college entry. Table 5 shows the changes in students' religious affilia-

Table 5. Changes in Religious Affiliation After College Entry

Denominational Preference	Average Freshman Percentage (1966-1969)	Percent Change				
		½ year (1969-1970)	1½ years (1968-1970)	2½ years (1967-1970)	3½ years (1966-1970)	4 years (1966-1970)
Protestant	50	−3.8	−3.4	−4.8	− 6.6	−11.0
Roman Catholic	29	− .9	−3.2	−3.7	− 4.1	− 5.7
Jewish	6	− .4	− .4	− .6	− .9	− 1.0
None	9	−1.7	+5.7	+8.3	+10.1	+14.9

Note: Students choosing "other" religions are not shown.

tions over five different periods from half a year to four years after college entrance. The pattern is consistent and clear-cut: the number of students with a conventional religious preference (Protestant, Roman Catholic, or Jewish) declines substantially, while the percentage with no religious preference shows a corresponding increase. These changes are not abrupt, but they become increasingly larger with time. By the end of four years, the number of students in each of the three major religious categories has declined by about 20 percent while the number with no religious preference has increased by more than 50 percent.

These findings are consistent with a large body of earlier research documenting the progressive secularization of students' religious beliefs after college entry (Feldman and Newcomb, 1969). What factors account for these changes? Are some students more likely to change their beliefs than others? Does the environment of the college contribute to such changes? To what extent are these changes maturational? The answers to these questions vary for each religious position.

Protestant Affiliation. Even though the Protestant category comprises many diverse religions, the correlation between pretest and posttest responses is relatively high ($r = .67$). (Since both measures are dichotomous, this coefficient is actually a phi coefficient.) Parents' religion can affect students' chances of changing their own religious preferences from pretest to posttest. Protestant students whose parents' religion was also Protestant are more likely to maintain their Protestantism over time (partial $r = .23$) than students whose parents professed other religions. Another freshman characteristic positively related to a posttest preference for Protestantism is the behavioral factor "religiousness," which involves such items as praying and reading the Bible (see Chapter Three). The student's chance of indicating Protestantism on the follow-up is also negatively related to the "hedonism" behavioral factor (see Chapter Three) and to college admission test scores. In other words, even when the religion of the student and the parents at college entry is considered, the brighter and more hedonistic students are less likely to choose Protestantism four years later.

Living with parents as a freshman increases the student's chances of indicating Protestantism on the follow-up, whereas living in a dormitory or private room is negatively associated with this preference. This suggests that parental influence on students' traditional religious beliefs is diminished by going away from home to attend college.

Since the ACE-Carnegie follow-up also contained a religious preference item, it was possible to replicate the analysis of college impact on religious preference in two separate follow-ups. The results were confirmed in both: Attending a Protestant college reduces the student's chances of changing from Protestant to some other religious choice. But the strongest association occurs with other institutional characteristics: The student's chances of giving a Protestant preference on the follow-up are substantially reduced by attendance at a prestigious institution. Other institutional characteristics positively related to a Protestant religious choice are colleges for men, predominantly black colleges, and a southern location. Characteristics other than prestige that are negatively associated with the Protestant choice are being Roman Catholic or nonsectarian and institutional size.

Roman Catholic Affiliation. The pretest-posttest correlation for a Roman Catholic religious preference is also high ($r = .74$), which suggests considerable stability in this choice. Being reared as a Roman Catholic reduces the student's chances of switching to some other religion. Other entering characteristics positively associated with maintaining Catholic identification are attending a private high school and being Mexican-American. Women are less likely than men to drop their Catholic preference. Living with parents or in a private room as a freshman increases the student's chances of maintaining a Roman Catholic preference over time, while living in a dormitory decreases these chances. Analyses of the effects of college characteristics produced a pattern that also resembles that for Protestant choice. Thus, Roman Catholic choice is strengthened by attending a Roman Catholic institution or a men's college and weakened by attending a prestigious institution or a Protestant college. A midwestern location is also associated with maintaining a Catholic preference.

Jewish Affiliation. The pretest-posttest correlation for Jewish preference is the most consistent over the four-year period ($r = .83$). The only other entering characteristic with substantial predictive weight is having parents who are also Jewish. The student's living arrangements do not appear to affect a Jewish preference one way or another. In fact, the only college characteristic that contributes significantly to the prediction is a northeastern location. Since a high proportion of Jews in the United States live in the Northeast, this finding suggests that attending institutions in areas where the Jewish population is substantial reinforces the Jewish student's religious identification. Another possibility is that a northeastern location may be a surrogate measure of the closeness of the college to the student's home. In other words, Jewish students who attend college far from home (in regions other than the Northeast) may have more difficulty maintaining their Jewish identification than students who attend college close to home.

No Religious Affiliation. Expressing no religious preference on the follow-up was much more difficult to predict than preferences for the three major religious groups. The pretest-posttest correlation was only .32, and the multiple correlation involving all entering freshman characteristics was only .44. Nevertheless, a number of variables entered the regression analysis. The most important positive predictors are having parents with no religious preference and college admission test scores. Other student characteristics with significant positive associations are smoking and having artistic interests. The only student characteristic with a substantial negative predictive weight is the behavioral factor "religiousness" (see Chapter Three).

The student's freshman residence produces a clear-cut pattern of effects: Living with parents reduces the chances that the student will express no religious preference on the follow-up, whereas living either in a private room or in a dormitory increases those chances. Having no religious preference is most affected by attending a prestigious institution. This effect is greatest at the highly selective, nonsectarian colleges, the so-called elite colleges (Astin and Lee, 1971) and is more pronounced among women than men. The only other institutional characteristic consistently related to no religious choice is attending a Roman Catholic institution, which has a negative impact.

Maturation versus College Impact. Once students enter college, the trend is clearly toward greater secularization of religious beliefs. Are these changes merely developmental for persons in this age range, or does the college experience contribute

to the changes? Results with age of the entering students suggest that secularization is in part maturational: Older students
showed less change, even after other entering characteristics and
college characteristics had been controlled. However, since staying at home is associated with maintaining a conventional religious preference (independent of age) and going away is associated with changing to no preference, possibly these maturational changes are accelerated by exposure to the college
experience.

Results with the involvement factors from the ACE-
Carnegie follow-up generally confirm this conclusion. Verbal
aggressiveness is negatively associated with both Protestant and
Roman Catholic preferences and positively associated with no
preference. Conversely, the two involvement measures that
would tend to isolate students from the interpersonal effects of
the campus experience—academic and athletic involvement—are
positively associated with all three religious preferences and
negatively associated with no preference. While these results
suggest that college attendance contributes to the secularization
of students, they also indicate that the *quality* of the collegiate
experience can be critical in determining how that experience
affects the student's values and beliefs. Thus, while leaving
home to attend college increases the likelihood that students
will abandon their traditional religious affiliations, these effects
can be counteracted if the student becomes heavily involved in
either academic work or athletics.

Attitudes

Between 1940 and the early 1950s, research on college
impact focused on students' attitudes (Sanford, 1962). Since
many people assumed that one purpose of a liberal education
was to help the student become more tolerant and open-
minded, social psychologists and psychometricians carried out
considerable basic research in attitude measurement. Among
other things, they believed that attitudes formed the basis for
much human behavior and that, therefore, behavioral change
was predicated on attitudinal change.

Every freshman survey since 1967 has included attitudinal items to which students respond on a four-point scale of
the type devised by social psychologist Rensis Likert (1932):
"strongly agree," "agree somewhat," "disagree somewhat," and
"strongly disagree." The 1967 freshman questionnaire contained fifteen attitudinal items that were repeated in both one-
and four-year follow-ups in 1968 and 1971. One additional item
from the 1967 freshman questionnaire was repeated after one
year but not after four years.

Table 6 shows the changes in these items over the one-
and four-year intervals. An analysis of the correlations among
these items revealed only one clear-cut factor, which has been
labeled "student autonomy." The other items are listed under
"other attitudes" in descending order of the degree of change
between pretest and posttest. Almost without exception, the
degree of change over the four-year interval is greater than that
over the one-year interval. As with religious identification, these
data show that change in student attitudes is a gradual process
and does not occur abruptly on exposure to the college environment. Changes in most items from pretest to posttest support
the assumption that students become more autonomous, liberal,
and open-minded after they enter college. With respect to college life, the percentage of students advocating institutional
control over student behavior decreases. On more general issues,
students are less inclined to see women in traditional roles, are
more favorable toward legalizing marijuana, and are more likely
to support the publication of all scientific findings. The only
attitudinal change that runs counter to these trends concerns
preferential treatment for disadvantaged students in admissions.
The percentage of students endorsing this idea decreased slightly over both the one- and four-year intervals.

While these trends confirm much earlier evidence about
the effects of college attendance on student attitudes (Feldman
and Newcomb, 1969), the interval during which these data were
collected (1967-1971) was one of political unrest and rapid
change on many campuses, as well as in society at large. Do
some of these attitudinal changes reflect larger societal changes
rather than the effects of attending college per se? The surveys

Table 6. Changes in Attitude One and Four Years After College Entry

Attitudinal Item	Pretest-Posttest Correlations		Percentage Agreeing "Strongly" or "Somewhat"		
	1967-1968	1967-1971	As Freshmen 1967	After 1 Year (1967-1968)	After 4 Years (1967-1971)
Student Autonomy[a]					
Student publications should be cleared by college officials.	.44	.32	52.6	−14.8	−22.4
College officials have the right to ban persons with extreme views from speaking on campus.	.40	.28	41.0	− 8.7	−14.4
Most college officials have been too lax in dealing with student protests on campus.[b]	.40	.28	47.8	− 2.0	− 4.6
Colleges have the right to regulate student behavior off campus.[b]	–	–	22.5	−16.9	–
Other Attitudes					
The activities of married women are best confined to the home and family.	.51	.31	56.4	− 3.0	−32.9
Parents should be discouraged from having large families.	.53	.28	43.1	+ 2.1	+32.9
Marijuana should be legalized.[b]	–	–	20.1	+28.5	–
College faculty are more competent than students to specify curriculum.	.23	.11	85.8	−15.3	−24.7
The chief benefit of a college education is that it increases one's earning power.	.45	.30	57.3	−10.5	−20.7
Faculty promotions should be based in part on student evaluations.	.34	.19	61.9	+ 7.6	+19.5
Colleges would be improved if organized sports were deemphasized.	.44	.33	20.3	+ 2.1	+14.3
My beliefs and attitudes are similar to those of most other college students.	.37	.22	71.3	− 6.2	− 9.9
Scientists should publish their findings regardless of the possible consequences.	.36	.23	43.5	+ 5.7	+ 8.6
Students from disadvantaged backgrounds should be given preferential treatment in college admissions.	.36	.20	43.2	− 2.8	− 6.8
Women should be subject to the draft.	.52	.35	25.3	+ 1.9	+ 5.9
Realistically, an individual person can do little to bring about changes in our society.	.30	.19	33.3	+ 7.6	+ 5.4

[a]The first three items under this heading formed the only identifiable factor with loadings greater than .4 (loadings were .62, .59, and .53, respectively).

[b]Item (– dash) not included in 1967 freshman survey. Data shown are from 1968 freshman survey and follow-up one and one half years later in winter 1969-1970.

of consecutive entering freshman classes conducted each fall during this four-year period provided an opportunity to examine this question. Since the longitudinal follow-ups of the 1967 entering freshmen were conducted during late summer and early fall, the one-year follow-up was carried out at approximately the same time that the 1968 entering freshmen were surveyed, and the 1971 follow-up was carried out at about the same time that the 1971 freshmen were surveyed. If certain longitudinal changes observed in the 1967 freshmen actually reflect societal changes rather than the college experience, there should be comparable changes between successive classes of entering freshmen.

Table 7 shows the results of this comparison. In many cases, changes between successive classes of entering freshmen are nearly as great as longitudinal changes observed in the 1967 freshmen, particularly for items about student autonomy and large families. Changes in at least two other attitudes—legalizing marijuana and traditional views of women's role—appear to be a mixture of societal and developmental changes in students while they attend college. Apparently, increases in the students' need for autonomy and support for student power in the institution largely reflect general changes that occurred in society during the same period, while liberalization of student attitudes about marijuana and the role of women reflects a mixture of societal and developmental changes. These findings highlight one limitation of much of the earlier research on changes in student attitudes: *Longitudinal changes in attitudes may represent societal changes rather than changes attributable to the educational experience.*

This caution is not intended to denigrate the role of academic institutions in fostering social change. Indeed, a comprehensive analysis of campus protest during the late 1960s (Astin and others, 1975) suggested that campuses were frequently the locus for the development of protest movements that led to many changes both on and off campus. Table 7 may be showing a "trickle-down" effect of attitudinal changes that began on college campuses and eventually affected students in the secondary schools. That each entering freshman class since 1971 has

Table 7. Longitudinal Changes in Attitudes, Compared with Changes in Successive Entering Classes, Over One- and Four-Year Intervals

| | Percentage Agreeing "Strongly" or "Somewhat" | | | | | |
| | 1-Year Interval (1967-1968) | | 4-Year Interval (1967-1971) | | | |
Attitudinal Item	Longitudinal Change, 1967 Freshmen	Successive Classes, 1967, 1968 Freshmen	Longitudinal Change, 1967 Freshmen	Successive Classes, 1967, 1971 Freshmen
Student Autonomy				
Student publications should be cleared by college officials.	−14.8	+ 4.2	−22.4	−19.7
College officials have the right to ban persons with extreme views from speaking on campus.	− 8.7	− 7.8	−14.4	−11.7
Most college officials have been too lax in dealing with student protests on campus.	− 2.0	+ 6.7	− 4.6	− 1.3
Other Attitudes				
The activities of married women are best confined to the home and family.	−10.5		−32.9	−14.4
Parents should be discouraged from having large families.			+32.9	+26.3
Marijuana should be legalized.			+28.5[a]	+15.3[b]
The chief benefit of a college education is that it increases one's earning power.	−10.5	+ 1.8	−20.7	+ 2.8
Faculty promotions should be based in part on student evaluations.	+ 7.6	+ 1.0	+19.5	+13.8
Colleges would be improved if organized sports were deemphasized.			+14.3	+ 5.2
My beliefs and attitudes are similar to those of most other college students.	− 6.2	+ .1		
Scientists should publish their findings regardless of the possible consequences.	+ 5.7	+10.5		
Students from disadvantaged backgrounds should be given preferential treatment in college admissions.	− 2.8	− 1.7	− 6.8	− 3.1
Realistically, an individual person can do little to bring about changes in our society.	+ 7.8	− .8	+ 5.4	+10.0

[a]Item was not asked in 1967 survey. Data are for 1968 freshman survey and follow-up in winter 1969-1970.

[b]Average of change between 1968 and 1969 survey (+6.2 percent) and 1968 and 1970 survey (+24.4 percent).

shown increasing support for student autonomy and legalization of marijuana and decreasing support for the traditional women's role (Astin, King, and Richardson, 1976) supports this view.

Analyses of personal and environmental factors affecting student attitudes were carried out with a one-fourth sample (N = 8,590) of the 1967-1971 longitudinal sample. The fifty-one entering freshman characteristics included freshman pretests on each attitudinal item in addition to the usual demographic and background data (race, religion, age, sex, educational aspirations, and high school achievements). Although this particular sample did not include data on residence and other involvement variables, it did include nineteen college variables: selectivity, enrollment size, control (public, private-nonsectarian, Roman Catholic, Protestant), level (two-year, four-year, university), race, curricular focus (liberal arts, teachers' college, technical institution), sex (men only, women only), and region (Northeast, Midwest, South, West-Southwest).

Are changes in attitudes different for students of different sex, race, ability level, and socioeconomic background? Do changes depend on particular college experiences or types of college? These questions are explored separately for change in attitudes toward student autonomy and other issues.

Student Autonomy. Students who showed greater-than-expected increases in support for student autonomy include those who were reared as either Protestants or Jews, those whose parents were highly educated, and those with relatively high educational aspirations. By far the most important characteristic affecting support for greater student autonomy is institutional prestige: Attending a large and highly selective institution substantially strengthens students' commitment to greater student freedom and autonomy. Greater-than-expected increases are also associated with attending a teacher's college or a private nonsectarian institution. Smaller-than-expected increases are associated with attending a two-year college or an institution located in the South or West.

Other Student Attitudes. Because of the numerous attitudinal items and the great variations in the associated independent variables, the results from these individual items can be only briefly summarized. The entering freshman pretest was always the most potent predictor of follow-up attitudes four years later. However, other freshman predictors entered many stepwise regressions. One of the most potent was the student's religious background. Students from Jewish families show greater-than-average attitudinal changes in a liberal direction: discouragement of large families, drafting women, preferential treatment for disadvantaged students, and opposition to traditional roles for women. Both Protestant *and* Catholic students also show increasing support for discouraging large families. Women changed more than men: They show increasing support for deemphasizing athletics and basing faculty promotions on student evaluations, and decreasing support for traditional roles for women, faculty control over curriculum, and publication of scientific findings regardless of consequences. Students with superior grades in high school show decreasing support for preferential treatment for disadvantaged students and for the idea that the chief benefit of the college experience is monetary.

A number of college characteristics are associated with changes in student attitudes. Attending a highly selective college is associated with much-larger-than-expected declines in support for the notion that the chief benefit of college is monetary and for traditional roles for women, together with a larger-than-expected increase in support for discouraging large families. These findings reinforce once again the notion that the selective or elite college fosters development of liberal attitudes toward social issues.

Universities and two-year colleges produced contrasting effects on students' attitudes. Attending a university is associated with increased support for preferential treatment for disadvantaged students and deemphasis on athletics and with decreasing support for a traditional role for women and for the idea that the chief benefit of college is monetary. Attendance at a two-year institution produces a pattern of findings precisely the opposite. Attendance at Roman Catholic institutions is associated with smaller-than-expected increases in support for the discouragement of large families and for the idea that the chief benefit of college is monetary. Attendance at a Protestant institution, however, is associated with smaller-than-expected increases in opposition to the traditional role for women. Attending college in the Northeast is associated with decreasing support for traditional women's roles, faculty control over curriculum, and the idea that the chief benefit of college is monetary, whereas attending college in the South is associated with the opposite pattern of changes. Again, these findings support the view that the Northeast is a liberal region and the South conservative.

College Impact versus Maturation. The absence of residence and other involvement variables in the 1967-1971 data precluded any direct examination of the relative importance of maturational and college effects.

Age at college entry contributed significantly to the prediction of only three attitudes: faculty being more competent than students to specify the curriculum (positively), publishing scientific findings regardless of consequences (negatively), and the chief benefit of college being monetary (negatively). These results suggest that changes in the first two items may be in part maturational but that maturation may impede change in the third item. Perhaps the best clue concerning college impact versus maturation is provided by the pattern of college variables that affect attitudes. Changes in what could be considered a more liberal direction are positively associated with attending a selective or prestigious institution and negatively associated with attending an institution located in the South. This result precisely duplicated the pattern shown by the effects of college characteristics on political liberalism. Moreover, the association between attending a two-year college and attitudinal changes in a *less* liberal direction may well reflect the effects of residence rather than two-year college attendance per se. In the analysis of college effects on political liberalism, two-year college attendance is associated with conservative political beliefs, but this relationship disappears when residence (dormitory versus parents versus private room) is controlled. Although residential variables were not available in the 1967-1971 longitudinal file, it is reasonable to assume that living at home (which applies to most two-year college students) is associated with smaller-than-expected attitudinal changes in a liberal direction.

Summary

These longitudinal analyses show clearly that students undergo a variety of changes in attitudes, values, and self-concept after they enter college. These changes include a more positive self-image reflected in a greater sense of interpersonal and intellectual competence, more liberal political views and attitudes toward social issues, and a decline in traditional religious affiliation, business interests, and needs for status. Student attitudes toward campus and national issues tend to become more liberal after college entry, although some of these changes, particularly those supporting women's rights and greater student power and autonomy, appear to reflect larger societal changes rather than changes associated with college attendance.

The amount of change sometimes varies considerably by sex, race, and ability of the students. For example, declines in business interests, status needs, and athletic interests are much greater among women than among men. Women show greater increases in artistic interests and self-criticism, while men show greater increases in intellectual and interpersonal self-esteem. Blacks, compared with whites, show greater decreases in conventional religious preferences (Roman Catholic and Protestant) and greater increases in political liberalism. Finally, high-ability students, in contrast to low-ability students, show greater increases in intellectual self-esteem and political liberalism and greater decreases in conventional religious affiliation, business interests, and status needs. In fact, with the exception of interpersonal self-esteem (where high-ability students show smaller increases), high-ability students show greater changes than low-ability students on nearly every measure of attitude, value, and self-concept.

The amount of student changes also depends on the type of college. Table 8 summarizes the major environmental effects on each outcome. Attending a selective or prestigious institution is associated with greater-than-expected increases in political liberalism, including support for student power and autonomy, and larger-than-expected decreases in conventional religious affiliations and business interests. Contrary to educational folk-

Table 8. Summary of Effects of College Environment on
Student Attitudes, Beliefs, and Self-Concept

Student Outcome	Positive Effects	Negative Effects
Self Concept		
Liberalism versus conservatism	Living on campus	Southern institutions
	Women's colleges	
	Universities	
	Highly selective private colleges[a]	
	Research involvement[a]	
Interpersonal self-esteem	Private institutions	Southern institutions
	Living on campus	Black institutions
	Social fraternities or sororities[a]	Two-year colleges
	Honors programs[a]	
	Research involvement[a]	
Intellectual self-esteem	Honors programs[a]	
	Research involvement[a]	
Self-criticism	Selective institutions	Southern institutions
		Black institutions
Values		
Altruism	Catholic institutions	Western institutions
	Protestant institutions	Northeastern institutions
	Research involvement[a]	
Artistic interests	Women's colleges	Black institutions
	Private institutions	
	Living on campus	
	Honors programs[a]	
	Research involvement[a]	
Athletic interests	Selective institutions	Black institutions
	Research involvement[a]	
Business interests	Men's colleges	Selective institutions
	Social fraternities or sororities	Black institutions
Musical interests	Living at home	Northeastern institutions
	Research involvement	
Status needs	Selective institutions	Black institutions
	Social fraternities or sororities	
	Research involvement[a]	
Religious Affiliation		
Protestant	Men's colleges	Two-year colleges
	Protestant institutions	
	Black institutions	
	Living at home	
Roman Catholic	Men's colleges	
	Catholic institutions	
	Living at home	
Jewish		

Table 8 *(Continued)*

Student Outcome	Positive Effects	Negative Effects
None	Selective institutions Living on campus	Men's institutions Midwestern institutions Social fraternities or sororities
Attitudes		
Student autonomy	Selective institutions[a] Large institutions Teacher's colleges	Two-year colleges[a] Western institutions
Woman's place at home	Protestant institutions	Northeastern institutions Universities Selective institutions[a]
Discourage large families		Roman Catholic institutions
Deemphasize college sports	Universities[a]	Black institutions
Monetary benefit of college		Midwestern institutions Selective institutions[a]
Preferential treatment for disadvantaged	Universities Southern institutions	Two-year colleges[a]

[a]Highly significant $(p < .001)$ findings.

lore, attending a highly selective institution does not have a negative impact on the intellectual self-esteem of bright students. Attending either a Protestant or Roman Catholic college seems to retard the decline in traditional religious preferences and to strengthen students' altruistic tendencies. Attending a private nonsectarian institution, however, is associated with greater-than-average declines in traditional religious preferences and larger-than-average increases in liberalism, interpersonal self-esteem, artistic interests, and intellectual self-esteem. Attending a college for women increases political liberalism and artistic interests, whereas attending a college for men increases traditional religious affiliation and business interests. Attending a southern institution is associated with smaller-than-average increases in political liberalism, interpersonal self-esteem, self-criticism, and support for student power and autonomy. Pre-

dominantly black colleges are associated with decreases in interpersonal self-esteem, artistic interests, business interests, athletic
interests, and status needs. Attendance at two-year colleges is
associated with decreases in interpersonal self-esteem and in
support for both student autonomy and preferential treatment
for disadvantaged students.

Earlier studies suggesting that students' values and attitudes can be affected by their major fields of study (Southworth and Morningstar, 1970; Feldman and Newcomb, 1969;
Franks, Falk, and Hinton, 1973) were confirmed. Intellectual
self-esteem is enhanced by majoring in mathematics or natural
sciences. Majoring in social sciences seems to magnify increases
in interpersonal self-esteem, artistic interests, and liberalism and
to accelerate declines in business interests, while majoring in
engineering appears to have the opposite effects.

Analyses indicate that many of these affective changes
may be attributed in part to the college experience rather than
simply to maturational factors. Students who go away from
home to attend college, for example, show larger-than-average
increases in liberalism, interpersonal self-esteem, and artistic
interests and larger-than-average declines in traditional religious
preferences. (See also the study by Chickering and Kuper,
1971.) In addition, students who become involved in campus
life tend to change more than students who are relatively uninvolved. Interpersonal self-esteem appears especially sensitive
to the college experience, since persisters show substantially
larger increases than dropouts. On the other hand, attending
college appears to retard the decline in status needs.

How does this pattern of college effects relate to educational policy? Although a definitive policy analysis must incorporate findings from all chapters, the results presented in this
chapter appear to be relevant to at least two policies that have
characterized American higher education during recent years:
the massive expansion of public higher education and the increased emphasis on commuter colleges. Findings from this
chapter indicate that affective changes facilitated by the college
experience (increased liberalism, interpersonal self-esteem, and
artistic interests, for example) are enhanced both by the residen-

tial experience and by attending a private rather than a public institution. Apparently, the impact of the college experience is diluted for commuter students and for students attending public institutions. Is it possible that the educational experience of many students has been watered down by public policies that have led to a proliferation of public commuter colleges and a diminished role for the private residential college? Are poor and minority students differentially affected by such policies? These issues will be considered at greater length in Chapter Nine.

III

Patterns
of Behavior

Human behavior covers an almost infinite range of phenomena. The behavioral counterparts of the affective outcomes in Chapter Two include extracurricular activities, personal habits, and patterns of interaction with others. Different college experiences affect these behavioral patterns to varying degrees.

Despite the plethora of psychological studies using affective outcomes, most behavioral studies have been limited to cognitive outcomes, such as academic performance and persistence in college, which are discussed in Chapter Four. Aside from the relative ease of measuring affective-psychological outcomes, researchers may have favored such outcomes over their behavioral correlates on the assumption that psychological changes are

72

usually accompanied by behavioral changes. Although it is not the purpose here to review the extensive literature on the relationships between attitudes and behavior (see, for example, McGuire, 1969), behavioral outcomes are worthy of study in their own right. Indeed, such outcomes as attitudes and beliefs are of little social significance unless they are associated in some way with behavior.

Data on behavioral outcomes were obtained by utilizing the students as observers of their own behavior. When they first participate in CIRP, freshmen are asked whether or not—and sometimes how frequently—they have done certain things prior to entering college. Follow-up questionnaires ask whether students have done these same things after entering college. Behavioral items are basically of two types: discrete events such as getting married or joining a social fraternity or sorority, and activities about which students report frequency of participation ("frequently" = three, "occasionally" = two, "not at all" = one). This latter group includes a wide range of activities developed from an earlier study of college environments (Astin, 1968a). These two types of items were used to study the impact of college on fourteen behavioral outcomes: religiousness, hedonism, drinking, smoking, marriage, joining a social fraternity or sorority, participation in honors programs, academic involvement, involvement in student government, participation in student demonstrations, student-faculty interaction, familiarity with faculty in a major field, athletic involvement, and verbal aggressiveness. (For a discussion of involvement factors, see Chapter One.)

General Behavioral Factors

Behavioral changes between college entrance and the various follow-ups are summarized in Table 9. A factor analysis of the longitudinal data from the 1969-1970 ACE-Carnegie follow-up of 1966 freshmen reduced the large number of items to a smaller number of general behavioral factors. This analysis (described in Chapter Two) did not include all items in Table 9, since only eighteen of the forty items were pretested and post-

Table 9. Student Behavioral Changes After College Entry

Factor[a]	Percentage Engaging in Activity Prior to College Entry	Change in Percentage Engaging in Activity Over:				
		½ year (1969-1969)	1½ years (1968-1969)	2½ years (1967-1969)	3½ years (1966-1969)	4 years (1966-1970)
Religiousness						
Attended church[b] (.67)	63.5					−34.7
Attended Sunday school (.43)	57.4					−31.0
Prayed (excludes grace)[b] (.68)	48.8					−15.6
Said grace before meals[b] (.65)	35.5					−13.9
Hedonism						
Drank wine (.44)	39.9					+35.3
Drank beer (.62)	56.5	+ 6.6	+16.9	+17.5	+21.9	+27.9
Overslept, missed class or appointment (.33)	20.0	+23.2	+35.7	+29.8	+32.0	+26.7
Smoked cigarettes[b] (.49)	36.6[c]	+ 4.7	+ 8.2	+10.0	+11.1	+ 9.8
Stayed up all night (.42)	59.0	−15.6	− 4.0	− 8.6	− 6.2	+ 7.1
Gambled with cards or dice (.37)	35.5					− .7
Other Activities						
Took a nap or rest during the day	70.6		+11.5	+ 8.6	+17.5	+18.6
Came late to class	53.0	− .4				
Drove a car[b]	74.0					+12.6
Participated in a protest or demonstration	13.5					+12.4
Took tranquilizers	9.0	− 1.7	+ 3.5	+ 3.0		
Took sleeping pills	6.5	− .8	+ 2.2	+ 2.0		
Tutored another student	48.2	− 1.1	+ 1.9	+ 1.8		
Discussed politics	90.1	− 7.3	− 3.9	+ 1.2		
Studied in the library	92.5	− 5.2	− 4.1	− 4.1	+ .7	

Typed a homework assignment	78.0	− 8.2	− 6.0	− 3.9		
Attended a concert[b]	14.8				+ .4	− 4.9
Checked out a library book or journal	83.2	−24.6	−15.8	−11.0	− 4.5	− 6.0
Arranged a date for another student	47.8	−13.8	− 5.4	− 5.9	− 6.3	
Argued with an instructor in class	51.8	−23.2	−12.1	− 6.5		
Asked instructor for advice after class	92.8	−13.6	−10.7	− 9.3		
Took vitamins	59.5	−11.1	− 8.5	− 8.7		
Discussed sports	89.8	−10.4	− 9.8	−10.5		
Did extra (unassigned) reading for a course	78.2	−19.6	−16.3	−10.7		
Went to the movies[b]	48.2					−13.0
Discussed religion[b]	90.7	−10.4	−10.1	−14.0		
Played a musical instrument	27.0				−12.9	−14.3
Voted in a student election	93.6	−36.7	−22.4	−16.7	−14.6	
Had a blind date	43.8				−14.7	
Played chess	43.0		−17.0	−17.2		
Visited a museum	72.3	−27.4	−21.6	−18.1		
Failed to complete a homework assignment on time	71.0	−29.3	− 9.5	−22.5		
Had vocational counseling	57.2	−19.9	−23.6	−22.9		
Was active in a school political campaign	47.0	−34.9	−24.2			
Attended a religious service[b]	56.0	−16.3	−25.1			
Missed school because of illness[c]	76.1	−39.1	−30.3	−26.6		

[a]Numbers in parentheses indicate factor loading.

[b]Percentage responding "frequently" only. Others include "frequently" and "occasionally."

[c]Declines from 39.0 in 1966 to 34.2 in 1969.

tested in the 1966-1970 sample. Two clear-cut factors—religiousness and hedonism—emerged from this analysis. Religiousness involves a homogeneous set of items reflecting various religious activities: praying, saying grace before meals, and attending church and Sunday school. Each religious activity shows substantial declines after college entry. Hedonism, or devotion to pleasure as a life-style, combines a heterogeneous set of items relating to pleasure, socializing, and impulse expression: smoking, drinking, staying up all night, oversleeping and missing classes, and gambling. Three other items with relatively high loadings were not used in scoring the factor, because they showed declines rather than increases in frequency of occurrence after college entrance. These items were arranging a date for another student (factor loading = .48), going to an overnight or weekend party (factor loading = .38), and having a blind date (factor loading = .38). Although an item on marijuana use was not included in the questionnaires, the fact that using alcohol and tobacco is related to marijuana use (Dvorak, 1971) suggests that hedonism is also related to marijuana use.

Students undergo marked decreases in religiousness and increases in hedonism after entering college. The absolute level of these changes is substantial: Attendance at church and Sunday school is reduced by more than half, while one third fewer students pray frequently or say grace before meals. The number of wine drinkers nearly doubles, and the number of beer drinkers increases by 50 percent. Katz (1968) also reported substantial increases in drinking between high school and college. Cigarette smoking increases by 25 percent and the number of students who oversleep and miss classes more than doubles. Hedonism appears to increase gradually, the frequency of each activity increasing regularly with time in college.

Other activities that increase after college entrance include taking naps during the day, coming late to class, driving cars, and participating in demonstrations. Although the absolute increase in use of tranquilizers or sleeping pills is small (3 percent and 2 percent, respectively), the relative increase is substantial: About one third more students use these drugs after entering college. Many behaviors also decline in frequency after college entrance: The number of students who miss classes because of illness drops by one third. Both interaction with instructors and the rate of failing to complete homework on time decline somewhat. Despite increased hedonistic behavior, dating and movie attendance decline.

In certain respects, the patterns of change in smoking, drinking, demonstrating, sleeping habits, and use of tranquilizers and sleeping pills suggest that college attendance is often accompanied by substantially increased stress. It is somewhat surprising that the frequency of academic behavior declines sharply after college entrance, as evidenced by a reduction in library use, typing assignments, doing extra reading for a course, and interaction with instructors and as evidenced by an increase in coming late and missing classes. The only exception to this trend is the reduced frequency of not completing homework assignments on time. For most of these academic behaviors, the reduction during the freshman year is the most pronounced: The frequency of the activity actually increases during subsequent years. This reversal of the freshman decline occurs for studying in the library, typing homework assignments, arguing with instructors, asking instructors for advice, and doing extra reading. Familiarity with instructors and academic involvement in general seem to be lower during the freshman college year than during the senior high school year, but both increase the longer the student stays in college.

In most respects, these behavioral changes are consistent with the psychological changes reported in Chapter Two: Declines in traditional religious preferences are accompanied by greatly reduced church attendance and praying. Liberalization of beliefs and attitudes is accompanied by increased drinking and drug usage, and increased support for students' independence and autonomy is accompanied by a greater tendency to come late or miss class and decreased interaction with instructors. That certain measures and their parallel follow-ups (religious preference and religious behavior, for example) are significantly related even after freshman pretests on both are controlled indicates that these psychological and behavioral changes are directly related. Changes in attitudes or beliefs, in other words, are associated with changes in behavior.

Religiousness. The pretest-posttest correlation between

religiousness at the time of college entrance and four years later is substantial ($r = .58$), suggesting certain stability in the *relative* religiousness of students, despite the marked overall decline after college entry. Greater-than-average declines in religiousness occur among Jewish students and students with high freshman ratings on hedonism and high scores on college entrance tests. Smaller-than-expected decreases occur among students who attend private high schools. Although students reared as Protestants or Roman Catholics show quite a high degree of religiousness on the follow-up, the amount of *decline* from freshman to follow-up is greater than that for other students. This effect is especially pronounced among men and middle- and high-ability students. Apparently, the degree of religiousness of some entering Roman Catholic and Protestant students is less a matter of personal commitment than of direct parental influence and control.

Living in a dormitory during the freshman year is associated with greater-than-expected declines in religiousness, whereas living with parents is associated with smaller-than-expected declines. These effects appear among both men and women and all except low-ability students. Once again it appears that change may be attributed in part to the experience of attending college. The comparative impact on religiousness of dormitory living and living with parents is dramatized by changes in the correlations between 1966 and 1970. The degree of religiousness of students at college entrance is uncorrelated with their residence. Students who live on campus are no more or less religious than those who live at home. Four years later, however, religiousness is negatively correlated ($r = -.12$) with dormitory living during the freshman year. In other words, dormitory residents are no less religious than students living with parents when they enter college, but they are substantially less religious four years later.

Declines in religiousness are accelerated by attending a prestigious institution and, in particular, a highly selective private college. However, declines are also greater than expected among students attending public two-year colleges and private nonsectarian colleges, particularly those that are highly selective. Among women, attending a private two-year college is associated with smaller-than-expected declines in religiousness. Most of these institutions, however, are either Roman Catholic or "finishing schools" for women. Declines in religiousness are retarded by attending both selective and nonselective Roman Catholic institutions. Attending Protestant institutions, however, has no effect on religious behavior. Declines in religiousness are greater than expected among students at Southern colleges.

These effects are consistent with the environmental effects on religious affiliation (see Chapter Two). Living on campus rather than at home and attending a selective rather than a nonselective college increase the students' tendency to express no religious preference and decrease the tendency to pray and to attend church. An opposite pattern of psychological and behavioral effects is associated with attending men's colleges and Roman Catholic colleges. However, although attending a Protestant college increases the students' tendency to express a Protestant affiliation, it does not curtail the decline in religious behavior that occurs among most students after college entry.

Hedonism. The pretest-posttest correlation between freshman and follow-up measures of hedonism is only moderate ($r = .47$). Larger-than-average increases in hedonism occur among men, Roman Catholics, highly able students, and students with well-educated parents. Smaller-than-average increases occur among women, older students, and students with high scores on religiousness. Although students reared as Protestants have relatively low follow-up scores on hedonism, their *increases* in hedonism are actually greater than average.

Living in a college dormitory as a freshman is associated with greater-than-expected increases in hedonism, whereas living with parents is associated with smaller-than-expected increases. Here again is evidence that increasing hedonism results in part from the college experience. Attending a large institution increases hedonism, whereas smaller-than-expected increases are associated with attending private two-year colleges and colleges in the South. Among women attending religiously affiliated institutions, selective Roman Catholic colleges appear to decrease hedonism, while selective Protestant colleges increase it. Apparently, the degree of behavioral control (in loco parentis) is considerably greater at selective Roman Catholic institutions than at selective Protestant institutions. This finding would also account for the differential impact of Protestant and Catholic colleges on religious behavior.*

The fact that younger students show significantly greater increases in hedonism than older students suggests that the increases that occur after college entry are in part maturational. Most freshmen, for example, are not of legal drinking age when they enter college. The minority of freshmen who are older, however, have probably been on their own and have experienced some of the behaviors making up the hedonism factor. Nevertheless, the fact that increases in hedonism are greater among residents than among commuters suggests that the college experience accelerates this maturational effect. Perhaps the strongest evidence that college attendance affects hedonism is the finding that, even after entering student, college environmental, and involvement variables were controlled, increases in hedonism were substantially larger for persisters than for dropouts. The results with involvement variables also support this conclusion: Involvements of an interpersonal nature, such as political and verbal aggressiveness and membership in social fraternities or sororities, are positively related to increases in hedonism, whereas academic involvement has a pronounced negative correlation ($r = -.29$) with changes in hedonism. Apparently, becoming heavily involved in academic work deters the student from experimenting with this behavior.

Drinking and Smoking. Even though the hedonism factor includes items on smoking and drinking, these behaviors are of interest in themselves, given their obvious relationship to public health. The pretest-posttest correlation of .54 indicates that smoking behavior is relatively consistent over time. Most changes from freshman to follow-up occur among nonsmokers

*Effects of involvement variables on religiousness could not be examined, because items of religious behavior were not included in the 1969-1970 ACE-Carnegie follow-up questionnaire.

who become smokers during the four college years. Increasing tendencies as an undergraduate are especially strong among younger students, blacks, drinkers, and students with high interpersonal self-esteem.

A measure of freshman and follow-up drinking behavior was obtained by summing the scores on drinking beer and drinking wine. Consistency with this behavioral factor over time is substantially less than with smoking: The pretest-posttest correlation is only .36. Greater-than-average increases in drinking occur among men, Catholics, younger students, smokers, and students with strong athletic or business interests. Smaller-than-average increases occur among Jews and students with high intellectual self-esteem and strong artistic interests.

The effects of residence patterns are identical for both drinking and smoking behavior. Dormitory living during the freshman year and fraternity or sorority membership are associated with greater-than-average increases in both behaviors, whereas living with parents is associated with smaller-than-average increases. These results duplicate the findings reported for hedonism. The association between smoking and membership in fraternities or sororities has also been demonstrated in a recent national survey at fifty colleges (Dilley, 1971).

Except for the fact that attending a two-year institution is associated with reduced drinking and reduced smoking, the effects of college characteristics are quite different for these two behaviors. Smoking is positively related to attending a midwestern institution and negatively related to attending a western institution. Drinking behavior, on the other hand, is positively affected by a number of institutional types: prestigious or selective institutions, public institutions, Roman Catholic colleges, and black colleges.

Age has small but statistically significant negative relationships with increases in both drinking and smoking, a finding that suggests the presence of a significant maturational effect on these behaviors. The pattern of effects with involvement variables closely parallels the results with hedonism with one major exception: Athletic involvement, which had only a borderline relationship with hedonism, is positively associated with increases in drinking but negatively associated with increases in smoking. Possibly this result reflects the behavioral mores of athletic subcultures, where drinking is common but smoking is discouraged. In any event, the pattern of relationships of both smoking and drinking with involvement variables once again indicates that college attendance has a significant impact on these behaviors.

Analyses of smoking and drinking behavior provided the first opportunity to examine the impact of both *intensity of exposure* and *time of exposure* to the college environment. The only longitudinal data containing detailed information on total time in attendance was the 1972 follow-up of the 1968 freshmen. After eliminating students who had attended more than one institution, two basic groups were created: those who began college living at home (commuters) and those who began college living in dormitories (residents). These groups were used to create a matched "commuter-resident" file and two matched "time-in-attendance" files. The time-in-attendance files were formed by first dividing commuters and residents separately into three subgroups on the basis of how much college they *completed*: less than two years, two years but less than four, and four or more years. The matched files were then created by selecting students so that any given college had equal numbers of students in each attendance category (usually this required randomly eliminating some students from the middle- and long-attendance categories). The matched commuter file comprised three groups of 590 students each, and the matched resident files included 558 students in each of the three groups. Next, a second independent "commuter-resident" file was created by using only students who had stayed at least four years and by selecting equal numbers of commuters and residents from each college. Note that this file, which contains 2,222 commuters and 2,222 residents, controls for time in attendance, and that time-in-attendance files control for commuter-resident status.

The arguments presented in Chapter One indicate that "true" college effects (as opposed to purely maturational effects or other artifacts) should be stronger with (1) longer exposure to the college environment and (2) more intense exposure.

Separate analyses of smoking and drinking behavior in all sets of matched files largely confirms these expectations. For example, the increase in both drinking and smoking behavior (from 1968 pretest to 1972 posttest) is greater among residents than among commuters and greatest among those who stay in college for four years. In fact, students who stay less than two years were the most frequent drinkers of the three groups when they first entered college and the least frequent four years later. Students who stay four years were the least frequent drinkers when they started college and the most frequent at the time of the follow-up. These differential changes occur among both commuters and residents.

Multivariate analyses produced similar results. The *importance* of college variables, as measured by increases in the proportion of smoking or drinking variance accounted for by college characteristics (after entering student characteristics had been controlled), was greater both for commuters and for students who stayed in college four years.

In short, these additional analyses of matched files provide strong support for the hypothesis that the college experience contributes significantly to the increased hedonism observed among young people after they enter college.

Marriage. Getting married is one of those behavioral outcomes that cannot be "pretested." Marriage-proneness at the time of college entry can, however, be estimated simply by inquiring about future marriage plans. Entering freshmen questionnaires over the years have asked students to make two estimates: chances of marrying while enrolled and chances of marrying within one year after leaving college. Both questions are answered on a four-point scale: "no chance," "very little chance," "some chance," and "very good chance."

The 1971 follow-up of the 1967 freshmen offered the best data for assessing college impact on marriage. In addition to providing the two entering freshmen estimates, these students responded four years later as to whether they were still single or whether they had been married prior to college entry, during college, or after leaving college. The following results were obtained after eliminating those students who were married at the time of college entry (only 2.4 percent of the total sample).

Table 10 examines the accuracy of the students' freshmen predictions. Results indicate that both estimates have some

Table 10. Marriage Predictions of 1967 Entering Freshmen
Followed Up in 1971 (in Percentages)

Marriage Prediction[a]	Percent Making Prediction at College Entry	Percent Married at Follow-Up	Percent Marrying	
			While in College	After College
While in college				
No chance	27.5	20.9	8.7	12.2
Little chance	44.1	27.7	12.8	14.9
Some chance	22.3	39.7	22.5	17.2
Very good chance	6.2	66.4	42.5	23.9
Within one year after college				
No chance	17.2	26.0	13.3	12.7
Little chance	25.4	25.4	12.5	12.9
Some chance	38.1	30.3	14.8	15.5
Very good chance	19.3	44.0	23.8	20.2

[a]Students married at college entry have been omitted.

validity: Among students who say their chances of getting married while in college are good, the percentage who actually do (42.5 percent) is nearly five times greater than the percentage of those who say they have no chance (8.7 percent). Predictions using a *combination* of the two items are not much better than predictions from either item used alone. For example, among students who say their chances of getting married are very good in response to *either* item, 47.9 percent get married after entering college. This result is only slightly better than the individual prediction about getting married within a year after college (44.0 percent) and worse than the prediction about getting married while in college (66.4 percent). Similarly, among students who say they have "no chance" of getting married in response to *both* questions, 16.9 percent are married at the time of the follow-up, as compared to 20.9 percent among those who say they have no chance of getting married while in college.

Which entering freshmen are most likely to get married after college entry? By far the largest predictive weight is associated with plans to get married while in college ($r = .26$). Plans for marrying after college carry only a small additional weight. Women are substantially more likely to get married than are men, even after initial marriage plans are controlled. Four other entering characteristics contribute negative weights: being black, being reared as a Jew, having a highly educated mother, and plans to participate in student demonstrations. One can only speculate about the possible meaning of these additional predictors. In the case of blacks, economic constraints may reduce the likelihood of marriage. As for students from highly educated parents or students whose parents are Jewish, family pressure to stay in college and to complete their studies may serve to deter them from early marriages.

Since the 1967-1971 data did not include information on the student's place of residence, it was not possible to assess the impact of residential variables on marriage. However, the fact that attending a two-year institution (where most of the students are commuters) does not significantly affect marriage chances suggests that living in a dormitory may not be a significant factor. As a matter of fact, the only institutional effects on getting married are of borderline significance ($.01 < p < .05$): Negative effects are associated with attending a highly selective institution, a liberal arts college, or an institution located in the Midwest or Northeast.

Perhaps the most notable result is the failure to replicate the finding that attending a coeducational institution rather than a single-sex college increases marriage chances. A similar result using CIRP data was reported recently by Bayer (1972). The studies thus conflict with an earlier study by Bayer (1969), which also controlled for a number of entering freshman characteristics but which did not include a measure of marriage plans at the time of college entry.

Is the negative finding in the current study attributable to the use of this additional control? To explore this possibility the simple and partial correlations among sex of college attended, initial marriage plans, and getting married were examined. Students entering single-sex institutions are (1) less likely to plan marriage during college than students entering coeducational institutions and (2) less likely to get married. When initial marriage plans are controlled, differences in marriage rates between students in single-sex and coeducational institutions disappear. Failure to control for initial marriage plans would lead to the conclusion that attending a coeducational institution increases the student's chances of getting married. In short, it appears that the positive findings of earlier studies were attributable to the lack of a measure of marriage plans at entry, rather than to the effects of coeducational versus single-sex institutions. Once again, these results underscore the importance of having adequate controls of entering freshmen characteristics in attempting to assess the impact of institutions on student behavior.

Joining Social Fraternities and Sororities. When the 1968 freshmen were followed up in 1972, nearly one third (32.8 percent) indicated that they had "joined a social fraternity, sorority, or club" while in college. Results with the 1967 freshmen were similar. Exactly one third reported joining in the 1971 follow-up. The students' freshman estimates of their chances of joining a social club were quite accurate: Of those who estimated their chances as very good, 52 percent actually did join a social fraternity or sorority, compared with only 14 percent of those who said they had no chance. These percentages were the same for both 1967 and 1968 freshmen.

Analyses of the effects of entering student and college environmental characteristics used longitudinal data from the more recent (1968-1972) sample. Plans to join a fraternity or sorority carries by far the most predictive weight ($r = .28$). Other entering characteristics with significant positive weights are being male and four measures of student accomplishment in high school: good grades, being a varsity athlete, being elected president of a student organization, and publishing original writing. These predictors suggest that social fraternities and sororities place a premium on academic and extracurricular talent in recruiting members. Negative predictors of joining a fraternity or sorority include plans to participate in demonstrations and having no religious preference. These student attributes reinforce the notion that "independents"—the popular designation for students who are not members of social fraternities or sororities—are nonconformists.

Students are most likely to join a fraternity or sorority if they attend a nonselective Protestant college, a highly selective nonsectarian college, or a college in the South. Students are least likely to join in public two-year institutions. Women are more likely to join sororities in coeducational than in women's colleges, and blacks are more likely to join fraternities or sororities in predominantly black than in predominantly white institutions. To a large extent, these institutional effects probably reflect the relative availability of social fraternities and sororities in different types of institutions.

Involvement Factors

The involvement measures derived from the 1969-1970 ACE-Carnegie follow-up of 1966 entering freshmen are basically behavioral in content. Although equivalent pretests from the entering freshman data are not available for all factors, the entering characteristics that predict various types of involvement can be identified. Analyses are presented for the following involvement factors: academic involvement, participation in honors programs, student-faculty interaction, familiarity with faculty in major field, verbal aggressiveness, involvement in student government and demonstrations, and athletic involvement.

Academic Involvement. By far the strongest predictor of academic involvement in college is the student's pretest score on hedonism (r = .23). Total dedication to academic pursuits usually requires a good deal of self-denial and the ability to postpone gratification. Students with strongly hedonistic tendencies may find it difficult to marshal the self-discipline necessary for heavy involvement in academic pursuits. Other positive predictors of academic involvement are good grades in high school, religiousness, and frequent use of the library during high school. Negative predictors include artistic interests, political liberalism, intellectual self-esteem, no religious preference, and being black. College characteristics had only weak relationships with academic involvement. Students are somewhat more likely to get involved academically if they attend a college for women or a two-year college, and somewhat less likely to get involved if they attend a teacher's college, a prestigious institution, or an institution located in the Northeast. The fact that academic involvement is more likely to occur in two-year institutions where opportunities for interaction with peers are usually limited underscores the interpretation that this particular form of involvement may insulate the student from peer and other kinds of interpersonal impacts during college.

Honors Programs. Students most likely to participate in honors programs in college are those with high grades in high school ($r = .24$). Other positive predictors include high intellectual self-esteem, artistic interests, aspirations for advanced degrees, and having a scholarship. Additional freshman predictors with small positive weights include being older than average at college entry, being president of a student organization in high school, and having highly educated and affluent parents.

Students' chances of participating in honors programs are increased at colleges for men and decreased at large and prestigious institutions and institutions located in the western states. The negative effects of institutional prestige no doubt reflect the high academic competition at a selective institution. A highly able student is more likely to stand out in a less selective institution. The negative effects of institutional size may indicate that honors programs are available to only a relatively small proportion of students in large institutions.

Student-Faculty Interaction. The strongest predictor of student-faculty interaction ($r = .18$) is the student's interpersonal self-esteem at college entry. The fact that this attribute has a substantial partial correlation with faculty-student interaction even after the other freshman and college characteristics enter the regression suggests that confidence in interpersonal skills leads to more contact with faculty, regardless of the type of institution. Other positive predictors of student-faculty interaction are frequent use of the library in high school, religiousness, musical interests, altruism, and artistic interests. Because the multiple correlation involving all these entering characteristics was only .26, student-faculty interaction appears to depend largely on factors other than student characteristics at college entry.

Students living in dormitories at the time of the 1969-1970 follow-up were much more likely to interact with faculty than were students living with parents. (The ACE-Carnegie follow-up did not inquire about the freshman residence.) However, by far the most important institutional characteristic affecting student-faculty interaction is size ($r = -.21$). Attending a four-year college, rather than a university or two-year college, is positively associated with student-faculty interaction, even after controlling for institutional size. Student-faculty interaction is also greater at single-sex colleges than at coeducational institutions, but it is somewhat below expectation at technological institutions. Student-faculty interaction is slightly above expectation at institutions in the South.

The negative association between institutional size and student-faculty interaction has been noted before (Astin, 1963b, 1968a). This outcome counters the folklore about student-faculty relations: The fewer students per faculty member, the greater the faculty-student interaction. In reality, student-faculty ratio has no direct relationship to interaction after institutional size and type have been controlled. At least two factors may be at work here. First is the considerable bureaucracy that characterizes many larger institutions. The complex administrative superstructure may create a formal or impersonal atmosphere that discourages direct contact between faculty and students. Second is the strong faculty emphasis on research and departmental affiliations in most large research-oriented institutions. In such institutions, paying attention to undergraduates often has lower priority than departmental research activities and concern with graduate students. Gaff's (1973) description of the faculty at the University of California at Berkeley is consistent with such a characterization. In this sense, the findings clearly confirm the stereotype of the large multiversity as an impersonal institution that discourages direct contact between faculty and students.

Familiarity with Faculty in Major Field. Entering student characteristics that predict familiarity with professors in the students' majors are similar to those for student-faculty interaction, although the relationships are generally smaller. Students are more likely to have a high degree of familiarity if they display high interpersonal self-esteem, religiousness, and frequent use of the library during high school. Other freshman characteristics with borderline positive relationships include high school grades, having a scholarship, aspiring to higher degrees, and participation in varsity athletics. Plans to marry in college are negatively related to this involvement factor.

Familiarity with professors in the major field is affected by a pattern of college variables that closely parallels that for faculty-student interaction. A high degree of familiarity exists in the smaller four-year colleges, whereas technological institutions show a low degree of familiarity. Two additional institutional characteristics are positively associated with familiarity but not with student-faculty interaction: high cost and prestige. The positive relationship with prestige is somewhat complex, given the fact that institutional size, which is negatively related to familiarity, is one ingredient in prestige. Thus, for institutions of a given size, students are on more familiar terms with professors in their major fields in the prestigious institutions.

This contrast involving institutional prestige provides material for speculation: After entering student characteristics are controlled, prestige correlates $-.07$ with overall student-faculty interaction but $+.07$ with familiarity with professors in the major field. When size is controlled, the negative relationship with student-faculty interaction disappears, but the positive relationship with familiarity remains. This result indicates that, even though the overall degree of student-faculty interaction in the more prestigious institutions is below average because of those institutions' larger size, the degree of familiarity between students and their major professors is above average. Perhaps students in the more prestigious institutions have little contact with professors outside their field, but contacts within the field are relatively frequent. Among other things, this result suggests that students in the more prestigious institutions are more strongly oriented toward their majors than are students in the less prestigious colleges and universities.

Verbal Aggressiveness. Once again interpersonal self-esteem proves to be the most potent predictor of an involvement factor ($r = .19$). Hedonism runs a close second ($r = .18$, partial $r = .15$). Significant positive weights are also associated with being male, being self-critical, having strong artistic interests, and using the library in high school frequently. Borderline positive weights are associated with being elected president of a high school organization, having highly educated parents, being politically liberal, having high intellectual self-esteem, and being Jewish or having no religious preference.

Verbal aggressiveness is influenced by a configuration of college characteristics similar to those that affected the preceding two faculty involvement measures. Students are most likely to display verbal aggressiveness if they attend small four-year colleges rather than large universities. Students also display more verbal aggressiveness if they attend colleges in the Northeast or colleges for women. The latter relationship raises some provocative questions: Given the stereotyped sex roles of male dominance and female submissiveness (apparently manifest in the simple correlation of .10 between verbal aggressiveness and being male), does the presence of men in the classroom inhibit women from asserting themselves? Are women more likely to be verbally aggressive in an all-female class?

Involvement in Student Government and Demonstrations. As with the three preceding involvement factors, involvement in student government is most strongly related ($r = .18$) to interpersonal self-esteem. Other positive predictors are being president of a high school organization, frequent use of the library, religiousness, and altruism. These latter two predictors reinforce the notion that aspiring to leadership is in part a manifestation of social or humanistic concerns. Other predictors with small positive weights are having affluent and highly educated parents, aspiring to higher degrees, being black, and having a Protestant or a Roman Catholic affiliation. Minor negative predictors include plans to marry in college, being a smoker, and being Jewish.

Interpersonal self-esteem is the best predictor of four involvement factors. These four—student-faculty interaction, familiarity with faculty in major, verbal aggressiveness, and involvement in student government—require substantially more interpersonal interaction on a verbal level than the other three factors (honors programs, academic involvement, and athletic involvement). Apparently, becoming personally involved with faculty and students in college is one behavioral manifestation of high interpersonal self-esteem. Clearly, involvement of this type requires a certain initiative and assertiveness by the student, regardless of environment. These results provide additional support for the notion that athletic and academic involvement, in contrast to other forms, are frequently not interpersonal and serve in part to isolate the student from effects of peers and faculty.

Students living in dormitories at the time of the 1969-1970 ACE-Carnegie follow-up were much more likely ($r = .22$) than students living with parents to be involved in student government. Similar findings have been reported by Baird (1969) and Chickering (1974a). Students in small four-year colleges are also more likely than those in two-year colleges or universities to get involved in student government. Participation in student government is positively related to attending an institution in the South but negatively related to attending a prestigious institution.

A behavioral outcome of considerable significance during the late 1960s was participation in college demonstrations. Table 9 shows that students in college demonstrated more frequently than those in high school, at least during the late 1960s. Are the personal and environmental factors that predict political activism similar to those that influence participation in traditional campus political organizations? To explore this question, longitudinal data from the 1971 follow-up of 1967 entering freshmen were utilized. This file contains an entering freshman self-prediction about plans to participate in demonstrations, as well as a follow-up question about actual participation in college. Plans to participate in demonstrations carry the largest weight ($r = .29$). Although this correlation seems modest, entering students who estimate their chances of demonstrating as "very good" are about five times more likely to participate in demonstrations (57 percent actually do) than students who say they have "no chance" at college entry (11 percent actually demonstrate in college). Other positive predictors of participation are being Jewish, being black, recognition in the National Merit Scholarship competition, having high educational aspirations, and having highly educated parents. Demonstrating is also related to support for student autonomy, as indicated by the *negative* predictive weights associated with three freshman attitudinal items: banning extremist speakers from the campus, clearance of student publications by college officials, and laxity of college officials in dealing with campus protestors. These results are consistent with earlier studies of student characteristics that predict participation in campus protests (Astin and others, 1975).

Three college variables entered the regression equation with positive weights after entering student characteristics had been controlled: selectivity, university, and northeastern location. Being located in the South had a substantial relationship that disappeared when three institutional characteristics were controlled. Again, these results are consistent with earlier studies showing that campus protests are much more likely to occur in large and highly selective institutions (Astin and others, 1975). Moreover, the findings provide additional evidence of the political contrast between the South and Northeast: Attending a southern rather than northeastern institution not only reduces the student's chances of becoming involved in protests but also attenuates the liberalizing trend in political beliefs (see Chapter Two).

Participation in demonstrations provides interesting similarities and contrasts to involvement in student government. Both outcomes are more likely to occur among blacks, students with high aspirations, and students from highly educated families. Involvement in student government, however, is closely associated with interpersonal self-esteem and religiousness, whereas involvement in demonstrations is related to political liberalism and support for student autonomy. Furthermore, being Jewish is positively related to demonstrating but *negatively* related to participation in student government. Even sharper contrasts occur in the effects of college characteristics. A given student is more likely to participate in demonstrations at a university or highly selective institution but *less* likely to become involved in student government. Similarly, whereas students are more likely in southern institutions and less likely in northeastern institutions to become involved in student government, these effects are reversed for demonstrating.

Athletic Involvement. By far the best predictor of athletic involvement ($r = .51$) is athletic interest at college entry. Other entering characteristics, however, add significantly to the prediction. Substantial positive weights are associated with winning a varsity letter in high school, being male, religiousness, and hedonism. Substantial negative weights are associated with artistic interests, being a smoker, and having no religious preference. This pattern of predictors supports the stereotype of the college athlete as masculine, conventionally religious, and pleasure seeking, although abstaining from cigarettes.

A number of institutional characteristics are related to athletic involvement after entering student characteristics are controlled. Institutional size is negatively related to athletic involvement: Any given student's chances of being on a varsity team are reduced if the student body is large. Athletic involvement is positively affected by attending a Protestant college or a college in the South, and negatively affected by attending a college in the Midwest. The most notable results occurred with single-sex institutions: Attending a men's college substantially increases a man's chances of becoming involved in athletics, but attending a women's college substantially decreases a woman's chances. Given the large sex differences in athletic interests and involvement, as mentioned before, it seems likely that these contrasting effects of men's and women's colleges can be traced to their dramatically different environments. A study of college environments (Astin, 1968a) has shown that all-male and all-female colleges differ most in terms of a bipolar factor labeled "cooperativeness versus competitiveness." There is no overlap between the two groups of this factor: Colleges for men cluster

at the competitive end and colleges for women at tl
tive end.

Summary

Students undergo a number of behavioral changes
entering college. Most dramatic is the decrease in religious behavior and the accompanying increase in hedonistic behavior
(drinking, smoking, partying, gambling, and so forth). Other
behaviors that increase in frequency are use of automobiles, participation in protests and demonstrations, coming late to class,
and using tranquilizers and sleeping pills. Behaviors that decrease in frequency after entering college include dating, missing
homework assignments, attending movies, playing musical instruments, and missing school because of illness. Interaction
with instructors and various indices of academic involvement
(typing assignments, doing extra reading, studying in the library)
decline sharply between high school and the freshman year but
then increase gradually in subsequent years.

Behavioral changes vary for different types of students.
Compared with women, men show larger declines in religiousness and larger increases in hedonism—particularly drinking.
Women, however, are more likely to marry. College men have a
greater propensity to be verbally aggressive and to get involved
in athletics. Women are slightly more likely to become heavily
involved in academic activities.

Compared with white students, blacks are more likely
to increase their smoking, to participate in demonstrations,
and to get involved in student government. Whites are more
likely to become involved with their academic work and to
marry. Highly able students, compared with less able students,
show much larger declines in religiousness and slightly larger increases in hedonism during the college years. These findings are
consistent with the relationships between ability and increases
in religious apostasy reported in Chapter Two. Highly able students are also much more likely to participate in honors programs and to become involved with their academic work. Again,
these findings are consistent with the positive relationship be-

tween ability and increases in intellectual self-esteem reported in Chapter Two.

The fact that older students show smaller increases in hedonism suggests that these increases are in part maturational. However, increases in hedonism are much greater among students who stay in college than among those who drop out and also greater among students who live on campus than among those who live at home (Table 11), which suggests that the

Table 11. Major Environmental Effects on Student Behavior

Behavior	Environmental Effects	
	Positive	Negative
Religiousness	Roman Catholic colleges[a]	Dormitory living[a]
	Southern institutions[a]	Prestigious institutions
	Living at home[a]	Large institutions
	Private two-year colleges	Public two-year colleges
		Private nonsectarian colleges
		Northeastern institutions
Hedonism	Fraternities and sororities[a]	Living at home[a]
	Dormitory living[a]	Southern institutions
	Involvement in student government[a]	Private two-year colleges
	Large institutions	
	Support from parents	
	Verbal aggressiveness	
Drinking	Fraternities and sororities[a]	Living at home[a]
	Dormitory living[a]	Private institutions
	Involvement in student government[a]	
	Athletic involvement[a]	
	Prestigious institutions	
Smoking	Fraternities and sororities	Prestigious institutions
	Dormitory living	Private institutions
	Verbal aggressiveness	Living at home
		Athletic involvement
Marriage	Southern institutions	Northeastern institutions[a]
	Western institutions	Midwestern institutions
		Liberal arts colleges
		Selective institutions
Participation in demonstrations	Universities[a]	Southern institutions
	Northeastern institutions[a]	Western institutions
	Selective institutions[a]	
Academic involvement	Colleges for men	Northeastern institutions[a]
	Colleges for women	Coeducational institutions
		Prestigious institutions
		Teacher's colleges

Table 11 *(Continued)*

Behavior	Environmental Effects	
	Positive	Negative
Participation in honors programs	Colleges for men[a]	Large institutions[a]
	Small colleges[a]	Selective institutions[a]
	Support from a scholarship	Colleges for women
Student-faculty inter-action	Private institutions[a]	Universities[a]
	Four-year colleges[a]	Coeducational institutions[a]
	Colleges for men[a]	Large institutions[a]
	Colleges for women[a]	Living with parents[a]
	Dormitory living[a]	Teacher's colleges
	Small colleges[a]	Technical institutions
	Religious colleges	Prestigious institutions
Familiarity with faculty in major field	Private institutions[a]	Technical institutions[a]
	Four-year colleges[a]	Universities[a]
	Small colleges[a]	Large institutions[a]
	Southern institutions	Western institutions
	Colleges for women	Two-year colleges
	Protestant colleges	
	High-cost colleges	
Verbal aggressiveness	Northeastern institutions[a]	Large institutions[a]
	Four-year colleges	Coeducational institutions
	Small colleges[a]	Two-year colleges
	Colleges for women[a]	Western institutions
	Colleges for men	
Involvement in student government	Southern institutions[a]	Western institutions[a]
	Private institutions[a]	Universities[a]
	Dormitory living[a]	Two-year colleges[a]
	Four-year colleges	Prestigious institutions[a]
	Colleges for women	Living at home[a]
	Religious colleges	Large institutions
	Small colleges	
Athletic involvement	Four-year colleges[a]	Colleges for women[a]
	Colleges for men[a]	Large institutions[a]
	Small institutions[a]	Two-year colleges
	Southern institutions	Midwestern institutions
	Protestant colleges	

[a]Highly significant ($p < .001$) findings.

college experience also contributes to this behavioral change. The positive association of hedonism with two interpersonal involvement variables—verbal aggressiveness and participation in student government—reinforces this conclusion. Students who join fraternities and sororities show larger increases in hedonism, whereas students who attend private two-year colleges or colleges in the South show smaller increases. Results with religiousness are similar: Students who live on campus show much larger decreases than students who live at home, whereas students who attend private two-year colleges, Roman Catholic colleges, or colleges in the South show the smallest declines in religious behavior.

Students attending institutions in the South or West are most likely to get married, whereas those attending an institution in the Northeast have decreased chances of marrying. Previous studies showing that attendance at a coeducational college increases the student's marriage chances were not replicated; apparently, this difference may be attributed to the inclusion in the present study of a control for the student's marriage plans at college entry. Students attending coeducational colleges are more likely to plan on earlier marriages than students attending single-sex institutions. Once these entering marriage plans are controlled, the sex designation of the institution shows no relationship to the student's chances of marrying.

Almost all forms of student involvement in campus life are increased by attending a small rather than a large institution. Students at small colleges are more likely to interact with faculty, to get involved in campus governance, to participate in athletics, to get involved in honors programs, and to be verbally aggressive in their classrooms. The only exception is student involvement in demonstrations, which is increased by attending large and selective institutions. Single-sex colleges, compared with coeducational institutions, increase the student's chances of becoming involved in academic pursuits, of being verbally aggressive in the classroom, and of interacting with faculty. Attending an all-male institution increases the man's chances of participating in honors programs and of becoming involved in athletics, whereas the opposite pattern occurs for women: Attending an all-female college decreases their chances of participating in honors programs or of becoming involved in athletics.

These findings lend further support to the policy issues mentioned briefly in Chapter Two. That is, students who attend private colleges and students who live in dormitories rather than at home are most likely to exhibit those behavioral changes that result from college attendance: decreased religiousness, increased hedonism, and involvement in campus life. These behavioral findings reported here are relevant to at least two other educational issues: the trend toward larger institutions and the recent conversion of most single-sex colleges to coeducational colleges. Large institutions, in contrast to small colleges, substantially reduce the student's chances of involvement in a wide range of activities: honors programs, student-faculty interaction, student government, and athletics. Single-sex colleges, in contrast to coeducational institutions, foster greater academic involvement, verbal aggressiveness, and student-faculty interaction. (For a fuller discussion of these issues, see Chapter Nine.)

IV

Competency and Achievement

Many educators and policymakers will argue that the principal purposes of higher education are to develop students' intellectual and vocational skills and to prepare them for the world of work. Indeed, of all the possible outcomes of higher education, learning and credentialing are probably given the most weight by students, parents, educators, and policymakers alike. This emphasis is reflected in the many studies predicting student grade-point averages and persistence.

This chapter examines the impact of the college experience on four areas of competency and achievement: academic achievement (traditional grade-point average, graduation with honors), educational attainment (persistence versus dropping

100

out, enrollment in graduate or professional schools, and aspirations for higher degrees), extracurricular achievements (leadership, journalism, science, creative writing, theater, and athletics), and specialized competencies and skills.

Academic Achievement

Academic achievement is surely the most researched topic in higher education. Hundreds of studies using various measurements and methodologies have yielded strikingly similar results: Undergraduate grades can be predicted with modest accuracy (multiple correlations around .55) from admissions information, and the two most potent predictors are the student's high school grade-point average and scores on college admissions tests. Grades almost always carry more weight than tests.

Few studies of undergraduate grades have involved more than one institution. Indeed, some researchers and educators will argue that predicting grade-point averages across different colleges simultaneously makes little sense, since grading systems and academic standards differ so much. Perhaps one of the most telling arguments against the use of grades is that they are *relative* indices and therefore are poor measures of student growth and development. Grades, it is argued, reflect only how the student is performing relative to other students at a given point in time, not necessarily what has been *learned* (Astin, 1974). There has been some pressure among educators and students to replace traditional grading systems with performance measures that reflect student growth and development through repeated pretesting and posttesting.

In spite of the advantages of measures that reflect student changes over time, institutions continue to rely heavily on traditional letter grades to assess student achievement. Even the students seem to have accepted the system, since the proposal to abolish college grades, relatively popular during the late 1960s (Astin and others, 1969), has declined rapidly and is now endorsed by only a small minority of students (Astin, King, and Richardson, 1976). Poor grades are still sufficient grounds for dismissal in many colleges, and high grades are necessary for admission to most graduate and professional schools. For these reasons, college grades continue to represent an important index of student accomplishment in college.

Grade-Point Average. Since information on cumulative undergraduate grade-point averages was obtained in all follow-ups, it was possible to replicate the analysis of environmental effects on grade-point average across several samples. The results were strikingly similar. High school grades are by far the best predictor of college grades; the simple correlation averages around .50. Even if one ignores college characteristics, high school grades are a reasonably accurate predictor of college grades.

How accurate are students' predictions about their chances of earning good grades in college? Table 12 shows these

Table 12. Students Earning at Least a B+ Average in College, as a
Function of Freshman Predictions and High School Grades
(in Percentages)

Average High School Grade	Entering Freshman Estimates of Chances for at Least an A— Average				
	None	Little	Some	Very Good	Total
A or A+	34.2	52.2	64.8	64.1	61.2
A— or B+	20.4	25.6	30.7	41.3	28.5
B	9.3	10.3	10.8	*	10.3
B— or C+	3.7	4.7	6.8	6.4	5.0
C	2.0	2.6	4.8	*	3.0
C— or less	*	.0	*	*	2.5
Total	6.3	10.8	21.5	38.9	14.2

Note: N = 34,344 freshmen in 1967, followed up in 1971; *indicates cell frequencies too small to compute reliable percentages.

predictions, separately for students with different grades in high school. Because A— and B+ grades were combined in the follow-ups, it was impossible to match exactly the cut-off points for actual and predicted college grades. However, freshman self-predictions are substantially accurate, regardless of the student's high school grades. Thus, for each level of high school grades, freshmen who say that their chances of getting an A average are very good are about twice as likely to obtain a B+ average or better in college than students who say they have no chance for an A. Nevertheless, high school grades are the more potent predictor: Regardless of self-predictions, students with A averages in high school are about *fifteen* times more likely to earn at least a B+ average in college than students with C averages in high school.

An additional finding, not shown in Table 12, concerns the absolute level of high school versus college grades. Using the six categories of high school grades in Table 12 as a standard, about one student in three (33.1 percent) obtains the same grades in college as in high school, only one in five (19.7 percent) obtains higher grades, and nearly half (47.2 percent) obtain lower grades. Clearly, it is unrealistic for most new college freshmen to expect to improve their academic performance in college; they should be prepared to obtain the same or lower grades than in high school (for details, see supplementary Table A5, available from the Higher Education Research Institute).

Another 1968 freshman prediction verified in the 1972 follow-up was whether the student would fail a course in college. Here again, students' predictions are valid: Of those who say their chances of failing a course are very good, 41 percent actually do fail one, compared with only 25.7 percent of those who say there is no chance they will fail a course. Even so, high school grades are the stronger predictor. One or more courses are failed by 45.3 percent of students with C averages in high school, compared with only 8.8 percent of those who have A averages (see supplementary Table A6, available from the Higher Education Research Institute).

A related measure of academic accomplishment, already discussed in Chapter Three, is participation in honors programs. Such participation is usually limited to students with outstanding academic abilities or prior accomplishment. Although the 1968 freshman survey did not contain a prediction about participation in honors programs, it did contain one about graduation with honors. This freshman estimate was a good predictor of participation in honors programs: Regardless of high school grades, those who estimate that their chances of graduating with honors are very good are about three times more likely to participate in honors programs than those who say they have no chance of graduating with honors. Again, high school grades are a better predictor: Regardless of freshman predictions, students with A averages are about *six* times more likely to participate in honors programs than those with C averages (see supplementary Table A7).

Freshman characteristics entering the regressions for predicting college grade-point average were very similar for men and women and for students of differing abilities. After high school grades (average $r = .50$), college admissions tests carried the largest weight (partial $r = .13$). Four other entering freshman characteristics, however, had weights in the final regression equation almost as large as the weight for admissions tests. These were intellectual self-esteem (positive weight), age (positive), hedonism (negative), and business interests (negative). This pattern of predictors was replicated in both male and female samples, as well as in the separate ability-level samples. The only exception was with the high-ability students, for whom age and intellectual self-esteem carried no weight. Apparently, regardless of ability and past achievement, mature students and students with a high regard for their intellectual capabilities will do better academically in college than younger, more pleasure-oriented students and students with strong interests in business and making money.

Women earn higher grades in college than men, even after their superior high school performance is considered. Other freshman characteristics that predict college grades include being Jewish, high status needs, and strong conservative politics. Predictors that operate only for women include a high parental income level and graduating from a private high school. The latter finding may reflect the more stringent grading standards of private high schools (Astin, 1971). For high-ability students, interpersonal self-esteem and religiousness have small positive weights, and plans to marry while in college and father's educational level have small negative weights. For low-ability students, two additional predictors carry positive weights: altruism

and plans to obtain a graduate or professional degree. The prediction for low-ability students is generally less accurate (multiple R = .45), than that for middle-ability (R = .52) and high-
ability (R = .55) students. In part these differences may reflect
the more restricted range in college grades among low-ability
students.

Students who become involved in either research or
honors programs earn relatively high grades. Students who
major in mathematics, engineering, or physical sciences, however, should expect somewhat lower grades in college than students who major in other fields. Majoring in these hard-science
fields is negatively related to college grades, even after high
school grades, ability test scores, and other entering characteristics are controlled. The positive weight associated with becoming a lawyer may well reflect easier grading standards in prelaw
fields, such as history and political science.

Support from a scholarship is associated with high grades
for women and students of average ability, while support from a
loan is associated with low grades. Living with parents is associated with low grades among men, whereas living in a private
room is associated with low grades among high-ability students.
Perhaps high-ability students who live at home or in dormitories
perform better because of pressure from parents or peers. Such
a conclusion is consistent with Blai's (1971) finding that high-
achieving roommates can positively affect students' grades in
college.

By far the most important institutional characteristic
affecting academic performance in college is the selectivity or
prestige of the institution: A given student will earn somewhat
lower grades in a highly selective than in a nonselective institution. This effect applies to men and women and to middle- and
high-ability students. The effect may not show up for low-ability students because so few attend selective institutions. That
the negative effects of college prestige or selectivity are true
effects and not statistical artifacts is supported by the *positive*
simple correlation (.27) between selectivity and college grades.
This correlation disappears and becomes negative (−.15) once
entering characteristics are controlled. These analyses show that

while selective colleges award higher grades than nonselective colleges, their grading standards, considering the caliber of their students, are actually more stringent.

Apparently, highly selective private colleges and public universities of all selectivity levels have especially stringent grading standards. Nonselective Protestant and Roman Catholic colleges, along with the public two-year colleges, have the least stringent grading standards. Grading also varies by region: Northeastern and southern institutions have relatively stringent standards, whereas institutions in the West and Midwest have the easiest grading standards.

Graduation with Honors. Of the 1968 freshmen, 13 percent graduated with honors. Freshman predictions of this outcome prove reasonably accurate: Of those who say their chances of graduating with honors are very good, 28 percent actually do, compared with only 6.4 percent of those who say they have no chance of graduating with honors. Among members of high school honor societies, predictions are even better: Fully 40 percent of the members who say their chances of graduating with honors are very good actually do graduate with honors, compared with 5.1 percent who are not in honor societies and say they have no chance for honors (for details, see supplementary Table A8, available from the Higher Education Research Institute).

While the freshman characteristics that predict graduating with honors closely parallel those that predict college grades, the relevant institutional characteristics are quite different. The student's chances of graduating with honors are substantially better at selective private and public universities, men's colleges, predominantly black colleges, and colleges in the Northeast. Chances of graduating with honors are somewhat reduced at public four-year colleges. Despite its negative effect on academic performance, institutional selectivity has a positive effect on the student's chances for honors. These contrasting patterns of college effects on grades and graduating have several explanations. For one, graduating with honors requires *both* high grades and completion of a degree program. Analyses of college effects on persistence show that certain types of institutions with relatively easy grading standards—the two-year colleges, for example—sometimes have poor holding power on their students. Many highly selective institutions also attempt to recognize the superior caliber of their students by graduating relatively large proportions with honors.

Educational Attainment

The various longitudinal data files were utilized to develop three measures of educational attainment: persistence versus dropping out, enrollment in graduate or professional schools, and aspirations for advanced degrees. In a sense, aspirations for higher degrees, obviously associated with academic attainment, represent a surrogate measure for actual attainment of higher degrees, a behavioral outcome that could be studied if longitudinal data were available for longer time intervals.

Persistence Versus Dropping Out. The concept of dropping out of college presents certain definitional problems: One is that classifying a student as a dropout is temporary. Since any dropout can, in theory, go back to college to complete the degree, no definition can be wholly satisfactory until all students have obtained their degrees or died without them. One approach to this problem in earlier studies was to define a third category of students: *stopouts,* those who leave college but intend to return to complete their degrees. Since stopouts resemble dropouts much more than persisters (Astin, 1975b), dropouts and stopouts can be combined.

Perhaps the simplest approach is to define as *persisters* all students who complete a degree program within a specified time. Among full-time freshmen entering college for the first time, about half earn baccalaureate degrees within four years. This number is similar for freshmen entering college in 1966 (49 percent), 1967 (47 percent), and 1968 (50 percent). Degree completion within five years is somewhat higher: 62 percent (El-Khawas and Bisconti, 1974). The only longer-term data are from 1961 freshmen followed up in 1971 (although these rates are inflated because they apply only to four-year college students): Baccalaureate completion rates after four, five, and ten years are 56 percent, 70 percent, and 80 percent, respectively. The number of additional students completing degrees drops off markedly to 2 percent in the seventh year after college entrance and to less than 1 percent in the tenth year (El-Khawas and Bisconti, 1974).

For the current study, a persister is defined as anyone who completed a baccalaureate degree within four years or who is still enrolled four years after entering college. All other students are considered dropouts. This definition classifies as persisters all stopouts who return to college within four years after entering; stopouts not enrolled after four years are included with dropouts. Regression analyses were carried out utilizing the 1966-1970 longitudinal file, primarily because separate files for men and women and for students of differing ability levels had already been created for other analyses. (For a detailed analysis of student and environmental characteristics affecting persistence in the 1968-1972 longitudinal sample, see Astin, 1975b.)

As in previous studies, the prediction of dropping out based on entering freshman characteristics produced only a modest multiple correlation ($r = .42$). By far the most potent predictor is the student's average grade in high school ($r = .29$). College admissions test scores carry little predictive weight once high school grades and other entering characteristics are controlled. Greater weight is associated with the student's degree plans at the time of college entry, with the higher degrees receiving positive weights and the bachelor's or lower degrees receiving negative weights. Greater weight is also associated with plans to marry while in college (negative weight) and hedonism (negative weight). These predictors have substantial weights for both men and women and for students of differing ability. High parental income and attendance at a private secondary school have small positive weights, while no religious preference has a small negative weight. This pattern of predictors suggests a stereotype of the college persister as a person with high grades, high aspirations, affluent parents, and the ability to postpone gratification. The potential dropout is an independent, pleasure-oriented individual with low aspirations and poor grades. The substantial negative weight associated with plans to marry in college is consistent with earlier studies suggesting that a major cause of dropping out is early marriage (Astin, 1975b; Bayer, 1969).

By far the most important environmental characteristic associated with college persistence is living in a dormitory during the freshmen year. After entering characteristics and other environmental measures are controlled, living in a dormitory, compared with living with parents or in private rooms, adds about 12 percent to the student's chance of finishing college. Chances of persisting are increased by about 6 percent if parents provide a major portion of financial support. The positive effects of support from parents and dormitory living apply to men and women and to students of differing ability.

Attending a public or private two-year college substantially reduces the student's chances of persisting. This negative effect is particularly strong among high-ability students. For women, however, the negative effect disappears when residence and region are controlled. In other words, the increased chance of dropping out that occurs in two-year colleges may be attributed to the lack of residential facilities in these institutions and to their preponderance in the West. For men, the negative impact of attending a two-year institution prevails even after residence and location are considered.

A man's chance of persisting is also reduced by attending a nonselective public university. Persistence among women, in contrast, is enhanced by attending a selective Protestant institution or a women's college. Persistence among low-ability students is enhanced by attending a nonselective Protestant college, whereas persistence among high-ability students is increased generally at a selective nonsectarian college but decreased slightly at a highly selective nonsectarian college.

Every form of involvement for which data were available in the 1966-1970 sample—research, honors programs, and social fraternities—is positively associated with persistence. The single variable most strongly associated with staying in college, however, is the student's undergraduate grade-point average, which has a partial correlation of .27 with persistence after all other variables are controlled.

The findings about environmental influences on student

persistence replicate almost exactly earlier findings from the 1968-1972 sample (Astin, 1975b). Thus, persistence is enhanced by living in a dormitory, by involvement in the campus environment, and by receiving major support from parents, and reduced by attending a two-year college and by poor academic performance. Both studies, as well as a recent multicampus study by Kamens (1971), failed to find a consistent relationship between institutional selectivity and persistence, once the effect of two-year institutions was controlled (most two-year institutions are of low selectivity). These studies also produced the somewhat paradoxical finding that attending a selective institution does not reduce the student's chances of persisting, even though it does increase chances of getting poor grades, a major correlate of dropping out.

Different studies have produced somewhat conflicting findings, however, concerning the impact of institutional size on persistence. Although an early study of 246 four-year institutions (Astin and Panos, 1969) found a clear-cut negative impact of size on persistence, a subsequent study of 99 institutions (Kamens, 1971) suggested a positive effect. This latter study, however, controlled fewer entering student characteristics and considered only three size categories ("large" institutions included all those with enrollments above 5,000). The recent study of 1968-1972 students (Astin, 1975b) showed that the effects of size were inconsistent: The poorest persistence rates occurred in the smallest (enrollments below 500) and the moderately large (enrollments of 10,000 to 20,000) institutions. The current study suggests a small negative effect of size on persistence, but the effect disappears when other institutional characteristics are controlled.

Enrollment in Graduate or Professional Schools. When they first enter college, about half the new freshmen say they intend to obtain an advanced graduate or professional degree (Astin, King, and Richardson, 1976). How successful are these freshmen in reaching this objective? How many actually enroll in graduate or professional school within four or five years after entering college? Do some with initially low aspirations change their minds and go to a graduate or professional school?

Table 13 shows the proportion of students with various initial degree plans who go to graduate or professional schools

Table 13. Graduate or Professional School Enrollment Four or Five Years After College Entry, by Freshman Degree Plans (in Percentages)

Highest Degree Planned as Freshman	Freshmen Planning Degrees		Graduate or Professional School Enrollment	
	1968	1969	Four Years (1968-1972)	Five Years (1969-1974)
LL.B. or J.D.	1.3	1.5	35.4	51.6
M.D., D.D.S., D.V.M.	4.2	4.5	34.6	49.2
Ph.D., Ed.D.	11.4	10.0	22.1	37.3
Master's	31.7	34.6	12.4	26.9
Bachelor's (others)	39.8	40.2	5.6	14.6
None	5.1	2.1	4.4	6.9
Associate	6.5	7.1	1.8	4.5
All students	100.0	100.0	10.9	22.3

four or five years after entering college. Students seeking law degrees are the most successful in implementing their plans for graduate study, but they are closely followed by a group aspiring to medical, dental, or veterinary degrees. More than 80 percent of this group aspires to medical degrees. About one third of those initially aspiring to either law or medical degrees is enrolled in professional schools within four years after entering college, and about half is enrolled within five years. Students planning master's degrees are the least likely to implement their plans within four or five years, although many of these students are probably schoolteachers, who frequently delay their graduate study by working a few years after receiving their baccalaureate degrees. Small percentages of students who initially do not aspire to graduate or professional degrees actually go to graduate or professional schools. The finding that students with no degree plans are more likely to go to graduate or professional schools than students aspiring to associate degrees may reflect the terminal nature of many associate degrees.

The data in Table 14 provide a clear illustration of how changes in students' aspirations can be affected by "floor" and

Table 14. Changes in Degree Plans of Students After College Entry
(in Percentages)

Highest Degree Planned as Freshman	Students Aspiring to Graduate or Professional Degrees			
	½ year (1969-1969)	1½ years (1968-1969)	2½ years (1967-1969)	3½ years (1966-1969)
LL.B. or J.D.	91.4	89.5	92.8	95.0
M.D., D.D.S., D.V.M.	88.6	87.9	86.0	88.1
Ph.D. or Ed.D.	92.3	89.7	89.4	83.7
Master's	75.4	76.5	75.4	77.2
Bachelor's	27.9	34.9	42.3	53.6
None	17.3	35.0	34.6	51.3
Associate	5.2	9.3	13.9	21.5
All Students	52.4	56.9	59.3	63.4

"ceiling" effects in the aspiration measure. Students most likely to lower their aspirations are those initially seeking Ph.D.'s or Ed.D.'s while those initially seeking bachelor's or no degree are the ones most likely to raise their aspirations. This type of artifact probably accounts for Fenske and Scott's (1973) observation that two-year college students raise their aspirations while four-year college students lower theirs. However, as far as college *effects* on aspirations are concerned, results of the current study suggest no systematic difference between two-year and four-year institutions (see later discussion).

The student's degree aspirations at the time of college entrance are the most potent predictors of enrollment in graduate or professional schools. Other predictors with substantial positive weights are being Jewish or black, being a high school science contest winner, and being a finalist in the National Merit Scholarship competition. Smaller positive weights are associated with being male or Oriental and with high grades in high school, and small negative weights are associated with plans to drop out temporarily or being a smoker. Clearly, the students' initial aspirations and racial or ethnic background are more important determinants than their past academic performance of whether they will enroll in graduate or professional school.

Environmental characteristics show only small relationships to enrollment in graduate school, once entering freshman

characteristics are controlled. Students are slightly more
to enter graduate or professional schools if they live in
tories initially rather than with parents. Women are more
to enter graduate or professional schools if they attend women's
rather than coeducational colleges initially, and students of
both sexes are more likely to enroll if they attend selective
Protestant colleges initially. The only other institutional characteristic significantly related to enrollment is location in a western state. This effect is somewhat puzzling, given the negative
impact of western institutions on persistence. These contradictory findings suggest that, among students who complete their
baccalaureate programs at western institutions, the rate of
attendance at graduate and professional schools is high.

Degree Aspirations. Students' aspirations for advanced
training increase after college entrance. Freshman surveys over
the years have shown that slightly more than half (an average of
51 percent) of the new freshmen aspires to postgraduate degrees
at the time of college entrance. This rate increases to nearly two
thirds (an average of about 65 percent) four years later. These
increased aspirations are remarkable, given that some students
leave college and abandon all plans for any degree.

Do these changes in aspirations occur at particular times
after college entrance, or are they gradual? Table 14 shows
changes in plans for advanced degrees over intervals from one
half to three and one half years after college entrance. Clearly,
changes in plans are gradual, with an average of about 4 percent
more students aspiring to advanced training each year. The
greatest increases occur among students who aspire to no degree
or to a bachelor's degree: Half these students say they intend to
earn some kind of graduate or professional degree three and one
half years after entering college. The greatest decline in plans
for advanced training occurs among students initially planning
master's or doctoral degrees. Students who plan law or medical
degrees show the smallest declines, which is consistent with the
finding that these degrees are most predictive of enrollment in
graduate or professional schools within four or five years after
college entry. Aspirations for advanced professional or doctoral
degrees can be predicted with modest accuracy (multiple R =

.54). Initial degree plans carry the largest predictive weights, and being male rather than female was second in importance as a predictor, with a partial correlation ($r = .24$) substantially larger than the partial correlation of sex with entry to graduate or professional school ($r = .05$). In fact, the increase in students' aspirations for graduate training is accounted for entirely by the men; women's aspirations actually decline slightly after college entry. In most other respects, the pattern of entering characteristics that predicts degree aspirations closely parallels the pattern of variables that predicts enrollment in graduate or professional schools. Substantial positive weights are carried by high school grades, admissions test scores, artistic interest, and interpersonal self-esteem (the latter two measures were unavailable in the analysis for predicting enrollment in graduate or professional schools).

Plans to become a doctor, lawyer, or a scientific researcher carry substantial positive weight in predicting degree aspirations, even after initial aspirations, ability, sex, and past achievements are considered. Majoring in physical science also carries a small positive weight, but majoring in engineering carries substantial negative weight. The large dropout rate from engineering (see Chapter Five) may steer many students into fields, such as business, that do not require advanced training. Engineering graduates, unlike graduates in many other fields, can find well-paying jobs that do not require advanced training. The availability of attractive employment immediately after graduation from college may tempt many engineering graduates to delay or perhaps give up plans for graduate study.

Living in a dormitory as a freshman has a positive effect on aspirations for advanced degrees. Increases in aspirations are greater than average among students at highly selective private colleges and smaller among students at large institutions and selective public universities. The negative effect of institutional size replicates an earlier study of high-ability students (Astin, 1973). For low-ability students, increases in degree aspirations are smaller than expected among those attending nonselective Protestant colleges. The most pronounced positive effect, however, occurs among women attending women's colleges.

Involvement in honors programs, high grades in college, and persistence are all positively related to increased degree aspirations. Involvement in research also produces a substantial positive effect (partial r = .14), but involvement in fraternities or sororities has no effect one way or the other. Similar findings have been reported previously by Thistlethwaite (1965).

Extracurricular Achievements

For many undergraduates, extracurricular activities provide some of the most significant consequences of college attendance. In certain respects, these activities offer an opportunity to develop skills that are more relevant to later life than the knowledge and cognitive skills acquired in the classroom. Undergraduate extracurricular activities may be the forerunner of adult achievement in a variety of fields: Many leaders in business, industry, and government were student leaders in colleges, many successful actors had their first experience with theater in college, and most professional athletes are selected from among the ranks of outstanding college athletes.

Which characteristics of the entering student predict subsequent extracurricular accomplishments? Are students more likely to experience extracurricular achievement in some colleges than in others? These questions are explored for six fields of extracurricular achievement: leadership, journalism, science, creative writing, theater, and athletics. Adequate follow-up data were not available for music, another potentially important area of extracurricular accomplishment.

Leadership. Two measures of leadership accomplishment were included in the analyses: being elected to a student office and being a member of a student-faculty committee. Both indices were considered evidence of significant leadership ability as recognized by other members of the campus community.

Approximately 16 percent of students is elected to a student office sometime during the undergraduate years. This election is clearly not a chance event, because many students who hold office expected to do so when they entered college. Some 43 percent of the students who enter college saying their chances of being elected to a student office are very good is actually elected, compared with only 7 percent of those who say they have no chance at all. Leadership from high school to college is also somewhat consistent: Of students who were elected president of an organization in high school, 24 percent is later elected to a student office in college, compared with only 12 percent of those who are not elected president of a student organization in high school. Although the prediction of this college outcome from all entering characteristics is modest (multiple R = .31), other freshman characteristics contribute significantly to the prediction. Positive weights are associated with being Oriental, aspiring to a law degree, having original writing published in high school, being a finalist in the National Merit Scholarship competition, and participating in regional or national speech or debate contests. Positive weights are associated with participation in demonstrations over racial issues or administrative policies in the high schools but negatively associated with participation in antiwar demonstrations. This configuration of predictors provides a clear-cut stereotype of the potential leader: a bright, verbally aggressive, political activist aspiring to a legal career.

The student's chances of being elected to a student office are substantially better if the student lives in a college dormitory as a freshman. The college characteristic most closely associated with being elected to a student office is institutional size, which has a partial correlation of −.13 with this outcome after entering student characteristics have been controlled. This result supports the finding that the student's chances of being involved in campus life are reduced at a large institution (Chapter Three). The chances of being elected to a student office are substantially better at most private four-year colleges, although chances are relatively poor at highly selective private universities and at private two-year colleges. Considering the relatively small size of most private two-year colleges, their negative effect on this outcome suggests that the number of student offices may be small.

A man's chances of gaining a student office are somewhat better at a coeducational institution than at a men's college, whereas a woman's chances are substantially better at a women's college. This finding suggests that women fare somewhat better in the competition for leadership positions if they are not competing with men. Are women less likely to attain leadership positions in coeducational institutions because they are less qualified than men? Or are they less likely to be aggressive when they are competing with men? The method of analysis in this study does not support the first question. That is, the students' objective qualifications for leadership positions are considered when their past leadership achievement and experiences are controlled statistically. The second question, however, is supported by the finding that women are less likely to be verbally aggressive in the classroom when they attend coeducational institutions (Chapter Three). In short, being in the presence of male students acts as a brake on a woman's tendency to compete, a finding that supports Horner's (1968) thesis that women experience a "fear of success" when they compete with men. Although the men's greater success in competing for leadership positions at coeducational institutions may be explained in the same way—that is, men will compete more aggressively if they are in the presence of women—this explanation is not supported by the results for verbal aggressiveness reported in Chapter Three. Men are not less likely to be verbally aggressive in men's colleges than in coeducational institutions. Sex bias may also be a consideration: Persons who elect or select student leaders may tend to favor men over women, independent of past accomplishments or qualifications.

The second measure of leadership achievement, being a member of a student-faculty committee, was reported by 11 percent of the 1968 freshmen when they were followed up in 1972. Although no identical pretest of this outcome was available from the entering freshman data, leadership accomplishments in high school predicted student-faculty committee membership in college significantly. Students elected president of a high school organization, for example, are twice as likely (18 percent) to become members of student-faculty committees in college as students not elected in high school (9 percent). Achievement in speech and debate also predict student-faculty committee membership: Of those who have participated in regional or state debate contests, 22 percent become members of student-faculty committees, compared with only 11 percent of those who have not achieved in speech or debate. Several other entering characteristics contributed independently to the prediction of student-faculty committee membership in college: Positive weights are associated with publishing original writing in high school, winning a varsity letter, participating in demonstrations against high school administrative policies, and plans to hold student office. Negative weights are associated with plans to obtain only an associate or bachelor's degree.

Environmental variables affecting membership on student-faculty committees closely parallel those affecting election to a student office. Thus, students are more likely to become members of student-faculty committees if they live in dormitories rather than with parents and attend small rather than large institutions. Women are more likely to be on student-faculty committees if they attend women's rather than coeducational colleges, whereas men are more likely to be on such committees in coeducational rather than men's colleges. The chances of being on student-faculty committees are especially poor in selective private universities.

Two additional characteristics unrelated to election to student office are positively associated with being on student-faculty committees: selective Catholic institutions and nonselective Protestant institutions. These positive effects were obtained even after institutional size had been controlled. Apparently, these two types of institutions are more likely to have students on committees.

Journalism. In the 1972 follow-up of 1968 freshmen, 8 percent of the students had worked on the staff of the college newspaper. The most comparable pretest item from the freshman questionnaire was "edited the school paper, yearbook, or literary magazine." Again journalistic achievement is somewhat consistent over time: Of those students who have been editors in high school (11 percent of all entering freshmen), 17 percent work on the college paper, compared with only 7 percent of other entering freshmen. The other entering characteristics that contributed to the prediction are publishing original writing in high school, *plans* to publish original writing in college, being a finalist in the National Merit Scholarship competition, winning an award in art competition (painting, drawing, or sculpture), plans to obtain a law degree, being Jewish, discussing politics frequently, and participating in demonstrations against the high school administration. This pattern of entering variables suggests that college journalists are to some extent political activists and that they also resemble student leaders. Being on the college paper is most strongly related to institutional size (partial $r = -.10$). Students' chances of participating in college journalism are better if they attend a relatively small institution. A southern location is also positively related to working on the college paper, which may indicate that southern colleges have larger newspaper staffs. Although numerous other college characteristics are related to working on the college paper after entering freshman characteristics have been controlled (public universities are negatively related and most types of private colleges positively related), these relationships disappear once institutional size and location are controlled.

Science. Only 1.3 percent of the 1968 freshmen indicated at the time of the 1972 follow-up that they had authored or coauthored an article in a scientific publication. This relatively rare achievement is predictable from entering freshman characteristics with only modest accuracy ($r = .29$). The most potent positive predictors are high grades in high school, attending a private high school, being Jewish, and aspiring to graduate or professional degrees. Negative weights are associated with being Protestant or Catholic, being an editor in high school, and receiving major financial support from parents. A somewhat unexpected finding occurred with being a finalist in the National Merit Scholarship competition: This entering characteristic has a significantly positive simple correlation with writing a scientific article but a significantly *negative* correlation when high school grades and college selectivity are controlled. Students who write scientific articles at the undergraduate level may be overachievers (that is, they have high grades and enter selective colleges but have relatively low test scores).

Students are more likely to write scientific articles if they
major in biological science or engineering or if they aspire to
careers as scientific researchers when they enter college. Aspiring to a legal career is negatively related to scientific authorship.
The environmental experience most closely associated with scientific authorship, however, is involvement in research (partial r
= .19). A student attending a highly selective institution is more
likely to be a scientific author, while a student attending an
institution located in the Northeast is less likely to write scientific articles.

Creative Writing. The 1972 follow-up of 1968 freshmen
contained another authorship item: "Was author or coauthor of
an article in another scholarly or literary publication." Some
4.8 percent, a substantially higher percentage, had published
such an article. The best predictor of creative writing achievement in college is publishing original writings (poems, articles,
or short stories) in high school. Other positive predictors are
being an editor in high school, artistic interests, hedonism, altruism, interpersonal self-esteem, aspiring to a professional degree,
being a man, winning a science contest, and being a finalist in
the National Merit Scholarship competition. Negative predictors
are plans to marry while in college, business interests, and being
Catholic. This complicated array of predictors suggests that college students who publish original writings are a highly versatile
and diverse group in terms of background characteristics.

Students are more likely to publish creative writing if
they major in the social sciences and less likely if they major in
the physical sciences. Creative writing has a different relationship to college characteristics than scientific writing. College
selectivity has a negative effect on creative writing while a
northeastern location has a positive effect, precisely the opposite of the effect these characteristics have on scientific writing.
Creative writing is least likely to occur in the large and prestigious institutions and most likely to be found in private institutions, particularly selective Roman Catholic colleges. One
possible explanation of the negative effects of size and prestige
is that creative writing at the undergraduate level may be published in college literary magazines and newspapers. The student

competition for space in these publications would be greater in larger institutions, and the caliber of the students would probably be higher in the more prestigious and selective institutions. Scientific authorship is more likely to occur in noncollege publications.

Theater. One follow-up item—"had a major part in a college play"—assessed achievement in theater. Only 4 percent of the students responded positively to this item, compared with 17 percent who responded positively to a comparable high school item at the time of college entry. Fifteen percent of those who had major parts in high school plays also had them in college plays, compared with only 2 percent of those who did not have a major part in a high school play. Other freshman characteristics positively related to subsequent achievement in college theater are achievement in high school speech or debate contests and musical competition, discussing politics frequently, and participating in either racial or antiwar demonstrations in high school.

As with most other extracurricular achievements, the size of the institution has a negative impact on the student's chances of having a major part in a college play. Several other college characteristics have small relationships to this outcome, but the relationships disappear when institutional size is controlled.

Athletics. The measure of athletic accomplishment in college was "playing on one or more varsity teams." Of the 1968 freshmen, 11 percent reported playing on a college team in the 1972 follow-up, compared with 31 percent that reported winning one or more varsity letters in high school. Prediction of athletic achievement from freshman characteristics is somewhat better than with other extracurricular achievements $(R = .43)$. After controlling for high school varsity letters $(r = .37)$, only a few additional freshman characteristics contribute to the prediction. Positive weights are associated with oversleeping and missing classes or appointments in high school, and negative weights are associated with being older than average, Jewish, smoking, being a finalist in the National Merit Scholarship competition, and extracurricular achievements in high school such as debate, theater, and editing the school paper, yearbook, or literary magazine. These negative weights for nonathletic accomplishments may reflect the substantial demand that college athletics makes on student time, which precludes participation in other time-consuming extracurricular activities. Athletic achievement in college correlates substantially less with achievement in leadership, journalism, and theater (average r = .04) than these achievements correlate with each other (average r = .17). Like most other achievements, athletic achievement is more likely to occur in small than in large institutions. In particular, attending selective private universities, nonselective public universities, or public two-year colleges reduces the student's chances of achieving in athletics. Athletic achievement is positively affected by attending prestigious institutions and institutions located in the Northeast. The negative effects of two-year institutions may reflect a relative lack of competitive intercollegiate athletic programs; the positive effects of institutional prestige and a northeastern location may reflect the relative lack of athletic competition at such institutions.

Competency

A number of studies suggest that students' basic skills and knowledge of academic material increase substantially after they enter college (Campbell, 1965; Learned and Wood, 1938; Lenning, Munday, and Maxey, 1969; Owens, 1953; Rossmann and others, 1975; Swanson, 1953). While no study has demonstrated unequivocably that these increases are entirely attributable to the effects of college, most point to the college experience as a major factor. In his twenty-five-year follow-up testing of persons who attended the University of Minnesota, for example, Campbell (1965) found that the amount of *gain* in general academic competency is directly related to the amount of formal education completed. Similarly, several studies have suggested that persons will gain more in those academic areas where they major or take the most courses (Astin, 1968b; Lenning, Munday, and Maxey, 1969; Rock, 1972).

College alumni often claim that the most significant skills

or competencies gained from the college experience were not learned in the classroom. These competencies may be acquired through extracurricular activities or through informal interaction with faculty and peers. To explore the possible impact of college on the development of skills, a heterogeneous list of competencies was included in the fall 1967 survey of entering freshmen. Students were asked to respond to thirty competency items (Holland and Astin, 1962) by indicating if they can presently perform each activity competently. The same list was repeated in a one-year follow-up in late summer 1968. Constraints on the follow-up questionnaire imposed by funding agencies precluded repetition in four- and five-year follow-ups (Bayer, Royer, and Webb, 1973; Cartter and Brown, 1976). One-year findings can only suggest the potential of colleges to affect nonacademic competencies.

Because of the many competencies, the analytic procedures were simplified by using factor analysis to combine 1967 pretest and 1968 posttest competencies into fewer, more general measures. Only four factors with substantial loadings from more than one item emerged from the analysis: general cultural knowledge, homemaking skills, sports knowledge, and musical competence (Table 15). (For the complete factor matrix, see supplementary Table A9, available from the Higher Education Research Institute.) In general, these four factors include most of the items that showed the largest changes during the freshman year. However, an additional seven factors defined by a single item were included in the analyses of college impact, either because of their intrinsic interest or because they showed relatively large changes during the one-year interval. These additional single-item factors were parliamentary knowledge, skill with a slide rule, skill in swimming, typing skill, computer-programming skill, foreign language skill, and physical fitness.

Table 15 shows changes in competency in the freshman year. Students change most in general cultural knowledge, sports knowledge, swimming skill, skill with a slide rule, and knowing the animal phyla. To some extent, these changes can be rationalized in terms of what we know about the freshman college experi-

Table 15. Changes in Competencies of Students During Freshman Year (in Percentages)

Competency	Factor Loading		Student Competence		
	Pretest	Posttest	1967	1968	Change 1967-1968
General cultural knowledge					
Identify many classical musical compositions by title and composer	.49	.49	12.2	20.6	+ 8.4
Recite long passages from plays or poems without notes	.41	.44	13.7	18.3	+ 4.6
Describe the personal freedoms guaranteed by the Bill of Rights	.34	.30	47.8	56.8	+ 9.0
Identify and describe examples from several architectural styles	.32	.32	13.7	24.1	+10.4
Identify most of the major constellations of stars	.27	.27	7.5	12.9	+ 5.4
Homemaking skills					
Bake a cake from scratch (no mixes)	.73	.76	44.5	48.7	+ 4.2
Use a sewing machine	.69	.71	40.1	44.5	+ 4.4
Set a table for a formal party	.49	.53	42.2	45.4	+ 3.2
Sports knowledge					
Name the starting players for a professional athletic team	.73	.72	32.6	36.8	+ 4.2
Referee one or more sporting events	.44	.47	38.1	49.4	+11.3
Musical competence					
Sight-read piano music	.67	.71	21.7	26.9	+ 5.2
Read music (singing)	.64	.67	31.9	37.0	+ 5.1
Parliamentary knowledge					
Use Robert's *Rules of Order*	.58	.70	16.2	24.5	+ 8.3
Skill with slide rule					
Use slide rule	.70	.81	35.9	44.1	+ 8.2
Skill in swimming					
Swim a mile without stopping	.80	.63	28.2	34.2	+ 6.0

Typing skills				
Type forty words or more per minute	.78	.79	43.5	48.3	+ 4.8
Computer-programming skill				
Program a computer	.18	.30	1.5	6.2	+ 4.7
Foreign language skill				
Speak a second language fluently	.68	.76	10.2	14.8	+ 4.6
Physical fitness				
Do at least fifteen push-ups	.63	.73	66.4	70.9	+ 4.5
Other competencies				
Name the animal phyla			9.0	25.4	+16.4
Score a tennis match			34.9	47.2	+12.3
Identify at least fifteen species of birds on sight			16.7	22.9	+ 6.2
Mix a dry martini			18.3	23.7	+ 5.4
Water ski			34.6	39.2	+ 4.6
Ski on snow			15.2	19.3	+ 4.1
Describe the difference between stocks and bonds			39.9	43.4	+ 3.5
Sketch people so they can be recognized			8.2	10.9	+ 2.7
Break 100 in golf			12.8	14.8	+ 2.0
Sail a boat			16.1	18.0	+ 1.9
Develop and print photographs (darkroom work)			7.7	9.3	+ 1.6

ence. Increases in general cultural knowledge and in knowledge of the animal phyla would be expected, because most entering freshmen take a general liberal arts curriculum (which frequently includes a course in introductory biology). Increased skill in using a slide rule would be expected from students majoring in engineering, mathematics, and statistics. These majors accounted for nearly 15 percent of all college freshmen in 1967 (Astin, Panos, and Creager, 1967). (With the widespread use of inexpensive electronic hand calculators in the early 1970s, results with slide rule competency might be different for contemporary college students.) Increases in sports knowledge and swimming skill may reflect the impact of freshman physical education programs. The heavy emphasis on intramural and intercollegiate athletics at many institutions may also contribute to the large increase in sports knowledge. Competencies showing the smallest increases—drawing, golfing, sailing, and photography—represent areas of endeavor excluded from most college curricular or extracurricular programs.

The data in Table 15 may also be viewed in terms of *relative* rather than absolute increases in competency. By far the largest relative increase occurs in computer-programming skills, with the number of students who can program quadrupling (from 1.5 percent to 6.2 percent) during the first year of college. Other competencies showing large relative increases are foreign language skill (40 percent), parliamentary knowledge (50 percent), knowledge of the animal phyla (200 percent), and most items of general cultural knowledge. All these changes can probably be attributed to the freshman undergraduate curriculum.

The limited data from the 1967-1968 longitudinal file precludes a sophisticated analysis of maturational versus college environmental effects. However, those competencies showing the greatest increases can be linked directly to the content of curricular and extracurricular programs, indicating that college may have a significant impact. Competencies showing the smallest changes have no obvious relationship to undergraduate programs. In all likelihood, one effect of the freshman year is to strengthen students' competencies in a wide range of fields.

Are these changes in competency different for different types of students? Competency at the time of college entrance is closely associated with competency one year later. The highest pretest-posttest correlations involve homemaking skills (r = .78), physical fitness (r = .68), and sports knowledge (r = .68); the lowest correlations involve computer-programming skills (r = .32), parliamentary knowledge (r = .49), foreign language skill (r = .53), and general cultural knowledge (r = .56). Although the relatively low pretest-posttest correlations may reflect unreliability in these simple competency measures, they may also reflect differential change and differential college impact.

Changes in competency are related to several entering freshman characteristics. After freshman pretests, sex is the most potent predictor for virtually all competencies. Women show substantially greater increases than men during the freshman year in homemaking skills, typing skill, skill in foreign languages, musical competence, and general cultural knowledge. Men show substantially greater increases in physical fitness, skill with a slide rule, sports knowledge, computer-programming skill, and skill in swimming. The only competency with no differential changes for men and women is parliamentary knowledge.

Changes on certain competencies also differ by race, ability, and age. Blacks show greater increases than whites in general cultural knowledge, sports knowledge, and physical fitness, while whites show greater increases in musical competence and swimming skill. High-ability students, compared with low-ability students, show greater increases in skill with a slide rule, in computer programming, and in foreign languages. Although students with good grades show larger increases in homemaking skills than students with poor grades, grades have a *negative* relationship to increases in homemaking skills once sex has been controlled. In other words, women with higher grades show smaller increases in homemaking skills than women with lower grades. Age at college entry is related to change in only one competency: Younger students show somewhat greater increases in sports knowledge than older students.

Once entering freshman characteristics have been controlled, institutional characteristics show several relationships to increases in competency. The most pronounced is the positive effect of college selectivity on foreign language skill (partial r = .11). (While this finding is consistent with Rock's [1972] study suggesting that selectivity facilitates achievement in the humanities, it may be that these effects are mediated by curricular differences between selective and nonselective institutions rather than by the effects of selectivity per se—see Astin, 1968b; Rock, Baird, and Linn, 1972.)

Both computer-programming and slide rule skills are positively affected by attending large institutions, nonselective private universities, men's colleges, and selective private nonsectarian colleges. Typing and homemaking skills are positively related to attending nonselective public universities. Typing skill is also positively associated with attending nonselective religious institutions. General cultural knowledge is positively affected by attending predominantly black institutions, small rather than large institutions, and public four-year colleges. Swimming skill is negatively associated with attending public two-year colleges or nonselective religious colleges.

This series of relationships suggests that the *curricula* and the *facilities* of institutions are important determinants of the particular skills and competencies students acquire during the undergraduate years. For example, selective institutions, which emphasize traditional liberal arts curricula more than nonselective institutions (Astin, King, and Richardson, 1976), are more likely to have a foreign language requirement for freshmen. Men's colleges and larger institutions are more likely to offer programs in engineering and computer science, fields where programming and slide rule skills are likely to be developed. Nonselective institutions are more likely to offer courses in business and secretarial studies, which could contribute to developing typing skill. Similarly, students in public two-year colleges and nonselective (presumably less affluent) sectarian colleges, which probably lack swimming pools and related physical education facilities, are not likely to develop swimming skills. The importance of curricula could be tested by introducing controls for the actual courses taken by students during the undergraduate

years. If controls were employed, many institutional effe
might disappear.

These results suggest that no single type of institution
facilitates the development of student competence across the
board. Rather, attendance at different types of institutions results in the development of different types of competencies.
The data suggest strongly that these institutional differences
may be accounted for by the different curricula and facilities at
each institution.

Summary

The impact of college on the student's intellectual skills
and attainments can be measured in various ways: grade-point
average, degrees, awards, extracurricular achievements, and the
acquisition of special skills and competencies. Although fewer
students achieve in college than in high school, the students
who display particular skills in secondary school are, generally
speaking, most likely to display the same skills during college.
Other factors, however, are important in determining intellectual and academic progress.

High-ability students move at a faster rate than students
of less ability, as indicated by their higher grades, more rapid
progress toward completion of a degree, and greater chance of
graduating with honors. High-ability students are also more
likely to acquire technical and scientific skills, to develop foreign language skills, and to publish original writing.

Men and women differ considerably in their educational
and intellectual development during the undergraduate years.
Although women earn higher grades than men, they are less
likely to persist in college and to enroll in graduate or professional school. Moreover, women's aspirations for higher degrees
decline, while men's aspirations increase during the undergraduate years. Compared with men, women are more likely to
acquire general cultural knowledge and skills in foreign languages, music, typing, and homemaking. Men are more likely to
achieve in athletics, to publish original writing, to acquire technical or scientific skills, to improve their knowledge of sports,

and to improve their skill in swimming and general physical fitness. Black students, compared with nonblacks of similar ability, are more likely to persist and to enroll in graduate school but less likely to graduate with honors.

Students' achievements can be affected by a variety of environmental experiences (Table 16). Majoring in engineering has a negative impact on grades and aspirations, whereas premedical and prelaw majors earn higher grades and generally

Table 16. Summary of Environmental Effects on Competency and Achievement

Outcome Measure	Positive Effects	Negative Effects
Academic Achievement		
College grades	Public two-year colleges Research involvement Honors programs Western or midwestern location	Selective and prestigious institutions Northeastern or southern location Majoring in engineering or natural science
Graduation with honors	Selective universities Colleges for men Predominantly black colleges Northeastern location	Public four-year colleges
Educational Attainment		
Persistence	Dormitory living Research involvement Honors programs Fraternities or sororities High college grades Financial support from parents	Living with parents Two-year colleges Nonselective public universities Western location
Enrolling in graduate or professional school	Dormitory living Colleges for women Selective Protestant colleges Western location	Living with parents
Degree aspirations	Dormitory living Highly selective private institutions Colleges for women Research involvement Honors programs High college grades	Living with parents Large institutions Selective public universities

Table 16 *(Continued)*

Outcome Measure	Positive Effects	Negative Effects
Extracurricular Achievement		
Leadership	Small institutions	Large institutions
	Dormitory living	Living with parents
	Private colleges	Private two-year colleges
	Coeducational colleges (men)	Selective private universities
	Women's colleges (women)	
Journalism	Small institutions	Large institutions
	Southern location	
Science	Majoring in engineering or biological science	Majoring in prelaw
	Research involvement	Northeastern location
	Selective institutions	
Creative writing	Majoring in social sciences	Majoring in physical sciences
	Northeastern location	Selective institutions
	Small institutions	Large institutions
	Selective Roman Catholic colleges	
Theater	Small institutions	Large institutions
Athletics	Small institutions	Large institutions
	Prestigious institutions	Selective private universities
	Northeastern location	Public two-year colleges
Specialized Competencies		
Foreign language skill	Selective institutions	
Computer programming, use of slide rule	Large institutions	Small institutions
	Nonselective private universities	
	Colleges for men	
	Selective private colleges	
Typing skill	Nonselective public universities	
	Nonselective religious colleges	
Homemaking skill	Nonselective public universities	
Swimming skill		Nonselective religious colleges
		Public two-year colleges
General cultural knowledge	Small institutions	Large institutions
	Predominantly black colleges	
	Public four-year colleges	

increase their aspirations during college. Being involved in research as an undergraduate is positively associated with grades, persistence, high aspirations, achievement in science, and publishing original writing. Living in a dormitory has a positive effect on aspirations and substantial effects on persistence. Residents are more likely than commuters to attain positions of leadership in college and to achieve in athletics, theater, and journalism. Persistence is also positively influenced by membership in social fraternities or sororities.

The most important environmental factor affecting academic achievement is the prestige or selectivity of the institution: Students attending the most selective institutions will earn lower grades than students of equal ability attending nonselective institutions. Prestige or selectivity does not decrease the student's chances of completing the baccalaureate degree, however. Indeed, the student's chances of persisting are poorest at public and private two-year colleges, which tend to be of low selectivity.

Selective Catholic institutions have a positive effect on the student's chances of attaining positions of leadership, publishing original writing, and enrolling in graduate school. Nonselective Protestant colleges positively affect the student's grades and undergraduate persistence but negatively affect the student's chances of attaining positions of leadership and of aspiring to higher degrees.

Men are more likely to get good grades, to achieve in athletics, and to graduate with honors at a men's college than they are at a coeducational institution. However, they are more likely to attain positions of leadership in a coeducational institution. The pattern for women is reversed: Although women are more likely to achieve in athletics at a coeducational institution, they are more likely to attain positions of leadership, to complete the degree, and to aspire to higher degrees if they attend a women's college.

Students are more likely to graduate with honors if they attend selective public or private universities. Attending a large rather than a small institution, however, has a substantial negative effect on the student's chances to achieve in a wide variety of extracurricular areas: leadership, athletics, journalism, and theater.

Policies that have guided much of the recent expansion of American higher education have favored the development of commuter institutions and, most recently, have discouraged expansion of residential facilities. The findings of this chapter suggest the net effect of these policies is to increase the likelihood that students will drop out before completing their baccalaureate degrees. Of course, commuter colleges and colleges that cannot accommodate all students in existing residence halls might argue that these data concerning the impact of the residential experience are irrelevant: Most of these institutions have no means to expand their residential facilities. From another perspective, these same data could serve as a challenge to the ingenuity and resourcefulness of the commuter college. It might be possible, for example, to devise ways to *simulate* the residential experience so students would spend more time on campus and interact more with faculty and fellow students. The strong association between involvement and persistence suggests that any programs that involve commuters more in campus life will have a positive affect on persistence. If nothing else, institutions should consider experimenting with such techniques on selected students.

V

Career Development

Many students attend college primarily to prepare for a career. Of new freshmen entering college in fall 1976, 71 percent reported that getting a better job was a "very important" reason in the decision to go to college (Astin, King, and Richardson, 1976). More than half (54 percent) also said making more money was a very important reason for attending college. Institutions attempt to facilitate this career development process in various ways, for example, by developing special skills and competencies, certification or awarding credits and degrees required to enter particular professions, and guidance and counseling to help students crystallize career plans.

This chapter focuses on two career outcomes: (1) implementation of the career plans expressed at college entry and (2) starting salaries of persons pursuing different careers. Analyses are limited to ten career fields: business, college teaching, engineering, homemaking, law, medicine, nursing, school teaching, scientific research, and social work. These fields account for nearly 60 percent of freshman career choices; if undecided students are excluded, they account for two thirds of the choices. Analyses examine several related questions: What characteristics of the entering students are associated with successful implementation of career plans during the undergraduate years? Are students more likely to be successful if they attend certain types of institutions? Are some institutions more successful than others in helping students achieve specific goals, such as admission to law or medical school? Which characteristics of students and institutions affect the student's starting salary in different fields?

Change in Career Fields During Undergraduate Years

A substantial literature on career development during the undergraduate years indicates that students frequently change their plans after they enter college (Astin and Panos, 1969; Davis, 1965; Fenske and Scott, 1973). These changes are more systematic than random: Students who change majors or career plans usually change to related fields. Fields differ markedly in their retention and recruitment of students, with business and law generally showing the greatest gains and science and engineering the greatest losses during the undergraduate years.

During the early years of the Cooperative Institutional Research Program (CIRP), entering freshmen specified their probable careers by choosing one of forty-four fields from a list on the freshman questionnaire. The list was repeated without change in the first three four-year follow-ups (1966-1970, 1967-1971, and 1968-1972). The five-year follow-up of 1969 freshmen in 1974 contained a different list because of requirements of the funding agency. Initial analyses of changes during the undergraduate years therefore utilize the 1968-1972 sample, which provides the most recent data with equivalent pretests and posttests.

Although it would have been useful to study all career-choice groups, the results for those other than the ten most popular careers would have been unreliable because of too few students. The ten careers account for about 61 percent of the entering freshman career choices in 1969 and for about 57 percent of the follow-up choices in 1974. These percentages increased to 68 and 64, respectively, when the undecided students (about 11 percent of the total group) were excluded.

Table 17 shows the changes in the ten choices during the undergraduate years. Careers with the largest absolute gain in popularity are listed first; those with the largest losses are listed last. Business, homemaking, and college teaching show the largest absolute and relative gains, whereas engineering and school teaching show the largest absolute losses. Substantial relative losses also occur for medicine and scientific research. These results confirm national surveys conducted during the late 1950s and the 1960s, which showed substantial increases for business and law and substantial decreases for scientifically oriented fields (Astin and Panos, 1969; Davis, 1964, 1965). These earlier studies did not, however, show such a large decline in the popularity of elementary and secondary teaching. That the discrepancy may reflect the decline in employment opportunities for schoolteachers that occurred during the late 1960s and early 1970s is supported by the CIRP freshman surveys during this same period. Successive classes of entering freshmen evidenced a steady decline in preference for careers as school-teachers between 1966 and 1976 (Astin, Panos, and Creager, 1967; Astin, King, and Richardson, 1976).

The next to last column in Table 17 shows the stability of the students' initial career choice. Students who plan to become either businesspersons or nurses are the most stable over time, whereas those who plan to become college professors, scientific researchers, social workers, and homemakers are most likely to change their minds after entering college. The last column shows the percentage of those choosing each career in 1972 who made the same choice as entering freshmen in 1968. Basically, this percentage shows how dependent the field is on students initially picking it. Engineering, school teaching, and

Table 17. Changes in Career Choice During the College Years
(1968 Freshmen Followed Up in 1972)

Career	Percentage Choosing in		Percentage Change Between 1968 and 1972		Of students choosing career in 1968, percentage choosing same career in 1972	Of students choosing career in 1972, percentage choosing same career in 1968
	1968	1972	Absolute	Relative		
Businessperson[a]	11.0	16.4	+6.4	+ 49	56	36
Homemaker	.7	3.9	+3.2	+457	23	4
College professor	1.2	3.6	+2.4	+200	19	6
Lawyer	3.4	3.8	+ .4	+ 12	40	36
Nurse	3.0	2.8	− .2	− 7	60	62
Social worker	2.8	2.5	− .3	− 11	23	25
Physician	2.9	2.2	− .7	− 24	40	51
Scientific researcher	3.1	2.0	− .9	− 35	22	35
Engineer	9.2	4.0	−5.2	− 57	32	74
Schoolteacher[b]	23.3	16.1	−7.2	− 31	45	64
All 10 Careers	60.6	57.3	−3.3	− 5.4	43	41

[a]Includes accountant, business executive, business owner, and business sales.

[b]Elementary or secondary.

nursing are most dependent on students retaining their initial choices, whereas college teaching and homemaking depend more on recruits from other fields.

Table 17 shows that engineering and schoolteaching lose many students to other fields during the undergraduate years, and that business and homemaking recruit many dropouts from other fields. What are the specific paths followed by students who change from one field to another as undergraduates? Are dropouts from given careers likely to change to particular fields? Are the changes systematic or random? Table 18 shows the results of the "traffic" between the four fields recruiting or losing the most students and the ten specific career fields. Each row in the table represents a different career. The first four values show the percentage of students who initially chose the career and changed to the four large fields. The last four values are based on students who chose the career at follow-up; they show the percentage *recruited* from each of the four large fields. Among freshman choosing a business career, for example, only 1.3 percent changed to engineering; by contrast, 13 percent of those choosing business four years later was recruited from engineering. Some traffic is two-way: Some 3.2 percent of those who initially chose engineering changed to school teaching, and 3 percent of those who chose engineering on the follow-up was recruited from school teaching. Similarly, 6.1 percent of those initially choosing college professor switched to business, and 6.7 percent of those choosing college professor on the follow-up was recruited from business.

The greatest "trade imbalances" involve the flows from teaching and nursing to homemaking and the flows from engineering to business, law, medicine, and college teaching. School teaching, although it suffers a net loss during the four undergraduate years, is involved in substantial two-way traffic. Thus, even though school teaching supplies many recruits for college teaching, social work, and homemaking, it also recruits many dropouts from these fields.

Considering the substantial drop in students' business interests during college, it is puzzling that the number of students planning to enter the field of business increases so much

Table 18. Career Flow Patterns During the Undergraduate Years
(1968 Freshmen Followed Up in 1972)

Career	Percentage of those choosing career in 1968 who changed to				Percentage of those choosing career in 1972 who were recruited from			
	Business	Engineering	Homemaking	School Teaching	Business	Engineering	Homemaking	School Teaching
Businessperson	—	1.3	1.4	4.8	—	13.0	.4	9.4
Homemaker	9.4	.0	—	14.7	4.1	.3	—	35.9
College professor	6.1	.8	.6	17.3	6.7	6.0	.7	33.3
Lawyer	18.7	.4	.0	2.1	10.9	5.7	.6	6.6
Nurse	2.2	.0	8.5	4.5	.8	.1	.5	8.4
Social worker	3.1	.8	3.8	14.3	5.3	3.9	1.0	18.8
Physician	7.7	.2	.7	2.5	2.7	6.7	.2	2.6
Scientific researcher	7.7	4.3	1.5	4.7	2.7	10.4	.4	5.9
Engineer	23.1	—	.1	3.2	3.8	—	.0	3.0
Schoolteacher	6.6	.8	6.0	—	3.3	1.8	.6	—

during and after college. Is it possible that many students go into business, in spite of minimal interest, simply because that is where the jobs are? Are the students whose interests decline most during the college years the same ones who are migrating into business from other fields? A closer inspection of the data shows that the initially high business interests of students who choose business as freshmen and maintain that choice over time decline somewhat, but the decline is less than among nonbusiness students. Students switching from business to other careers show by far the largest declines (more than a full standard deviation). Students who switch into business, however, actually show a slight increase in business interests, although their follow-up scores are still far below the scores of students who chose business as freshmen. These results show that most of the overall decline in business interests is accounted for by students who switch from business to other careers and by students who never choose business. The large influx of students with only moderate business interests suggests that the field of business may be less a magnet attracting students from other fields than a haven for people who, for various reasons, are not able to carry through initial plans to enter other fields. Compared to most other fields of employment, business is probably much more flexible in matters such as course and degree requirements.

Successful Implementation of Career Plans

The frequency of change in career plans during the undergraduate years suggests that some students are much more able to realize their initial aspirations than others. Factors affecting implementation of career plans were assessed using the 1969-1974 longitudinal file, the most recent longitudinal data available, which covered a five- rather than four-year span. Since many undergraduates take five rather than four years to complete their programs (see Chapter Four), the file with the additional year provides a better measure of educational and career progress than the four-year file.

One problem with previous research on undergraduate

career choices is that the analyses of the effects of personal and environmental factors were made with undifferentiated samples. For example, in the multiinstitutional study by Astin and Panos (1969), many career outcomes were used as dependent variables, and predictions of these outcomes were made for all students at the time they entered college as freshmen. While such a design may be valuable for manpower forecasting, the results are of limited use for individual students, since they apply only to students in general, not to those who begin college with specific career aspirations. Moreover, using undifferentiated groups for predicting career outcomes implicitly assumes that students will be influenced by the same environmental factors regardless of initial career aspirations.

To overcome these difficulties, students were separated initially into homogeneous groups based on their career plans at time of college entry. Thus, the 1969-1974 longitudinal sample was sorted into groups by data provided in 1969. (Because of limitations in the 1974 follow-up questionnaire, two career groups—homemaker and college teacher—were studied using the 1968-1972 sample.) Freshmen were classified into groups by three criteria: initial career choice at college entry, highest degree planned, and estimates of chances that they would change their career plans after entering college (Table 19). The chances of changing plans were estimated on a four-point scale ("no chance," "very little chance," "some chance," "good chance"). Students who estimated that they had a "good chance" of changing plans were eliminated. Students who said there was "some chance" of changing plans were eliminated from the school teaching and social work groups. Additional criteria were used to screen two other groups: Students were included in the business group only if they checked "being very well off financially" as an essential or very important career goal, and students were included in the nursing group only if they checked "helping others in difficulty" as an essential or very important goal. The basic purpose was to define a set of freshman career groups in which people had homogeneous aspirations, as well as degree plans and life goals that were consistent with their stated career goals.

Table 19. Freshman Career Groups and Attainment of Career Goals After Five Years

Career Group	Freshman Criteria (1969) for Group Membership[a]		Criteria for Attainment of Career Objective After Five Years (1974)[b]	Percentage Attaining Objectives
	Career Choice(s)	Highest Degree Planned		
Business[c] (N = 895)	Accountant Business Executive Business Owner Business (sales)	Bachelor's or higher	Have bachelor's degree, employed in business or enrolled in graduate school	50
Engineering (N = 1,448)	Engineer	Bachelor's or higher	Have bachelor's degree, employed as engineer or enrolled in graduate school	51
Law (N = 384)	Lawyer	LL.B. or J.D.	Enrolled in law school	38
Medicine (N = 863)	Physician	M.D.	Enrolled in medical school	31
Nursing[d] (N = 413)	Nurse	Bachelor's or higher	Have bachelor's degree, employed as nurse or enrolled in graduate school	69
School teaching (N = 378)	Elementary teacher Secondary teacher School counselor Principal	Bachelor's or higher	Have bachelor's degree, employed as teacher or enrolled in graduate school	59
Science (N = 378)	Scientific researcher College teacher with science major	Ph.D. or M.D.	Enrolled in graduate or medical school, pursuing Ph.D. or M.D.	42
Social work (N = 150)	Social worker	Master's or higher	Have master's or enrolled in graduate school and pursuing master's or higher	21

[a]All freshmen who estimated their chances of changing career plans as "very good" were eliminated; for school teaching and social work, students estimating "some" chance were also eliminated.

[b]Students had to be pursuing the same career at follow-up.

[c]Includes students who checked "being very well off financially" as an essential or very important goal.

[d]

Attainment of appropriate career outcomes was defined somewhat differently for each group (Table 19). Attainment for a student in any group involved several criteria: stability in expressed career choice during the five years after matriculation, attainment of the bachelor's degree, and employment or enrollment in graduate or professional school. At first it was assumed that imposing a bachelor's degree would confound the analysis of factors influencing successful implementation of career plans. That is, if one set of factors affects the student's chances of completing a baccalaureate degree within five years and if a contrasting set affects career plans, including nonbachelor's recipients in the analysis would confound the two effects. To test this possibility, a preliminary set of analyses was conducted in which all nonbachelor's recipients were excluded. The only major changes in the findings concerned the impact of two-year colleges (see following discussion). Since the results otherwise proved similar to those using all students in each group, only the analyses involving larger, unselected samples are reported.

The effects of freshman and environmental variables on successful implementation of career plans were assessed separately for each career group with stepwise regression analyses. Because the career outcomes were unique, several additional freshman characteristics were included in the analyses: student's freshman major, father's occupation, and a set of items from the 1969 questionnaire about attitudes of parents. Additional college variables included the percentage of baccalaureate degrees awarded by the institution in various fields, the percentage of women, and the percentage of graduate students in the student body. Degrees awarded by field was an important determinant of career outcomes in an earlier longitudinal study (Astin and Panos, 1969). Percentage of women was included because of the strong association between sex and career choice, and percentage of graduate students was included because of the possible effects of a substantial graduate program on career choice. The large number of predictor variables required that the regression analyses involving each career be done in two stages. In the first stage, two independent regressions were conducted to screen variables; in the second stage, variables entering either regression in the first stage were included in the final analysis.

While it would have been desirable to perform separate analyses by sex for each career group, the sex distribution was such that separate analyses were possible only for medicine and school teaching. Business, college teaching, law, engineering, scientific research, and social work had fewer than 100 women; nursing and homemaking had fewer than 100 men.

Because of limitations in the 1974 follow-up questionnaire, analyses of the careers of homemaker and college teacher were carried out with the 1968-1972 longitudinal sample. Peculiarities in the change patterns from freshmen to follow-up for both fields required several special analyses. For example, among students indicating, in the 1972 follow-up, that they wanted to be college professors, 93.8 percent was recruited from other careers. The corresponding percentage for homemaker was 95.7 percent. In other words, students who pursue these careers initially account for less than 10 percent of those who pursue them ultimately. These low percentages result from two conditions: (1) the low stability of choice among students initially pursuing the careers (18.6 percent for college professor and 23.3 percent for homemaker) and (2) the large growth in popularity in both careers during the undergraduate years.

The undergraduate flow patterns for these two careers prompted a decision to establish three groups to analyze the career of college teacher and two groups for homemaker (Table 20). The two additional groups to study the college teacher included students who initially chose elementary or secondary school teaching (dropouts from these fields account for one third of all students who wanted to be college professors in 1972), and all students with doctoral degree aspirations who started out pursuing a career other than college professor (primarily physician, lawyer, scientific researcher, and "undecided"). The additional group to analyze homemaking included all students initially pursuing elementary or secondary teaching, nursing, or business-clerical (primarily secretarial) careers. Dropouts from these careers account for more than half (51.3 percent) of all students who ultimately pursue careers in homemaking. Since more than 99 percent of these students were women, the handful of men pursuing homemaking was excluded from both groups.

Table 20. Special Groups for Analyses of College Teaching and
Homemaking (1968 Freshmen Followed Up in 1972)

Career Group	Freshmen (1968) Criteria for Group Membership	Follow-Up (1972) Criteria for Attainment of Career Outcome	Percentage Attaining Career Outcome
College Teaching— Stables (N = 138)	*Career:* College Teacher *Degree Planned:* Ph.D.	*Career:* College Teacher *Degree Planned:* Ph.D. Enrolled in graduate school	10.1
College Teaching— Recruits from precollege teaching (N = 5,460)	*Career:* Elementary or Secondary School Teacher *Degree Planned:* Bachelor's or higher	Same as Above	1.8
College Teaching— Recruits from other graduate fields (N = 5,859)	*Career:* All except college teacher *Degree Planned:* Ph.D., M.D., D.D.S., LL.B., or J.D.	Same as Above	3.1
Homemaking— Stables (N = 353)	*Career:* Homemaker *Degree Planned:* Bachelor's or higher *Sex:* Female	*Career:* Homemaker	17.3
Homemaking— Recruits (N = 3,483)	*Career:* Elementary or Secondary School Teacher, nurse, business-clerical *Degree Planned:* Bachelor's or higher *Sex:* Female	*Career:* Homemaker	7.6

Results of the regression analyses of the effects of entering freshman and institutional characteristics on career choice are presented separately for the ten career fields.

Business. Attainment of career objectives in business was predicted with modest accuracy ($R = .40$) from entering freshman and institutional characteristics. Students are most likely to succeed in pursuit of a business career if their undergraduate major is in business (partial $r = .24$), if their father's occupation is in a business field, and if their parents have high aspirations for them. Publishing original writing in high school carries a negative weight for a business career (partial $r = -.11$). The chances of successfully implementing a career plan in business increase if students attend a prestigious institution, a private institution, or a university and substantially decrease if they attend a public four-year college or a public or private two-year college. The positive effect of prestige is consistent with Sharp's (1970) study of college alumni, which found that graduates of the more prestigious institutions are particularly likely to pursue careers in business.

After controlling for entering freshman and institutional characteristics, the student's undergraduate grade-point average (GPA) was significantly related to the business career objective (partial $r = .08$). Additional analyses indicated that this relationship may be attributed to the effect of GPA on degree completion. That is, when the criterion of completing the bachelor's degree is not imposed on the measure of career attainment, undergraduate GPA shows no relationship to the attainment of a business career.

Engineering. Students are most likely to become engineers if they have good grades in high school, major in engineering initially, or have a father who is an engineer. Other positive predictors are wanting to make a theoretical contribution to science and viewing parents as highly religious. Significant negative predictors are being elected to a student office in high school, winning a varsity letter in high school, planning to change major fields in college, showing interest in the performing arts, and having parents with a low income.

The likelihood of implementing an engineering career is strongly associated with the sex ratio in the student body and with the distribution of undergraduate major fields. The concentration of undergraduates in engineering is strongly associated (partial $r = .17$) with an engineering career, whereas concentrations of students in all other undergraduate fields, particularly the humanities (partial $r = -.19$), is negatively associated. Similar effects have been reported by Skager, Holland, and Braskamp (1966). Despite the strong association between the sex ratio of the student body and the engineering objective, noncoeducational colleges do not have a significant effect on this outcome. In short, engineering majors who find themselves in the company of many students and faculty members in the humanities and other nonengineering disciplines may be less likely to maintain their career plans than engineering majors in technological institutions. This effect confirms Astin and Panos' (1969) hypothesis of "progressive conformity" and Feldman and Newcomb's (1969) hypothesis of "accentuation of initial differences." These hypotheses state that students in the company of similar students will be better able to maintain their unique characteristics than students in the presence of those with different characteristics.

Students also have a better chance of realizing an engineering career if they attend a selective institution or a public four-year college, whereas their chances are reduced by attending a nonselective Protestant or nonselective nonsectarian college. Undergraduate GPA is substantially associated with becoming an engineer (partial r = .21), independent of entering student or institutional characteristics. This effect is not dependent on completing the bachelor's degree. That is, even among bachelor's degree recipients, achieving an engineering career is substantially related (partial r = .15) to the career outcome.

Law. Attaining the career objective in law—enrollment in law school—was predicted with greater accuracy (R = .58) than any other career outcome. By far the best predictor is the student's score on college admissions tests (r = .35; partial r = .23). A smaller positive weight is associated with high school grades and substantial negative weights with plans to marry at college entry, age, and having a father who is a college teacher. (Having a father who is a lawyer is not related to attaining this career objective.) Why older students should have less chance than younger students to enter law school within five years is not entirely clear. It seems unlikely that law schools would discriminate against older students in their admissions policies. It is more likely that older students may delay or change plans after college entry because of family or other responsibilities.

The strong association between college admissions tests and being in law school may reflect the strong dependence of law schools on the Law Scholastic Aptitude Test (LSAT). Because of the crush of applications, many law schools have been forced to rely on relatively mechanical procedures with formulas based on college grades and LSAT scores. This interpretation is supported by the substantial partial correlation ($r = .33$) between *college* GPA's and entry to law school that is obtained after entering freshman and college characteristics are controlled. This partial correlation changes little when nonbachelor's degree recipients are excluded.

Attending a men's college substantially increases the chances of attaining the career objective in law, a finding that replicates the earlier results of Astin and Panos (1969). Chances are substantially reduced, however, by attending a prestigious or selective institution. This negative effect is especially pronounced in Protestant institutions: Chances are substantial in the nonselective institutions and reduced in the selective institutions. Selective private universities also substantially reduce the student's chances of entering law school. Why selectivity should have such an effect is not clear. The lower grades that students receive at selective institutions (see Chapter Four) may be one explanation; however, the impact of selectivity does not disappear when undergraduate GPA is controlled. Another explanation may lie in the extreme diversity in the quality of law schools. Possibly students who attend selective institutions—private universities, in particular—develop high aspirations about the kind of law school they want to enter. If they fail to gain admittance to one of the most prestigious schools, they may be unable to settle for a less prestigious school and, instead, switch their career to other fields, such as business or teaching. Students attending a less selective institution, however, may be willing to settle for a less elite law school.

Admission to law school is also related to the distribution of undergraduate major fields. Increased chances of admission are associated with attending an institution that emphasizes social science fields, biological science, or humanities; chances of entry are reduced at institutions that emphasize education, business, physical sciences, and engineering.

Medicine. Being in medical school after five years was also predicted with substantial accuracy ($R = .56$) from entering student and institutional characteristics. As with law, the strongest predictors for medical admission are high school grades, college admissions test scores, and undergraduate college grades. The relative weights assigned to high school grades and admissions tests are different for men and women: Among men, high school grades carry more weight, whereas among women, college admissions tests carry more weight. For women, receiving an award in a National Merit Scholarship (NMS) competition (based primarily on high college admissions test scores) was strongly associated (partial r = .35) with entry into medical school. Other predictors for men include plans to raise a family (positive), winning a varsity letter in high school (negative), plans to change initial career aspirations (negative), and interest in creative writing (negative). Black men have a better chance of admission to medical school (r = .09) than white men with comparable abilities and aspirations. For women, admission is positively associated with attending a private high school (partial r = .21) and negatively associated with being reared as a Catholic (r = −.32). Having a physician for a father significantly increases chances of entering medical school for both sexes. Chances of entry are increased by attending a selective private university and decreased by attending a public four-year college. Institutional size produces opposite effects for men and women: Men increase their chances of entering medical school by attending small institutions, whereas women increase their chances by attending large institutions.

Nursing. Students planning to become nurses show the highest rate of attainment of their career objectives (69 percent), although prediction of this outcome was only moderately accurate (R = .46). High school grades carry a substantial positive weight (partial r = .23), but this weight disappears when students who fail to complete the bachelor's degree are excluded. Apparently, high school grades are important only in increasing the student's chances of completing the baccalaureate degree. Other positive predictors of becoming a nurse include being reared as a Catholic and being a member of a high school honor society. Negative weights are associated with plans to change major fields of study and being black.

Chances of attaining a career objective in nursing are substantially increased by attending a selective or prestigious institution (partial r = .22) and substantially reduced by attending a two-year public college (partial r = −.16). Chances are also improved by attending a nonselective Catholic college or a selective Protestant college. For black students, chances of becoming a nurse are better at a black than at a predominantly white college. The distribution of undergraduate major fields shows no systematic relationship to nursing. Nursing is also the only one of the ten careers in which attainment of the objective is not related to undergraduate GPA. As long as they complete college, students are equally likely to go into nursing regardless of their undergraduate grades.

School Teaching. Successful attainment of the career objective of schoolteacher was more difficult to predict (R = .31) than any other career outcome. Predictors carrying the largest positive weights include majoring in education as a freshman and good grades in high school and college. The impact of college grades was not diminished appreciably by excluding students who had not completed bachelor's degrees at the time of the follow-up. Being a woman also carries substantial positive weight: Of the women, 61 percent, compared with only 47 percent of the men, become schoolteachers. The lower rate of attainment for men is due primarily to the large number switching into business and college teaching. Negative predictive weights are associated with interest in making a theoretical contribution to scientific knowledge and estimated chances of dropping out. For men, positive weights are associated with being elected president of a student organization in high school and plans to raise a family, whereas a negative weight is associated with intention to change career plans at time of college entry. Among women, positive weights are associated with interest in the performing arts and becoming an expert in finance, whereas negative weights are associated with interest in creative writing, father's educational level, and estimated chances of obtaining an A average in college. Why women who are optimistic about their chances of academic success in college should be less likely to follow through on plans to become elementary or secondary school teachers is not clear. Possibly many of these women decide to switch into career fields, such as science or law, that require postgraduate training.

The environmental variable with the strongest effect on a teaching career is getting married in college: Women are substantially less likely to become teachers if they get married as undergraduates. Marriage has no effect, however, on a man's chances of implementing a teaching career. A woman's chances of teaching are enhanced by attending a college for women or a public four-year college (many such institutions are former teacher's colleges). Students in institutions in which a relatively large proportion of other students are majoring in education are more likely to become teachers. These results are, once again, consistent with the positive impact of teacher's colleges on plans to go into teaching reported by Astin and Panos (1969). Students attending a public community college are less likely to become teachers; this effect is especially pronounced among men. A man's chances are somewhat greater at northeastern institutions and somewhat less at midwestern institutions.

Scientific Research. Attainment of the career objective in scientific research (enrollment in graduate school for a doctorate) was predicted with only modest accuracy ($R = .41$). The most potent predictors are good grades in high school, high scores on college admissions tests, and, in particular, good grades in college (partial $r = .34$). Students are more likely to obtain a career objective in scientific research if they are black or relatively young, or if their fathers are engineers. Attending a private college—in particular, a private nonsectarian four-year college—increases the student's chances of having a career in science, whereas attending a college with a high proportion of students majoring in education reduces these chances. Among black students, the chances of attaining their objective are greater at predominantly black colleges.

Social Work. Because of the small size of this career sample, only a few freshman and institutional characteristics contributed significantly to the prediction. Students are more likely to implement plans for a career in social work if they value raising a family at the time of college entry and if they were reared in a nonreligious family. Nonimplementation is related to being black and to an interest in keeping up to date with political affairs. Social work is the only career in which neither high school nor college grades carries significant weight in the prediction. College characteristics have only borderline effects. Attending a college in the Northeast is positively related to this career outcome, whereas attending a community college or a college in the Midwest is negatively related.

College Teaching. Because of the low percentage of students choosing college professor as a career on the 1972 follow-up of 1968 freshmen, the predictions of this career outcome were not accurate: The multiple correlations were .38 for the group that initially chose college teaching, .17 for the school-teaching group, and .14 for the group pursuing other professions but planning doctoral degrees. Nevertheless, the entering freshman characteristics predicting attainment of college teaching were similar across the three samples. Positive predictive weights are associated with high academic attainment in secondary school (election to an honor society, high school rank, average high school grades, and recognition in NMS competition). Among students initially planning to be schoolteachers, changing plans to college teacher is also associated with aspiring to the Ph.D., being editor of the high school paper, and political interests (discussing politics and demonstrating against the war in southeast Asia). Among freshmen aspiring to doctoral degrees but to some other career, white students and students who had authored original writing in high school are most likely to switch to college teaching, whereas students aspiring to medical degrees are less likely to switch.

The importance of academic accomplishment in predicting entry into college teaching raises interesting possibilities for speculation. Is high academic achievement simply a requirement for entry to graduate school, or are more subtle motivational processes at work? Does the student's sense of mastery over academic material stimulate the pursuit of subject matter in greater depth? Does succeeding in the academic setting reinforce the student's tendency to stay in that setting? Do professors single out their best students for special attention, and does the student reciprocate by identifying with and wanting to emulate the professor?

College selectivity or prestige appears to increase the student's chances of pursuing college teaching. Among blacks who want to be schoolteachers, those attending black colleges are more likely to switch to college teaching than those attending white colleges. Again, this result suggests the presence of motivational factors: Black students may find it easier to identify with professors in black colleges than in predominantly white colleges. Among students who aspire to other doctoral-level careers, students attending selective Protestant colleges and colleges in the Northeast are most likely to change to college teaching.

The low rate of attainment of a college teaching career may be attributed in part to the stringency of the criteria for this outcome: Pursuing the Ph.D. four years after college entry does not apply to a substantial proportion of students who take five years to complete their baccalaureate work (see Chapter Four). Longitudinal data over a longer time are necessary to study those who take more than four years to complete their baccalaureates and enter graduate school. Future studies using this career outcome should use data encompassing a minimum of five years after initial college entry.

Homemaking. The prediction of this career outcome with data from 1968 freshmen followed up in 1972 was not particularly accurate, probably because few students in both groups aspired to be homemakers at the follow-up. The prediction among those who initially wanted to be homemakers produced a multiple correlation of .26; prediction among those who aspire to other related careers (nursing, school teaching, business-clerical occupations) produced a correlation of only .19. The most potent predictor for both groups is low degree aspirations as entering freshmen (bachelor's or "other" degree). Students in both groups were less likely to choose homemaker as their career on the follow-up if they planned to join in demonstrations at the time of college entry. Among women who wanted to be homemakers, those who held elected offices in high school are more likely to persist in their choice after entering college. Among women who aspired to other careers, those who planned to marry while in college or within a year after college are likely to switch to homemaking. White women are substantially more likely than black women to switch to homemaking; business majors are most likely and social science majors least likely to make that switch. College characteristics show only borderline effects on pursuit of a homemaking career. This career choice is most likely to result from attending small, nonselective institutions (particularly Roman Catholic). Women who attend institutions in the Northeast are most likely to change from homemaker to some other career.

Effects on Income

Can the student's income in the first job after college be predicted from entering freshman characteristics? Does the type of college attended have any impact on income? Are the predictors of income different for different careers? To explore these questions, analyses were conducted with students who indicated that they were employed full-time at the five-year follow-up. Four fields—business, engineering, nursing, and school teaching—had sufficient persons to permit an analysis. Table 21 shows the size and income level of each group. Engi-

Table 21. Prediction of Annual Salary for Full-Time Employees
Five Years After College Entry

| Career Group | N | Annual Salary 1974 | | Stepwise Regression | |
		Mean	Standard Deviation	Final R	Number of Predictors
Business	525	9,964	3,159	.42	17
Engineering	782	11,185	3,297	.40	12
Nursing	282	8,968	2,214	.39	6
School Teaching	1,203	7,375	2,209	.37	20

neers command the highest salaries and schoolteachers the lowest salaries. Nurses and students in business fall in between. What is perhaps most remarkable in Table 21 is the size of the multiple-correlation coefficients (range from .37 to .42). Many chance factors can influence salary levels. Considering that this is the student's first job (a level at which one would expect only a small variation in salary), the predictions are quite accurate.

Business. The strongest positive predictors of salary for students in business fields are parental income, Catholic religious preference, ratings of parents as financially comfortable, and aspirations to be more successful than others and to obtain recognition from colleagues. Men and blacks command higher salaries than women and whites. The only negative predictor is aspirations to achieve in the performing arts. This complex of predictors suggests that high needs for recognition and status may directly affect the salary a student is able to command at the time of college graduation. The positive effect of parental income and of having parents who are financially well off is subject to several interpretations. Affluent parents could stimulate the student to seek the highest-paying job at graduation. By the same token, affluent parents may be in a position to assist the student in finding remunerative employment. Indeed, some wealthy parents may actually help their children secure a high-paying job.

Although high school grades carry only a borderline weight in predicting salary for students aspiring to business careers, college grades carry a substantial weight (partial $r = .15$). Employers may be willing to pay somewhat more money to students with better grades. The high-achieving student may also be more diligent in searching for the best-paying job. Salary in business is also substantially related to the student's residence as an undergraduate. Students living at home as freshmen earn substantially less than students living in dormitories or apartments. Perhaps getting away from home broadens the potential job contacts for students when they complete college.

With multiple-regression analysis, the regression weights make it possible to estimate the actual dollar value associated with various predictors. Being a man, for example, is worth about $1,900 in additional salary during the first year on the job. Being black is worth about $1,300. Each additional letter grade in college is worth approximately $900: students with A averages usually earn about $1,800 more than C students.

That blacks can command higher salaries than whites is perhaps to be expected, given the strong affirmative action pressures on business and industry to recruit more racial minority members. Why women should receive lower salaries than men with comparable characteristics, however, is not entirely clear. One explanation is outright sex discrimination: Business and industry may be less willing to pay women comparable salaries. Another possibility is that women may be more willing to settle for lower salaries, particularly if their job options are limited because of their husbands' mobility. Or women may seek lower-paying jobs. Men, for example, may be more interested in sales jobs, which probably pay more, whereas women may be more likely to select office jobs. Whatever the explanation, this large discrepancy merits much more intensive study to assess the relative importance of motivation, sex discrimination, and other factors.

Only one college characteristic significantly affects the student's business income: attending a men's college. After considering the effects of college grades and other student characteristics, the men's college is worth an additional $700 in income. Possibly the environment of an all-male college reinforces the student's interest in making money. Or men's colleges may have more effective relationships with potential business employers; students who attend these colleges may be in touch with better-paying jobs.

Engineering. Several entering characteristics carry positive weights in predicting salaries in the engineering field: good grades in high school, high parental income, parents rated by their children as financially comfortable, aspirations to raise a family or to be successful in business, interest in contributing to scientific knowledge, a father who is a farmer, and an engineering or fine arts major. Negative weights are associated with winning a varsity letter in high school, highly educated parents, plans to change careers after college entry, parents interested in politics, and interest in developing a meaningful philosophy of life. This pattern of predictors suggests that students will obtain better-paying jobs if they are strongly committed to either business or engineering and if their interests are more pragmatic than philosophical. Sex and race do not carry significant weights for engineers' salaries, although the small number of minorities and women (less than 1 percent) virtually eliminates any possibility of a significant predictive weight.

As with business, engineers with high grades in college earn better salaries. The additional salary associated with higher grades in engineering is almost identical to that found in business: approximately $900 for each letter grade. The only college characteristic with a significant weight is midwestern location: Students attending institutions in the Midwest earn, on the average, about $900 more than students in other regions. (A northeastern location carries a borderline negative effect equivalent to approximately −$700 in salary.) In all likelihood, these regional differences reflect labor market conditions. That is, starting salaries for engineering baccalaureates may be higher in the Midwest than other regions—in particular, the Northeast. That students from farm families should make approximately $1,000 more than students from nonfarm families may also reflect the labor market: A paucity of engineers in rural areas may create a local market where higher salaries are paid to persons willing to work there.

Nursing. Age carries the strongest weight in predicting salaries for nurses (partial $r = .23$). Students nineteen years or older at college entry are earning close to $2,000 more, on the average, than students eighteen years or younger when they entered college. Possibly, older students have already had some experience in nursing (practical nursing, for example) before they enter college. This experience could presumably translate into higher salaries once they complete their undergraduate training. The only other positive predictors of nursing salaries are good grades in high school and being reared as a Roman Catholic. College grades have no impact on salary for nurses, although each additional letter grade in high school is worth approximately $500. The only college characteristic that significantly affects salary for nurses is northeastern location, which is associated with approximately $600 in additional salary compared with other regions. Possibly this difference also reflects labor market factors: Nurses may be in greater demand in the Northeast than in other regions.

School Teaching. By far the most important predictor of salaries for schoolteachers is sex: Being a man is worth approximately $1,100 in additional salary. Although this finding provides evidence of sex discrimination, other explanations are possible: Men, for example, may be more likely than women to train in higher-paying specializations, such as physical education. Being a varsity athlete in high school, for example, has a positive effect on teaching salary after college. Men may also be more interested in higher-paying schools (secondary versus elementary, for example). Lacking any definitive test of these explanations, the strong association between sex and teacher's salaries warrants more intensive study.

Being black is worth approximately $1,000 in additional salary for teachers. Once again, this discrepancy may reflect the pressure on schools for affirmative action and the consequent high demand for minority teachers. Other positive predictors include high school and college grades, interest in raising a family, plans to change career at college entry, and parents interested in politics. Negative predictors include being raised in a small town or a father who is a farmer, aspirations to publish original writing, and majoring in the humanities. The negative impact of humanities (a salary approximately $750 lower) may reflect an oversupply of teachers trained in fields such as English, history, and foreign language. The negative effect of being raised in a rural or farm family may reflect labor market conditions: Teachers in rural communities may receive lower salaries than those in urban areas because of an oversupply. The dollar value of college grades is somewhat lower than with business and engineering: One letter grade difference is worth approximately $500.

The only college characteristic with a significant impact on teacher salaries is enrollment size: Students who attend large institutions tend to earn more as teachers than students who attend small institutions: The average difference between the largest and the smallest institutions is approximately $700. Again, labor market conditions may explain this difference. Since students from rural areas tend to enroll in small institutions (Astin, 1975a, p. 139), graduates from small institutions may be more likely to seek jobs in rural or other relatively low-paying regions.

Summary

While many students change their career plans during college, the changes are frequently systematic. Dropouts from engineering, for example, frequently change to business or science, while dropouts from school teaching and nursing frequently change to business and homemaking.

Perhaps the most important factor influencing career outcomes is sex. Women are more likely than men to leave traditionally masculine careers, such as medicine and law, and men are more likely to leave the traditionally feminine career of teaching. Perhaps more significant is the dramatic impact of sex on starting salaries in business and teaching. Even after background factors such as interests, high school and college grades, and fields of study are considered, men earn better than $1,000 more in salary than women in both these fields.

Being black produces a pattern of effects different from that for women. After other student characteristics are controlled, blacks are more likely to implement plans for a medical career. Being black is also associated with larger starting salaries in business and teaching. Blacks are less likely than whites, however, to implement plans for a nursing career.

Another student characteristic strongly associated with career outcomes is academic ability. Able students have a better chance than average students to implement career plans in law, medicine, nursing, engineering, and scientific research. College grades are strongly related to successful career implementation, as well as to starting salaries. Getting an A rather than a C average in college is worth at least $1,000 in additional income in nursing and engineering. These results clearly contradict the claim (Hoyt, 1966) that grades are not an important determinant of subsequent career outcomes.

Major field of study is closely related to career outcomes in two ways. First, students whose major fields are closely associated with their career objectives are more likely to realize these objectives than students without declared majors or in unrelated fields. Thus, students pursuing careers in business,

school teaching, and engineering are more likely to obtain their
objectives if they start out as freshmen majoring in these same
fields. Students planning to become engineers also receive
higher starting salaries if their initial major is engineering. The
second effect of major fields is environmental: Students are
more likely to implement their initial career plans if relatively
large numbers of fellow students are majoring in the same fields.
This mutually reinforcing effect adds further support to the
theories of "progressive conformity" (Astin and Panos, 1969)
and "accentuation of initial differences" (Feldman and Newcomb, 1969).

Table 22 summarizes the major environmental factors
influencing career outcomes. In general, students are less likely

Table 22. Summary of Environmental Effects on Career Outcomes

Career Outcome	Positively Affected by	Negatively Affected by
Successful Implementation of Plans To Become a		
Businessperson	Selective institution	Two-year college
	College for men	Public four-year college
College teacher	Selective institution	
	Selective Protestant college	
	Northeastern location	
Engineer	Public four-year college	Private two-year college
	Selective institution	Private university
	High percentage of men	Nonselective private college
		High percentage of women
Lawyer	College for men	Selective institution
	Highly selective private college	Public four-year college
	Nonselective Protestant college	Northeastern location
Homemaker	Nonselective Catholic college	Selective institution
		Northeastern location
Nurse	Selective institution	Two-year college
	Black college	Public four-year college
	Nonselective Catholic college	College for women
	Northeastern location	Western location

Table 22 *(Continued)*

Career Outcome	Positively Affected by	Negatively Affected by
Physician	Selective private university	Public four-year college
	Black college	
Schoolteacher	Public four-year college	Getting married (women only)
	College for women	Public two-year college
Scientific researcher	Highly selective private college	Western location
		Nonselective Protestant college
Social worker	Northeastern location	Two-year college
	Nonselective private college	
Salary in		
Business	College for men	Living with parents
Engineering	Midwestern location	Northeastern location
Nursing	Northeastern location	Midwestern location
Schoolteaching	Large institution	Small institution

Note: Good grades in college are positively related to successful implementation of careers in all fields except nursing and social work and to salaries in all fields except nursing.

to implement career plans if they attend a two-year college initially. With the possible exception of careers in nursing and business, this negative effect may be attributed entirely to the reduced chance of completing a baccalaureate that confronts students in a two-year college. Public four-year colleges produce mixed effects: The chances of implementing career plans for college teacher or engineer are facilitated by attending public four-year colleges, but chances of implementing plans for business, medicine, law, or nursing are reduced.

College selectivity or prestige has mixed effects on career outcomes. The chances of successfully implementing career plans in business or nursing are reduced by attending a nonselective institution, but the chances of becoming a lawyer are substantially increased. The chances of getting into medical school are enhanced by attending selective private universities. Apparently, college prestige or selectivity does not give students an advantage in competing for salaries in business, engineering, nursing, and teaching. It remains to be seen whether institutional prestige has significant impact on salaries in fields requiring graduate training.

The data did not support earlier studies showing a positive effect of college selectivity on income (Daniere and Mechling, 1970; Solmon, 1975). Many explanations for the discrepancy are possible: The current study controlled more student characteristics and performed analyses separately, by field; most subjects in the current study were not yet in the labor market, whereas these earlier studies covered longer periods of time. These issues are discussed in more detail in Chapter Seven.

The analyses also failed to confirm Kamens' (1971) finding that college size positively affects student interest in engineering, law, and medicine. Although Kamens' study was longitudinal and involved ninety-nine institutions, he controlled only a few entering characteristics and used much less stringent outcome criteria. The earlier study by Astin and Panos (1969), which used more elaborate freshman input controls, also failed to find a positive effect of size on these three career choices.

Some of the most pronounced effects involve colleges for men. The male student's chances of becoming a lawyer are substantially increased by attending a men's college. The chances of implementing a career in business are also increased, as is the salary level for men pursuing business careers. Colleges for women, however, produce less clear-cut effects. Attending a women's college increases a woman's chances of becoming a schoolteacher, but reduces her chances for a career in business. Women's colleges increase chances for a career in nursing, but graduates of women's colleges tend to get lower starting salaries than graduates of coeducational institutions.

That the region in which the college is located is significantly related to salaries suggests the presence of local labor market factors. Students pursuing careers in nursing, for example, receive higher salaries if they attend colleges in the Northeast and lower salaries if they attend institutions in the Midwest. Salaries for engineers show the reverse pattern. In general, attending institutions in the Midwest increases the students' chances of implementing career plans (careers in law are the major exception) and leads to reduced starting salaries. The negative effect may well reflect the negative impact of western institutions on persistence: Students may be less able to implement career plans because they have reduced chances of completing the baccalaureate degree required to enter the profession.

These findings have obvious implications for career guidance and counseling. For example, it would be useful for students to have access to some of the major empirical findings: that the proportion of students who manage to implement initial career plans is relatively low, that success in implementation varies considerably from one field to another, and so on. Students could also benefit from a knowledge of various personal qualities, such as sex and ability, that affect their chances of implementing career plans in different fields. From the standpoint of maximizing the students' opportunities to implement career plans successfully, the most important findings concern the effects of environmental factors, such as the type of college attended and the choice of a major field of study.

Satisfaction with the College Environment

Current discussions of accountability or the "outputs" of higher education frequently overlook student satisfaction. This area covers the student's subjective experience during the college years and perceptions of the value of the educational experience. Given the considerable investment of time and energy that most students make in attending college, the student's perception of value should be given substantial weight. Indeed, it is difficult to argue that student satisfaction can be legitimately subordinated to any other educational outcome.

This chapter focuses on student satisfaction and ratings

of the college environment. The analyses treat the students' overall satisfaction with the total undergraduate experience, as well as with specific aspects of that experience such as quality of instruction, contacts with faculty and fellow students, curriculum, college administration, reputation of the institution, and intellectual environment. The student's subjective response to the college environment can be assessed in at least two ways: The first is to ask the student directly about the degree of satisfaction with various aspects of the college. The second, utilized previously in several studies of college environments (Astin, 1968a; Pace and Stern, 1958), is to obtain the student's perception of such environmental factors as academic demands, social life, faculty-student relations, and so forth.

Student Satisfaction

The most detailed information about student satisfaction was available from the 1969-1970 ACE-Carnegie follow-up of 1966 freshmen. This follow-up questionnaire contained a measure of overall satisfaction based on a five-point scale (five = "very satisfied," four = "satisfied," three = "on the fence," two = "dissatisfied," one = "very dissatisfied") and seven ratings of satisfaction with specific aspects of the college based on a four-point scale (one, two, four, and five under overall satisfaction). Table 23 shows the mean ratings by students on each measure. Most students were midway through their senior year when they responded to the follow-up questionnaire, although the sample included dropouts. Students were asked to rate the institution they entered as first-time freshmen in the fall of 1966.

Table 23 suggests only a moderate degree of satisfaction with the overall college experience: the mean score (3.7) falls between "on the fence" and "satisfied," somewhat closer to "satisfied." The most satisfaction is with friendships with other students (see Fenske and Scott, 1973) and with the college's academic reputation (both means fall between "satisfied" and "very satisfied"). That all correlations are positive and statistically significant suggests an overall sense of satisfaction or dissatisfaction that affects students' ratings in all specific areas.

Table 23. Student Satisfaction with the Undergraduate Experience
(N = 17,771 Undergraduates 3½ Years After College Entry)

Satisfaction Measure	Mean Score	Intercorrelations						
		1	2	3	4	5	6	7
How satisfied are you with the following at your college?[a]								
1. The college's academic reputation	3.2							
2. The intellectual environment	2.8	.54						
3. Faculty-student relations	2.9	.24	.38					
4. The quality of classroom instruction	2.7	.34	.42	.50				
5. The variety of courses I can take	2.6	.25	.32	.25	.37			
6. Friendships with other students	3.3	.17	.23	.24	.18	.17		
7. The administration	2.6	.27	.34	.36	.32	.27	.17	
What is your overall evaluation of your college?[b]	3.7	.42	.54	.45	.49	.40	.31	.44

[a]Four-point scale: "Very satisfied" (4), "satisfied" (3), "dissatisfied" (2), "very dissatisfied" (1).

[b]Five-point scale: "Very satisfied" (5), "satisfied" (4), "on the fence" (3), "dissatisfied" (2), "very dissatisfied" (1).

That overall satisfaction correlates, on the average, more with specific areas of satisfaction than the specific areas correlate with each other supports this interpretation. Student friendships and variety of courses have the least in common with other satisfaction areas. The two highest correlations among specific satisfaction areas involve the college's academic reputation and intellectual environment ($r = .54$) and the quality of classroom instruction and faculty-student interaction ($r = .50$).

Because students were still enrolled at the time of the follow-up in 1969-1970, the most turbulent years on many college campuses, the degree of overall satisfaction with the college (midway between "on the fence" and "satisfied") could represent an underestimate of true student satisfaction with the undergraduate experience. To explore this possibility, the overall satisfaction ratings obtained during the 1972 follow-up of 1968 freshmen were tabulated along with the results from the five-year (1974) follow-up of the 1969 freshmen. Both follow-up questionnaires contained an identical item tapping overall satisfaction. Both follow-ups produced weighted means of 3.8—almost identical to the weighted mean in Table 23. This result suggests two conclusions: First, that overall student satisfaction with the undergraduate experience has remained relatively stable during the past decade, and second, that satisfaction ratings obtained from college seniors during the time of greatest campus unrest in the late 1960s do not produce spuriously low degrees of satisfaction.

Determinants of Satisfaction

Procedures for assessing the impact of entering student and environmental characteristics on student satisfaction were similar to those for assessing outcomes in earlier chapters. With each satisfaction measure as an outcome or dependent variable, stepwise regression analyses were used to control characteristics of the entering student. The entering freshman, institutional, and involvement measures were identical to those in the study of student involvement (Chapter Three). Analyses were identical for each satisfaction measure, except that, for overall satisfaction, analyses were repeated separately for men, women, and students of differing abilities.

Overall Satisfaction. The student's degree of overall satisfaction can be predicted with moderate accuracy (R = .49). Unlike most other outcome measures, however, entering student characteristics account for relatively little of the variance (R = .12). The addition of institutional characteristics increases the multiple correlation substantially (R = .25); the addition of involvement measures increases it further (R = .49). This pattern, replicated for all satisfaction measures, suggests that the student's satisfaction with college is much more dependent than other outcome measures on the characteristics of the institution and the student's involvement in the institutional environment. Small positive weights for overall satisfaction are associated with attending a private high school, religiousness, and frequent use of the library in high school. Small negative weights are associated with being hedonistic, self-critical, having artistic interests, and no religious preference. This pattern suggests that rebellious, nonconforming students are more likely to be dissatisfied with their colleges. For women, satisfaction is positively associated with intellectual self-esteem and parental income, whereas dissatisfaction is associated with being Jewish or black. Among men, satisfaction is positively associated with good grades in high school, interpersonal self-esteem, and interest in business; it is negatively associated with musical interests. For low-ability students, satisfaction is greater among white Protestants from highly educated families who attend private high schools and had high intellectual self-esteem; low satisfaction is associated with being black, attending a public high school, and being a smoker. For high-ability students, satisfaction is greater among women, political conservatives, and students with business interests. Overall satisfaction is likely to be greatest if the student attends a selective, affluent, high-cost institution. Satisfaction is enhanced by attending a men's college but decreased by attending a technological institution.

The positive effects of affluence and selectivity on satisfaction can be interpreted in several ways. That overall satisfaction correlates substantially with the college's reputation suggests that students may be more satisfied in a highly selective institution simply from knowing that the institution has a good reputation and that having a degree from that institution may be useful in later life. Since the correlation is far from perfect, however, it would appear that other factors are at work. The positive effects of tuition and institutional affluence provide additional clues. "Educational and general" expenditures, which form the basis for the affluence measure, are used to support items such as faculty salaries, library, laboratories, and physical plant. Students may thus report more satisfaction at affluent institutions in part because such institutions have superior faculties and educational resources. The positive effect of high tuitions on satisfaction may involve somewhat more subtle effects: Is it possible that students may value their educational experience more simply because it costs more?

Several involvement factors add significantly to the prediction of overall satisfaction: The most potent correlates are academic involvement (partial $r = .29$) and student-faculty interaction (partial $r = .21$). The positive effects of interacting with faculty have been noted by several other investigators (Gaff, 1973; Wood and Wilson, 1972). Small additional positive effects are associated with athletic involvement and familiarity with faculty in the major field. Students who are verbally aggressive in class tend to be less satisfied with their institutions. Involvement in student government or in honors programs is not related to satisfaction after other forms of involvement are considered. These strong associations of satisfaction with student-faculty interaction and academic involvement suggest that the student's undergraduate college experience might be much more meaningful if there were more personal contact between faculty and students and if students devoted more time and effort to their studies.

But what of the nonconformist? Are such students simply more inclined to be critical and to express dissatisfaction, regardless of their environment, or is it possible that colleges provide inadequate learning opportunities for such students? While this question cannot be adequately answered with existing data, the fact that nonconformity and independence is also related to dropping out (Astin, 1964, 1975b) suggests that colleges may reward certain types of conformity to the point where the more independent students become alienated.

Academic Reputation. Satisfaction with the academic reputation of the college is likely to be greater among students with better grades in high school and high scores on religiousness and interpersonal and intellectual self-esteem. Dissatisfaction with the reputation is somewhat greater among highly able students, Orientals, students with no religious preference, drinkers, and students with artistic interests. College characteristics show a pattern of relationships similar to that for overall satisfaction. The strongest correlate of satisfaction with academic reputation is selectivity (partial r = .18), with highly selective private colleges and universities generating the highest ratings. Satisfaction is greater at colleges for men and private institutions with high tuition. Satisfaction is lower at institutions in the South. Although northeastern institutions are associated with greater satisfaction with academic reputation, a northeastern location is negatively related to satisfaction after selectivity is controlled. In other words, northeastern institutions produce less satisfaction with academic reputation than comparable selective institutions elsewhere. Conceivably, this finding reflects the high concentration of selective or prestigious institutions in the northeastern United States. Because of this concentration, students attending institutions in the Northeast may develop higher subjective standards about what constitutes academic excellence.

Students are more likely to rate their institutions high in academic reputation if they show a high degree of academic or athletic involvement or if they interact frequently with faculty. These relationships are not as strong (partial r between .07 and .11) as those for overall satisfaction. Satisfaction with academic reputation is lower among verbally aggressive students and students participating in honors programs. The latter effect may mean that students in honors programs develop relatively stringent standards for their institutions' academic reputation.

Intellectual Environment. Satisfaction with the intellectual environment has small positive relationships with being white, religious, and having high grades in high school. Satisfaction is lower among students with artistic interests, drinkers, and students from highly educated families. As with the two previous measures, satisfaction with the intellectual environment is greatest at selective and prestigious institutions. Students express the least satisfaction at teacher's colleges, technological institutions, and institutions located in the South. A northeastern location again shows a reversal after other college characteristics are controlled. Being located in the Northeast, viewed by itself (after controlling for student characteristics), has a positive partial correlation of .15 with satisfaction with the intellectual environment. The correlation reverses to —.07, however, when other characteristics (prestige and selectivity, in particular), are controlled. Again, it appears that students attending institutions in the Northeast have more stringent standards for academic quality than students attending institutions elsewhere.

Academic involvement shows the strongest partial correlation (.21) with satisfaction with intellectual environment. Apparently, students are more likely to perceive the intellectual environment favorably if they become involved in it. The direction of causation here is not entirely clear, since having a favorable impression of the intellectual environment may also prompt students to become more involved in academic pursuits. Whatever the explanation, the students' own involvement is a more important determinant of satisfaction with the intellectual environment than any objective characteristics of the institutions themselves. Other involvement variables positively related to satisfaction with the intellectual environment are student-faculty interaction and athletic involvement. Satisfaction with the intellectual environment is negatively related to involvement in student government and verbal aggressiveness.

Student-Faculty Relations. Satisfaction with student-faculty relations is less dependent on entering student characteristics ($R = .08$) than is any other satisfaction measure. Institutional characteristics add some to the predictability ($R = .17$), but involvement measures add by far the most ($R = .45$). Men and students with high intellectual self-esteem are most likely to be satisfied with student-faculty relations. Satisfaction is lowest among women, political liberals, and students high in hedonism or artistic interests. The pattern of institutional characteristics affecting satisfaction with student-faculty relations is markedly different from that obtained with the first three measures. By far the most important institutional attribute is size: Students in small colleges are much more likely to be satisfied with student-faculty relations than those in large institutions. High satisfaction with student-faculty relations is also associated with high tuition, and low satisfaction is associated with teacher's colleges and technological institutions. Men are more satisfied with student-faculty relations in colleges for men than in coeducational institutions, and blacks are less satisfied in black than in predominantly white colleges.

The negative effect of size on satisfaction with student-faculty relations is clearly not the result of student-faculty ratios: Large institutions, if anything, have slightly lower ratios than small institutions. The most likely explanation is in (1) the neglect of undergraduate teaching that characterizes faculties in many large research-oriented universities (Astin, 1963b, 1968a) and (2) the impersonality that often results from the highly bureaucratic structures needed to run large institutions.

The involvement factor showing the strongest association with satisfaction with student-faculty relations is student-faculty interaction. This measure produces the highest partial correlation (.40) between any satisfaction and any involvement measure. This association shows that students are much more likely to be satisfied with their relationships with faculty if they interact frequently. Distance, it would seem, leads to dissatisfaction. Satisfaction is also positively associated with academic involvement and negatively associated with verbal aggressiveness.

Classroom Instruction. Men and students high in intellectual self-esteem are most likely to be satisfied with the quality of classroom instruction. All other entering student characteristics have only marginal predictive value. Students are more likely to be satisfied if they attend selective institutions and single-sex colleges. Satisfaction is lowest in universities and teacher's colleges. With the exception of two-year colleges, which produce a slight positive effect on satisfaction with instruction, public institutions in general produce substantially lower satisfaction than private institutions. Students are much more likely to be satisfied with classroom instruction if they show a high degree of academic involvement (partial $r = .28$) or student-faculty interaction (partial $r = .26$). Small negative relationships are associated with involvement in student government and verbal aggressiveness.

Friendships with Other Students. By far the greatest satisfaction with student friendships occurs among white Protestant women with high interpersonal self-esteem. Dissatisfaction with student friendships is greatest among blacks, Jews, and students with financial concerns, high educational aspirations, and artistic interests. Satisfaction is highest among students attending men's colleges or teacher's colleges, and lowest among students attending two-year colleges or colleges located in the West. But the strongest environmental correlate of satisfaction with student friendships is living in a dormitory rather than with parents. Here is further support for the assumption that going away from home and living on campus provides students with more opportunities to interact and to develop friendships.

Satisfaction with student friendships is most strongly associated with involvement in student government ($r = .14$), student-faculty interaction ($r = .13$), and athletic involvement ($r = .12$). Participation in honors programs shows a slight negative association with satisfaction with friendships, possibly because students who become involved in special academic programs find themselves isolated from most other students.

Variety of Courses Offered. White students and those with high intellectual self-esteem are most likely to be satisfied with the variety of courses offered at the institution. Other entering student characteristics show only borderline relationships. Students are most likely to be satisfied with curricular offerings if they attend an affluent, prestigious, high-cost institution. Such institutions would probably have the resources to offer a varied curriculum. Satisfaction with curricular variety is also higher at single-sex institutions but lower at Roman Catholic colleges. Teacher's colleges and technological institutions produce lower satisfaction with curricular offerings, although these effects disappear when affluence and cost are controlled. Students are most likely to be satisfied with the variety of curricular offerings if they are heavily involved academically (partial $r = .21$) and if they have frequent interactions with faculty (partial $r = .11$).

Administration. Satisfaction with the administration is highest among students who are white, varsity athletes in high school, religious, and high in interpersonal self-esteem and business interests. Dissatisfaction with the administration is greatest among political liberals and students with strong artistic interests or hedonistic tendencies. Satisfaction with the administration is greatest at high-cost or selective institutions, single-sex institutions, two-year colleges, and institutions located in the West. Dissatisfaction is strongest among students attending institutions in the Northeast. Although the public-private dichotomy does not show a significant simple relationship to dissatisfaction, public institutions produce much less dissatisfaction than private institutions once other characteristics are controlled. In other words, students at coeducational private colleges are likely to be more critical of the administration than are students at public colleges of comparable selectivity, but private institutions as a group produce no more dissatisfaction with the administration than public institutions because they are more selective and include most of the single-sex colleges. Satisfaction is highest among students who become involved in athletics or academic pursuits or who interact frequently with faculty and is lowest among those who are verbally aggressive in class. This latter effect may well reflect the greater critical tendencies of verbally aggressive students.

Rating the College Environment

The 1970 follow-up of 1966 freshmen contained two sets of items on the college environment. The first set—nineteen environmental descriptions—assessed the students' subjective impressions of the environment as part of an earlier large-scale study of college environments (Astin, 1968a). The items had been completed by the students when they entered college as freshmen in 1966, and they were repeated four years later in the follow-up survey. The second set concerned students' impressions of the adequacy of various aspects of their undergraduate experience. These items were included only in the summer 1970 follow-up, not in the 1966 freshman survey.

How do students' perceptions of the college environment change once they enter college? Table 24 shows the percentage of students that endorsed each of the nineteen environmental

Table 24. Changes in Students' Perceptions of the College Environment During the Undergraduate Years

Environmental Description	Agree with Description		
	Percentage in 1966 (entering freshmen)	Percentage in 1970[a]	Absolute Percentage Change
The student body is apathetic and has little "School Spirit"	9.3	64.3	+55.0
There isn't much to do except to go to class and study	13.8	35.5	+21.7
Most students are treated like "numbers in a book"	25.2	43.0	+17.8
The students are under a great deal of pressure to get high grades	44.7	54.5	+11.5
Athletics are overemphasized	4.4	15.4	+11.0
I felt "lost" when I first came to the campus	35.1	45.2	+10.1
Snobbish	1.6	4.7	+ 3.1
Victorian	1.9	3.8	+ 1.9
The classes are usually run in a very informal manner	51.2	51.9	+ 0.7
Most of the students are of a very high caliber academically	50.4	42.0	− 8.4
There is a keen competition among most of the students for high grades	55.5	46.2	− 9.3
Freshmen have to take orders from upperclassmen for a period of time	32.1	16.1	−16.0
Liberal	35.6	14.7	−20.9
Intellectual	30.4	9.2	−21.2
Being in this college builds poise and maturity	84.2	59.1	−25.1

(continued on next page)

Table 24 *(Continued)*

Environmental Description	Agree with Description: Percentage in 1966 (entering freshmen)	Percentage in 1970[a]	Absolute Percentage Change
Social	53.2	21.0	–32.2
Practical-minded	58.7	18.7	–40.0
Warm	59.1	17.5	–41.6
Realistic	64.5	16.8	–47.7

[a]Single adjectives, which were obtained from the summer 1970 follow-up, are answered on a three-point scale. Percentages shown are based on "very descriptive" ratings ("not descriptive" and "in between" not shown.) Other items, obtained from 1969-1970 ACE-Carnegie follow-up, use a two-point response ("agree"-"disagree").

descriptions as freshmen and again four years later. Many items show marked changes between freshman and follow-up surveys. For the most part, these changes reflect a much more negative or critical attitude at follow-up than at college entrance. Berdie (1967) and Pervin (1966) have reported similar findings. While it may be tempting to conclude that students become increasingly "disillusioned" with their college as they learn more about it, other interpretations are possible: The typical entering freshman is not likely to have much valid information about the campus atmosphere. Lacking this information, the student may be inclined to project the most favorable image. There are wide variations among institutions in the percentages of students that will endorse any one item on a follow-up survey. This is particularly true for items where the overall endorsement is nearly 50 percent. Most such items vary widely, say from 10 percent to 90 percent endorsement, from one institution to another (Astin, 1968a). Items for which the percentages are nearer to zero or 100, however, vary much less among institutions. For example, few students at any institution see their colleges as either snobbish or Victorian.

Table 25 shows the second set of environmental ratings reported by students in the 1970 follow-up. Items are grouped with the most favorable ratings first and the least favorable last. Most students say they had "just about the right amount" of required work in courses and personal contact with classmates.

Table 25. Satisfaction with Specific Aspects of the Undergraduate
Experience (1966 Freshmen Followed Up in 1970)

"How much of the following did you receive from your undergraduate college?"	Degree of Satisfaction (Percentage)		
	(Not Enough)	(Just About the Right Amount)	(Too Much)
Work required of you in courses	8.6	83.5	7.9
Personal contacts with classmates	16.1	82.1	1.8
Social life	20.1	75.4	4.4
Personal contacts with faculty	26.1	73.2	.7
Freedom in course selection	22.5	72.9	4.5
Outlets for creative activities	30.0	69.0	.9
Advice and guidance from faculty and staff	30.2	68.8	1.0
Personal contacts with family	36.9	59.4	3.7
Sleep	55.3	42.6	2.2
Exercise	60.4	38.0	1.5

"Rate the following at your most recently attended college":	(Unsatisfactory or Very Unsatisfactory)	(Excellent or Good)[b]
Science[a] equipment and facilities	8.9	65.7
The variety of science courses	7.4	64.3
The quality of science instruction	7.2	63.2
Opportunities to discuss your work outside the classroom with professors in your major field of study	15.6	62.9
The overall quality of instruction	8.5	59.0
Facilities for library research	17.9	58.3
The variety of courses in humanities	9.2	58.2
The quality of instruction in the humanities	9.4	56.6
How well your undergraduate training has prepared you for your future career	17.2	40.2
Opportunities for extracurricular science activities and projects at your school	12.9	29.1
Opportunities you had to do scientific research as an undergraduate	18.0	19.0

[a]"Science" refers to both natural and social science.

[b]Omitted middle category is "unsatisfactory."

Most feel they received "not enough" sleep and exercise. In services rendered by the college, the most student dissatisfaction occurs over outlets for creative activities and advice and guidance from faculty and staff. Nearly one third of the students feels that these services are insufficient. The second set of items in Table 25 concerns the adequacy of specific facilities, programs, and services at the institution. (The large number of items pertaining to science instruction was included at the request of the National Science Foundation, a cosponsor of the survey.) Students seem most satisfied with science facilities, courses, and instruction and seem least satisfied with opportunities for extracurricular science activities and independent research. An item of special interest is how well undergraduate training prepares the student for future careers. Less than half (40.2 percent) of the students feels this preparation has been excellent or good, an equal number thinks it has been satisfactory, and one student in six (17.2 percent) states flatly that it has been unsatisfactory or very unsatisfactory.

How does the type of college affect these various environmental descriptions and ratings? Are certain types of students more likely to see the environment in certain ways, regardless of their actual college experience? To explore these questions, the forty items in Tables 24 and 25 were first reduced to a smaller number of more general measures by factor analysis. The analysis yielded seven identifiable factors. (For the complete factor matrix, see supplementary Table A10 from the Higher Education Research Institute.) Two factors almost exactly duplicate the environmental ratings discussed earlier: overall satisfaction and quality of instruction. The five remaining factors—academic demands, closeness to faculty, emphasis on social life, quality of the science program, and practicality—were analyzed by regression analyses involving entering freshmen and institutional characteristics. As with the earlier satisfaction items, these regressions produce relatively small multiple-correlation coefficients (between .25 and .31). Moreover, entering freshman characteristics carry much less predictive weight than do institutional characteristics.

Academic Demands. The academic demand factor was defined by five items in Tables 24 and 25: pressure to get good grades, keen competition for high grades, high-caliber students, intellectual environment, and work required in courses (a high score was "too much," a low score "not enough"). Freshman characteristics with the largest predictive weights include high school grades (positive) and smoking (negative). Men, blacks, and older students are more likely than women, whites, and younger students to feel that the academic demands are severe. The most important environmental characteristic affecting the student's perception of academic demands is prestige (partial r = .22). In particular, the environments of selective private universities are seen as exerting very strong pressures for academic performance. Pressures at selective private colleges are only slightly greater than average. Academic demands are also high at colleges for women and, in particular, at colleges for men. Academic demands are perceived as being lower at two-year colleges, but these effects disappear when institutional prestige is controlled. A northeastern location, which produced no simple correlation with academic demands, is negatively related after institutional prestige is controlled. Once again it appears that the student develops more stringent subjective "norms" about academic quality and competition in institutions by attending an institution in the Northeast.

Closeness to Faculty. Relationship with faculty was defined by three items: personal contact (a high score was "too much," a low score "too little"), advice and guidance from faculty and staff (scored the same), and being treated like "numbers in a book" (scored negatively). Older students and women feel closest to faculty; smokers and students with artistic interests are least likely to feel close to faculty. The most important institutional characteristic affecting this rating is size (partial r = −.19). Primarily because of their small size, private two- and four-year colleges of all types produce feelings of closeness to faculty among most students. Among the private four-year colleges, however, closeness is greatest among the most selective ones. Students feel closer to faculty if they live away from home. Black students are less likely to feel close to faculty in black than in predominantly white institutions. Closeness is high in religious colleges and low in universities and colleges located in the West, but these relationships disappear when institutional size is controlled. Students also feel closer to faculty if they become involved in research or in honors programs.

Here again is evidence that institutional size produces distance between faculty and students. While there may not be much large institutions can do to get smaller, the other variables affecting closeness to faculty suggest a number of ways in which large institutions can counteract the impersonality of their environments: expand honors programs, increase opportunities for undergraduates to get involved in research, and expand residential facilities.

Emphasis on Social Life. This factor was defined by three items: social, social life (a high score was too much, a low score not enough), and little to do except go to class and study (scored negatively). White students are likely to report greater emphasis on social life than black students. That this may reflect the isolation and alienation experienced by many black students at predominantly white colleges, which the majority of black students attend, is supported by the positive effect of black colleges on the black student's impression of the social life of the institution. Women, students with high test scores, and students from highly educated families are also likely to report more emphasis on social life. This emphasis is greatest at the public universities and lowest at four-year colleges and colleges for men (this is one of the few cases where men's colleges are perceived negatively). Students report considerably more emphasis on social life if they become involved in social fraternities or sororities, but they report considerably less if they live with parents. Universities have more social life than other types of institutions, but the effect of universities on social life becomes negative when institutional size is controlled. In effect, universities have more social life simply because they are larger, but they have considerably less social life than nonuniversities of comparable size. Apparently, the student is likely to encounter maximum emphasis on social life by going away from home to a large coeducational institution (other than a university) and by joining a social fraternity or sorority.

Quality of the Science Program. This factor was defined by five ratings from Table 25: variety of science courses, opportunities to do scientific research as an undergraduate, quality of science instruction, science equipment and facilities, and opportunities for extracurricular science activities. Students most likely to rate the quality of their science program positively tend to be white and to have good grades, high aspirations, and highly educated, affluent parents. Hedonistic students tend to rate science programs negatively. Science programs are rated highest in selective institutions, universities, and men's colleges; ratings are lowest in Catholic colleges. Although ratings are somewhat below average in two-year and black colleges, these two types of institutions receive relatively high ratings after institutional selectivity is controlled. In other words, black colleges and two-year institutions have science programs that are rated somewhat higher than those of institutions of comparable selectivity. Students involved in research and in honors programs are much more inclined to rate their science programs positively. Students are also more likely to view their science programs positively if they live away from home during college.

Some additional differences of interest emerged when the five items making up this factor were examined separately. Universities—both public and private—received higher ratings than four-year colleges on variety of science courses and quality of equipment and facilities, but the colleges (particularly the highly selective nonsectarian colleges) received higher ratings in quality of science instruction and opportunities for undergraduate research and extracurricular science activities. Apparently, when it comes to undergraduate instruction in science, the universities do not take full advantage of their superior curriculum, equipment, and facilities.

Practicality. Practicality was defined by three ratings from Table 24: practical-minded, warm, and realistic. The factor closely resembles that from an early study of the college environment (Astin, 1968a) called "snobbishness"; that is, institutions low in practicality tend to be snobbish. Catholics and students from highly educated families and with plans to marry in college see their environments as relatively practical. Low ratings on practicality are associated with hedonism, high aspirations, no religious preference, and political liberalism. Two- and four-year colleges and institutions located in the South are most likely to be considered practical, whereas the lowest practicality

gs occur in universities and prestigious institutions. Stu-
ts who join social fraternities or sororities tend to see their
vironment as more practical.

Another way of looking at this factor is in terms of its
negative end—snobbishness. Although the "snobbish" rating was
not used in the scoring of the factor, it produced substantial
differences among institutions. The least snobbish institutions
are the public four-year colleges and the private two-year colleges, and the more snobbish are the private four-year colleges
and universities—in particular, the highly selective private universities. Although the selective private colleges were seen as
snobbish, they also received a higher rating than any other type
on warmth. (This inconsistency—with both snobbish and warm
being high rather than at opposite poles—is the principal reason
why the snobbish rating was not used in scoring the practicality
factor.)

Summary

Students in general report relatively high satisfaction with
most aspects of their college experience. There are, nevertheless,
substantial minorities of students who report significant dissatisfaction with particular aspects of the collegiate experience.
Unlike most other student outcomes, satisfaction depends less
on the characteristics of the individual student than on those of
the institution. Women tend to be slightly more satisfied than
men with their collegiate experience (particularly with student
friendships), and whites tend to be somewhat more satisfied
than blacks. Institutional characteristics show pronounced relationships with satisfaction.

The most important institutional characteristics affecting
student satisfaction are academic selectivity, prestige, and institutional size (Table 26). Selectivity and prestige are associated
with greater student satisfaction in almost all areas: classroom
instruction, variety in the curriculum, quality of the science
program, academic reputation, and the student's overall evaluation of the college. The environments of large and highly selective institutions are especially noted for their stringent academic

Table 26. Summary of Institutional Characteristics Affecting
Student Satisfaction and Perceptions of the College Environment

Student Rating	Positively Affected By	Negatively Affected By
Satisfaction		
Overall	Selective institution	Technological institution
	Affluent institution	
	High-cost institution	
	College for men	
	Academic involvement	
	Student-faculty inter-action	
Academic Reputation	Selective institution	Southern institution
	Private institution	Northeastern institution
	College for men	Verbal aggressiveness
	High-cost institution	Participation in honors program
	Academic involvement	
	Athletic involvement	
	Student-faculty inter-action	
Intellectual Environment	Prestigious institution	Teacher's college
	Academic involvement	Technical institution
	Student-faculty inter-action	Southern institution
		Verbal aggressiveness
	Athletic involvement	Involvement in student government
Student-Faculty Relations	Small institution	Large institution
	High-cost institution	Teacher's college
	College for men	Technical institution
	Student-faculty inter-action	Predominantly black college
	Academic involvement	Verbal aggressiveness
Classroom Instruction	Selective institution	Coeducational institution
	College for men	
	College for women	Teacher's college
	Private institution	Public institution
	Academic involvement	
	Student-faculty inter-action	
Friendship with other students	College for men	Two-year college
	Teacher's college	Western institution
	Living in a dormitory	Living with parents
	Involvement in student government	Participation in honors program
	Student-faculty inter-action	
	Athletic involvement	

(continued on next page)

Table 26 *(Continued)*

Student Rating	Positively Affected By	Negatively Affected By
Variety of Courses offered	Prestigious institution Affluent institution High-cost institution College for men College for women Academic involvement Student-faculty inter- action	Roman Catholic college Teacher's college Technical institution
The Administration	Selective institution High-cost institution Two-year college Western institution Academic involvement Athletic involvement Student-faculty inter- action	Northeastern institution Verbal aggressiveness
Perceptions of the Environment		
Academic Demands	Prestigious institution Selective private univer- sity College for women College for men	Two-year college Northeastern institution[a]
Closeness to faculty	Small institution Living on campus Religious institution Involvement in research Involvement in honors program	Large institution Living at home Predominantly black in- stitution University Western institution
Emphasis on social life	Large institution Predominantly black college Public university Membership in social fraternity or sorority	Small institution College for men
Quality of science programs	Selective institution University College for men Involvement in research Involvement in honors program Living on campus	Roman Catholic college Predominantly black in- stitution Two-year institution Living at home
Practicality	Two-year college Four-year college Southern institution Membership in social fraternity or sorority	University Prestigious institution

[a]After control for selectivity.

demands on students. The environments of selective institutions
—particularly the private universities—tend to be rated somewhat low in practicality and high in snobbishness. Large institutions are noted for a strong emphasis on social life, high-quality
science programs, varied curricula, and good academic reputations. The most significant negative correlate of institutional size
concerns faculty-student contacts. Students are much closer to
faculty and express much greater satisfaction with relationships
in small institutions. Large institutions tend to be downrated in
quality of classroom instruction and in practicality of environment.

Teacher's colleges produce high satisfaction with student
friendships, but low satisfaction with student-faculty relations,
classroom instruction, and intellectual environment. Overall
satisfaction, as well as satisfaction with student-faculty relations
and intellectual environment, is lower at technological institutions. Two-year colleges foster relatively high satisfaction with
intellectual climate, college administration, variety of curriculum, quality of the science program, and emphasis on social life.
They tend to produce below-average satisfaction with student
friendships. They are seen as having relatively low academic demands. The environments of black colleges produce high satisfaction with social life and quality of science programs and relatively low satisfaction with student-faculty relations.

Private institutions, while rated somewhat low in social
life, foster more frequent faculty-student contact and produce
greater satisfaction with faculty relations. They are also noted
for the quality of their classroom instruction and their academic
reputation. In particular, Roman Catholic and Protestant institutions are characterized by high faculty-student contact and
student satisfaction with relationships with faculty. Most of
these traits may be attributed to relatively small size and high
selectivity.

Some of the most distinctive patterns of satisfaction are
associated with the environments of men's colleges. Compared
with men attending coeducational institutions, those at men's
colleges are much more satisfied with virtually every aspect of
their undergraduate experience. Men attending men's colleges
report a higher degree of satisfaction with the college's aca-

demic reputation, quality of instruction, faculty-student relations, friendships with other students, administration, and curriculum. The quality of the science program is also highly regarded, and the environment is seen as placing strong academic
demands on students. The only area where men's colleges
receive low ratings is in emphasis on social life, which is substantially downrated. The environments of women's colleges are
also regarded favorably by women, compared with the environments in coeducational institutions, although the differences are
not as pronounced.

Student satisfaction is not strongly related to geographic
region, with the possible exception of institutions located in the
Northeast. Students attending these institutions apparently
develop relatively stringent subjective "norms" for overall quality, quality of instruction, academic reputation, and academic
demand. Considering the high selectivity of northeastern institutions, their students rate them relatively low in these areas.

The student's ratings of the undergraduate college experience and environment are strongly influenced by various forms
of involvement. The greater satisfaction associated with being a
resident rather than a commuter has been reported by several
other investigators (Baird, 1969; Chickering, 1974a). Being active in a social fraternity or sorority also leads to a higher degree
of satisfaction with the undergraduate experience, as well as
to greater satisfaction overall with institutional quality and a
higher emphasis on social life. Involvement in undergraduate
research projects leads to greater satisfaction with quality of science programs, quality of instruction, and faculty-student contacts. Students are also much more likely to be satisfied with
virtually all aspects of their undergraduate experience if they
live in a dormitory or private room rather than at home. While
satisfaction is much greater among persisters than among dropouts, the direction of causation is not clear: Does dissatisfaction
lead to dropping out, or is expressed dissatisfaction a kind of
rationalization for dropping out, or both?

Involvement in particular types of activities during the
undergraduate years is associated with enhanced satisfaction in
related areas. The most clear-cut example of this relationship is
student-faculty relations. Students who interact more fre-

quently with faculty report a much higher degree of satisfaction with student-faculty relations than students who do not interact with faculty. At the same time, students who are heavily involved in their academic pursuits are much more satisfied with quality of the instruction, student-faculty relations, curriculum, institutional reputation, and college administration. Students who are heavily involved in student government are much more satisfied with student friendships but generally less satisfied with other aspects of the institution. Involvement in athletic activities produces a high degree of satisfaction, particularly with student friendships.

These findings suggest a number of intriguing causal questions for future research. Does interacting with faculty result in greater satisfaction with faculty, or are more satisfied students more likely to interact? Does heavy involvement in academic pursuits lead students to be more satisfied with the quality of instruction, or does good teaching motivate students to study harder? Does involvement in student government make students more critical of their institutions, or does dissatisfaction lead students to become more involved? While such questions cannot be fully resolved without further research, the fact that these associations remain even after entering freshman characteristics are controlled suggests strongly that the student's general satisfaction with the undergraduate experience can be enhanced by more direct involvement in various aspects of the college environment.

The matter of how to get students more involved in campus life poses an interesting challenge for college faculty and administrators. Some of the more obvious approaches would be to expand the size and number of student organizations and extracurricular activities and to promote or facilitate student participation. Another approach, which has been shown to enhance student persistence (Astin, 1975b), is to expand opportunities for part-time student employment on campus. Still another method would be to develop recreational facilities, cultural events, and other programs to encourage students to remain on campus during nonclass hours and weekends. These possibilities are explored in greater length in Chapter Nine.

VII

Permanence
of College
Effects

There is no doubt that students change in a variety of ways while attending college and that these changes can be attributed in part to the college experience. The direction and extent of change depend not only on the student's characteristics at the time of college entry but also on the type of institution. Because most of these college effects have been measured over relatively short periods—four to five years after entering college—it is important to know something about the permanence or stability of these outcomes. Are college effects

188

transitory phenomena that dissipate once students leave campus, or do certain impacts persist and perhaps even grow with time?

From a purely theoretical view, there are forces that operate to diminish, as well as to preserve or even strengthen, the impact of college over longer periods of time. Factors limiting the permanence of college impact include such phenomena as forgetting and competition from rival environmental influences. Studies of student learning usually show that the greatest impacts occur immediately following exposure to the learning environment and that the apparent effects of particular learning experiences dissipate with time. Students are most likely to recall the details of a Shakespearean play, for example, when they have just completed a course in English literature; as time passes, recall is likely to worsen. The same kind of "forgetting" may apply to nonacademic outcomes. For example, students may become increasingly supportive of particular values and behaviors while they are in college, because of peer-group effects, but such support may diminish after they leave college, because of changes in peer-group and other environmental experiences. In short, the uniqueness of the college experience and the competing environments that confront many students when they leave college may counteract some changes in values and behaviors that occur while students are attending college.

A process that tends to extend rather than diminish college impacts is the "channeling" effect of college attendance. The impact of college can be extended over a long period because the student is steered into certain unique career paths and living patterns. Simply going to college and obtaining a baccalaureate or postgraduate degree channels the young person into an environment where the options in available jobs and general life-style are radically different from those that confront the typical high school graduate. The mere act of attending and completing college exposes the undergraduate to an array of experiences and opportunities that are never available to the dropout or the person who does not attend college. At the same time, the college graduate is insulated from the stresses of succeeding with limited educational credentials.

Any given college outcome can be affected by channeling and forgetting forces. Take, for example, religious behavior. Data in Chapter Three show clearly that such formal religious behavior as praying, attending church, and reading the Bible declines substantially during the college years and that this decline may be attributed in part to the direct effects of attending college. This decline in religious behavior is accompanied by a weakening of religious beliefs. Since it is greater among dormitory residents than among commuters, it is probably related to the lessening of parental control and supervision. Still another factor may be the questioning of traditional religious values that often occurs during this period of life and the reinforcing effect of such mutual questioning in undergraduate bull sessions. For some students, these effects may be temporary: Formal religious behavior may increase when students move away from these peer-group influences and are once again exposed to the more conventional values that usually accompany employment, raising a family, and living in an adult community. Channeling could have the opposite effect. For example, some students, by virtue of their undergraduate friendships and the careers open to them because they have a college education, may be exposed to coworkers and social relationships that involve people who engage in little formal religious activity. University teaching, journalism, and scientific research are examples of such careers. Under these conditions, religious apostasy developed during the college years would probably be strengthened.

Which effects are most likely to prevail after students leave college? Do students tend to change back to their original precollege attitudes and behaviors, or are college effects maintained or strengthened over longer periods of time? Do different student outcomes have different long-term consequences? Answers to such questions are, unfortunately, somewhat ambiguous because of conceptual problems, methodological issues, and—most important—limitations in available data. Before discussing the different long-range impacts, it is important to review these other issues.

Conceptual and Methodological Problems

Although economists and some sociologists have emphasized the importance of long-range impacts of college on such outcomes as income and occupational level, a strong case can be made for the importance of relatively short-range impacts on behavior and attitudes. The importance of short- and long-term effects is discussed in Chapter One. The issue here is the *usefulness* of evidence on long-range effects. For example, in a rapidly changing society, it is risky to assume that long-term effects observed during, say, the past twenty years will apply to the next twenty years. If convincing data were available to show that the average World War II veteran who entered college in 1946 realized a given increment in earnings over the next twenty-five years compared with a veteran who did not attend college, would there be any reason to believe that a similar difference would occur for a student entering college today? Such inferential problems are further complicated because higher education in the United States has undergone dramatic changes in recent years. Not only has the system changed from a predominantly private to a largely public system of relatively low-cost institutions but the proportion of secondary school students going to college has also increased. At the same time, the system during the past twenty-five years has become much more selective in terms of the student's academic ability (Taubman and Wales, 1975b). One little-recognized consequence of the greater selectivity of the American higher educational system is that the intellectual caliber of persons who enter the *non*college world of work has probably diminished over time. One could argue that, for the highly able person, competition in fields that require intellectual skill but not formal education, such as business ownership, has deteriorated to a point where the economic returns from a college education may be nil. Before colleges became as expert as they are today in identifying and recruiting the most capable students, many highly able persons probably went directly into the labor force without considering college.

A related problem in generalizing results from older long-term studies to the future concerns the dramatic changes in the structure of the higher educational system that have occurred during the past thirty years. More than one third of all new college freshmen now enroll at public community colleges (Astin, King, and Richardson, 1976). Most colleges have dropped parietal rules, fewer students live in dormitories, curricular programs have changed, such specialized institutions as technological schools and teacher's colleges have virtually disappeared, and many single-sex colleges have become coeducational. These and other changes make it difficult to be sure that effects observed in earlier long-term studies will apply to the future.

Data Requirements

Another problem with assessing the permanence of college effects is the paucity of adequate data. Ideally, investigators should be able to tap sources that include longitudinal data from students at a wide variety of institutions, beginning at initial college entry and including follow-ups at graduation and many years later. Although such data will be forthcoming from the Cooperative Institutional Research Program (CIRP) in future years, there are now limited amounts of data to use for obtaining definitive information on long-term effects. Therefore, evidence presented here must be considered tentative and, in many instances, highly ambiguous.

Some of the best available data on long-term college effects involve only one institution. While such data provide some evidence on the permanence of changes that occur during college, there is no way to determine if similar long-term effects would occur at other institutions or among students who never attended college. Still other data showing long-term changes are limited because the initial assessment involved college seniors rather than freshmen.

Probably the more useful long-term studies involve national samples of data collected for other purposes. One problem with these data is that the investigators have frequently oversimplified the issue of college impact in terms of simplistic variables, such as "years of schooling." Preceding chapters have shown that the *type* of institution and the conditions of attendance (commuter versus resident, for example) can substantially alter changes that occur during the undergraduate years. Although some investigators using long-term data have attempted to introduce measures of college type, these measures have usually been limited to such variables as college quality (selectivity). They have made no attempt to examine the importance of the conditions of attendance.

Notwithstanding these limitations, several data bases provide clues of varying quality about the permanence of college effects. Because each data base is referred to several times in the review of evidence, a brief description of each is provided here.

Perhaps the most widely used source for studying long-term educational effects is the so-called National Bureau of Economic Research-Thorndike (NBER-Thorndike) data involving a large sample of white men who entered pilot training during 1942. A major strength of these data is the availability of a large battery of aptitude and ability measures obtained in 1942 and follow-up data obtained twenty-six years later in 1968. Assuming that most who entered college began their undergraduate education in 1945 or 1946, these data provide information on the permanence of college effects over more than twenty years.

A second sample involves 1961 entering freshmen who were followed up ten years later in 1971 as part of CIRP. Although this sample does not include ability tests at the time of college entry, it does include substantial questionnaire data obtained at three time points: 1961 (entering freshmen), 1965, and 1971. These data are useful primarily in assessing the permanence of college effects on career plans and occupational attainment (H. S. Astin, El-Khawas, and Bisconti, 1973).

A third longitudinal source is a national sample of 1961 college graduates. These students were followed up seven years later in 1968 (Spaeth and Greeley, 1970). Although this source, called the National Opinion Research Center (NORC) sample, includes no college dropouts and only retrospective data from the time of college entry, it provides an opportunity to examine changes in attitudes and political beliefs in the seven years following college graduation.

A fourth data base provides evidence on the permanence of college impact over twenty years (Pace, 1974). Although the data are not longitudinal, they involve simultaneous surveys of the class of 1970 and the alumni of 1950 from a diverse sample of institutions. If alumni of different colleges show differences in attitudes or other outcomes that resemble the differences shown by incumbent undergraduates, one can argue that some college effects are permanent. However, if alumni do not show the same differences as incumbents, one cannot make a case for permanence. However, because the data are not longitudinal, both lines of reasoning involve serious qualifications (see Chapter One). This source is called the Pace alumni survey.

The final major data source for information on permanence of college impact is a remarkable long-term study of students who entered the University of Minnesota in 1933 and 1936 and were followed up some twenty-five years later in 1962 (Williamson and Bordin, 1940; Campbell, 1965). This sample originally included 768 freshmen who took several aptitude tests both in high school and after they had been exposed to some undergraduate instruction. More than 80 percent of the original group were located in 1962 and persuaded to retake a college admissions test and to complete an extensive personal questionnaire that repeated many questions that had been asked in the 1930s. Although few investigators are aware of these data, they provide some of the most convincing evidence on the permanence of college effects. This sample is called the Campbell data.

The evidence on long-range impacts of college follows the organization of the preceding five chapters: attitudes, beliefs, and self-concept; behavior; competency and achievement; career development; and satisfaction.

Attitudes, Beliefs, and Self-Concept

Much evidence on the permanence of college effects on affective-psychological outcomes concerns political beliefs. Using the NORC seven-year follow-up of college alumni, Spaeth and Greeley (1970) found that the predominantly liberal beliefs of graduates when they received their baccalaureates tend to persist. Subjects reported that their parents' political beliefs favor conservatives over liberals by better than three to two. Their own beliefs, measured three years after they left college in 1964, favor liberals over conservatives by approximately four to three. Between 1964 and 1968, conservatives were slightly more likely to shift to liberal (34 percent) than vice versa (32 percent of liberals switched to conservative). However, because the liberals substantially outnumbered the conservatives in 1964, these changes led to a net decline in the total number of liberals during the four years. Spaeth and Greeley speculated that "perhaps the erosion of democratic strength . . . is part of the natural change in the economic and social perspective of the college alumni or is related specifically to the confusing political situation in 1968" (p. 102). (The 1968 survey was conducted after President Lyndon B. Johnson announced his decision not to run but before the assassination of Senator Robert F. Kennedy.) Whatever the correct interpretation, these data show that the predominantly liberal identification of students at college graduation does not decline substantially for at least seven years. Missing from these data, of course, is information on the relative stability in political preference of those who do and do not change beliefs during the college years. Spaeth and Greeley also attempted to determine if political attitudes differ by college selectivity, grade-point average, and other factors. They found that more liberal students attend more selective institutions, have higher grade-point averages, and spend more years in graduate study than students with conservative attitudes. Other studies have produced similar findings. For example, in his twenty-five-year follow-up of freshmen at the University of Minnesota, Campbell (1965) found a strong relationship between liberalism, college completion, and high school and college grades. Pace (1941) found a similar relationship between college completion and liberal attitudes in a thirteen-year follow-up of an earlier group of Minnesota freshmen who entered the university in the 1920s. In his later alumni study, Pace (1974) found that graduates of the more selective institutions, like incumbent students in those institutions, take a more liberal view on a controversial issue (freedom of speech on the campus) than graduates and incumbent students at less selective institutions. Similarly, Beaton (1975) found more liberal attitudes among persons with higher ability and levels of educational attainment in a longitudinal analysis of the NBER-Thorndike data. The most recent longitudinal evidence comes from a ten-year follow-up of students who were political activists in college during the early 1960s (Fendrich, 1974). Compared with groups of uninvolved students and members of student government, activists still had a radical commitment to political and economic change at the follow-up.

Although these studies suggest that political attitudes of college attenders persist over time and that the better students and those at more prestigious colleges remain relatively liberal over long periods, they do not provide direct evidence on the stability of changes during college. Two other studies provide some evidence on this matter: In a longitudinal study of 221 students who entered college in the early 1930s, Bugelski and Lester (1940) showed substantial increases in political liberalism during the college years but little change during the first few years after graduation. In a much longer study, Newcomb and others (1967) showed that students who change from conservative to liberal during the college years tend to maintain their liberalism twenty years after leaving college. Students who start and remain liberal throughout college are only slightly more likely to be liberal on the follow-up, whereas students who remain conservative during college are substantially less likely than the other two groups to express liberal views twenty years later. This study involved relatively small samples of students attending a single unique undergraduate institution (Bennington College). Because these data do not include comparisons with persons at different colleges or those who are not attending college, there is no way to determine if the changes *specifically attributed* to college persist over time.

One national survey of political beliefs and educational attainment yields what seem to be highly contradictory findings. Taylor and Wolfe (1971), in a review of national surveys of voting behavior over the past three decades, showed a posi-

tive association between Republican party preference and educational attainment. According to their findings, college-
educated persons also express more conservative views on such
matters as low-cost medical care or efforts to combat under-
employment, although they are neutral on school integration
and more favorable than noncollege-educated persons on student protests. If, as the longitudinal studies suggested, persons
of higher ability and those who attain high levels of education
tend to be more politically liberal, how can a cross-section of
the adult population show a consistent preference for the Republican party and, at best, a mixed attitude on controversial
social issues among the college educated? Whatever the explanation, this discrepancy highlights the differences that can be obtained from cross-sectional polling techniques and longitudinal
studies, and underscores the need for better longitudinal data to
understand the longer-term impacts of college.

How stable is the decline in religious attitudes and beliefs
that occurs during college? Here the evidence is even more
sketchy. A recent twenty-five-year longitudinal study suggested
that declines in religious beliefs during the college years may
continue into adult years (Arsenian, 1970). Two other long-
term studies (Bender, 1958; Nelson, 1956), however, suggest
that declines in religious values during the college years may be
reversed in subsequent adult years. Also, Argyle (1959) reported that college graduates are more likely than nongraduates
to attend church. (The effect was more pronounced among
Protestants than among Catholics.)

Other relevant works include Freedman and Bereiter's
(1963) study on the persistence of personality characteristics in
the immediate postcollege years and Stouffer's (1955) study
showing that the association between tolerance and education is
stronger among younger than among older people. This latter
finding has been interpreted by some (Jacob, 1957) to indicate
that societal values are changing, but it could also indicate that
the liberalizing effect of college declines over time.

In short, available evidence on the permanence of college
effects on affective-psychological outcomes suggests that the
positive association between political liberalism and educational

attainment persists over long periods, but the underlying causal reasons for this persistence are unclear. Data on other affective outcomes are inadequate to assess long-term impact.

Behavior

Long-term longitudinal studies have provided limited evidence on the permanence of college effects on behavior. Most relevant data concern marriage. Starch (1969) reported a lower rate of marriage among women who attend graduate school but a higher rate among those who complete college than among those who drop out. Marriage and educational attainment show no relationship among men. These findings seem to contradict those in preceding chapters and in a related longitudinal study of dropouts (Astin, 1975b), which showed that marriage significantly decreases a woman's chances of completing college. Perhaps the simplest explanation of the discrepancy is that the *timing* of marriage is critical to whether women complete college but that college completion itself increases the woman's chances of marrying eventually, provided that she does not go to graduate or professional school.

Perhaps more relevant are the long-term results concerning childbearing. Michael (1975) showed a clear-cut relationship between the married woman's level of educational attainment and the number of her children. Again, the man's educational attainment and number of children shows no relationship once the woman's educational level is controlled. At least two factors may be involved here: The first is the obvious occupational handicap experienced by women who fail to complete their undergraduate training. Such women are much less likely to be employable later on. The second is the more subtle effect of higher levels of education on decisions about family size and birth control. Both factors are probably at work. Whatever the mechanism, these data provide evidence that one long-term effect of attending college is to decrease family size: The average family size in the United States has continued to decline as the percentage of college-educated women has risen.

Scattered evidence on other behavioral outcomes is available from the NORC sample and the Pace alumni data. Spaeth and Greeley (1970) reported a positive association between alumni giving and the quality of the college. Pace (1974) reported a positive association between selectivity and participation in community affairs twenty years later among alumni of liberal arts colleges, but the association was not replicated among alumni of universities.

One major behavioral change noted in Chapter Three was the increase in hedonism (drinking, smoking, gambling). Are such changes temporary, a kind of "sowing wild oats" that accompanies the students' first experience of being on their own? Does hedonistic behavior decline once the student leaves college and is confronted with the realities of making a living and raising a family? Freedman and Bereiter (1963) provided some tangential evidence on these questions: They found a significant increase in such traits as "impulse expression" and "psychopathology" during college but a decline in the years immediately after college. The generality of these findings is open to question, however, because they involve only high-ability women at a single, unique institution (Vassar College).

Competency and Achievement

Chapter Four showed that college attendance is accompanied by a general increase in competency as well as in performance on standardized tests. Do such changes persist once the students leave college? In the twenty-five-year follow-up of students from the University of Minnesota, Campbell (1965) showed that persons gain significantly in performance on achievement tests during the college years and that these gains are maintained over a period of twenty-five years. Some individuals lose and others gain over this time span, but the performance of the group as a whole on the follow-up was equivalent to its performance immediately after college. Moreover, the gain was greatest for those who had the most years of college or graduate education. Campbell concluded: "These data . . . demonstrate that growth in these abilities is associated with college attendance, though they do not prove which is cause and which effect. Education may foster this increased growth or, alternatively, people who develop most may seek more education. From this study, it is impossible to tell which is happening, but some combination of factors would seem most plausible" (p. 16).

One of the most ambitious attempts to assess the long-term impact of college on knowledge and intellectual competence is the study by Hyman, Wright, and Reed (1975). Persons of different ages and levels of educational attainment were polled on their knowledge of a wide range of facts. Since the data came from cross-sectional surveys at several different times, it is possible to determine if the relationship between education and knowledge "endures" across different age groups and from the earlier to the later surveys. The authors concluded that education, including higher education, "produces large, pervasive, and enduring effects on knowledge" (p. 109). The authors controlled for the effects of such variables as race, religion, and socioeconomic status, but the absence of a control for initial ability weakens their major conclusion.

Even if one accepts the causal conclusion that the superior knowledge of college-trained people may be attributed directly to college attendance, are the college trained simply demonstrating the greater knowledge acquired during college, or has "channeling" been an important factor? One can assume that much specific knowledge gained from college courses will be forgotten, particularly by the majority of college graduates who go into fields that do not require such knowledge. However, attending college may reinforce certain knowledge-acquiring habits, such as reading books, papers, and magazines, participating in intellectual arguments and discussions, travel, and attending particular kinds of motion pictures, plays, and other cultural events. Such habits would be reinforced among those college graduates who mingle on their jobs and in their communities with similarly trained persons who provide greater intellectual stimulation than the associates of non-college-trained persons. These alternative explanations offer challenging hypotheses that need to be tested in future research.

Career Development

Perhaps the greatest research effort on the long-term impact of college attendance has focused on career outcomes, particularly two aspects: occupational level or attainment and earnings or income. Practically every study, regardless of data or methodology, has supported the idea that education substantially increases the student's chances of entering a high-level occupation. Such findings are hardly surprising, because most high-level occupations require at least an undergraduate education, and such prestigious professions as law and medicine require postgraduate training.

A more pertinent issue is the permanence of *changes* in career plans which occur during the undergraduate years. Do these changes persist in the years following graduation, or do career preferences change back once the student confronts the world of work? The four- and ten-year follow-ups of the freshmen who entered college in fall 1961 show changes in students' career choices separately for men and women (Table 27). With few exceptions, the data strongly support the notion that career changes occurring during the undergraduate years extend into the postgraduate years. These trends are perhaps best exemplified by the career of business executive: During the undergraduate years, the percentage of men choosing this career increases from 5 percent to 12 percent, then spurts to 27 percent six years later in the 1971 follow-up. Comparable figures for women rise from near zero to 2 percent during the undergraduate years, then to 6 percent six years later. A similar continuation of trends during the undergraduate years occurs for the career of college teacher, which, for both sexes, more than doubles in popularity during the undergraduate years, then again in the postgraduate years. Among men, the career of engineer declines in popularity from 15 percent to 10 percent during the undergraduate years, then continues to decline to 6 percent during the next six years. For women, the career of housewife increases in popularity from 2 percent to 6 percent during the first four years after college entry, then nearly doubles to 11 percent in the next six years.

Table 27. Changes in Distribution of Career Choices (1961 to 1965
to 1971) by Sex: 1961 Cohort (in Percentages)

Career	Men			Women		
	1961	1965	1971	1961	1965	1971
Physician	7	4	4	2	1	1
Dentist	2	2	1	*	*	*
Biological scientist	1	1	2	1	1	1
Physical scientist	4	3	2	1	1	*
Mathematician	1	1	1	1	1	*
Social scientist	1	1	1	1	1	1
Social worker	*	1	1	2	4	3
College teacher	1	4	9	1	2	8
Engineer	15	10	6	*	*	*
Lawyer	5	6	6	*	1	2
Health professional	*	1	*	9	7	7
Elementary or secondary school teacher	14	17	8	44	46	30
Business executive	5	12	27	*	2	6
Artist, writer	3	3	2	4	3	3
Housewife	*	*	*	2	6	11
All others	21	25	26	16	14	22
Undecided or none	22	11	4	15	10	5
Total Percent	100	100	100	100	100	100

*Indicates less than 1 percent.

Source: Astin, El-Khawas, and Bisconti, 1973.

The only significant exception to this trend occurs with the elementary or secondary school teacher, which shows a slight *increase* during the undergraduate years, then declines substantially during the next six years. The problem here seems to be with the slight increase observed during the undergraduate years, a trend inconsistent with the data in Chapter Five. This increase may have occurred when teachers were in short supply —the early 1960s—and federal and state efforts were made to encourage students to pursue teaching careers. Other possible explanations are methodological: The 1961 sample did not include students entering two-year institutions. Also, the career-choice question was an open-ended response rather than a checklist of careers as in the two follow-ups. Whatever the reason for the discrepancy, recent CIRP data provide more consistent findings for collegiate and postcollegiate trends for the career of schoolteacher. Thus, the 1970 follow-up of 1966 freshmen showed a *decline* in the popularity of teaching from 12 percent to 10 percent for men and 38 percent to 37 percent for women. This decline extended into the next year, according to an additional follow-up in 1971: Some 8 percent of the men and 32 percent of the women in this one-year postgraduate follow-up intended to become schoolteachers.

These results show clearly that changes in career interests during the undergraduate years are not reversed during the postgraduate years. Rather, these changes tend to continue, at least during the six years following graduation. The most dramatic trends are increasing interest in business, college teaching, and homemaking and decreasing interests in engineering and school teaching. The number of students undecided about their careers also decreases progressively during and after college.

Although these results show that the changes in career choice during the college years persist over time, they provide no evidence on the permanence of the effects of different *types* of institutions. Only a handful of studies provide any evidence on this issue. Sharp's (1970) national alumni study suggested that pursuit of a business career is enhanced by attending a prestigious institution, a result that confirms one finding in Chapter Five. Spaeth and Greeley (1970) in their seven-year alumni follow-up of 1961 graduates found a positive association between occupational prestige and quality of the institution. College grades and ability, which also carried significant weight, were controlled in this particular study. Although the analyses in Chapter Five do not order occupations along a prestige continuum, results do not support any clear-cut relationship between quality and prestige. For example, admission to medical school is positively associated with attending a prestigious private university, but admission to law school is negatively associated with institutional prestige. Similarly, attending a prestigious institution increases the student's chances of implementing career plans in business and nursing, two relatively low-prestige fields. Reasons for this discrepancy are not clear. Spaeth and Greeley (1970) used quite different methodology: Because all dropouts were excluded, some of the most important college impacts may be missing from their data. Their control of freshman characteristics also involved retrospective reporting by graduating seniors of their career plans and aspirations at college entry. That such reporting is subject to systematic bias has been shown in other studies (Astin, 1962). It is possible, of course, that a significant effect of college quality on occupational prestige would show up in longer-term follow-ups of the various CIRP samples, a possibility that underscores the need for future follow-ups.

The most heavily researched long-term outcome of college is income or earnings. Longitudinal studies beginning as early as the 1920s (Pace, 1941) and continuing to the present have documented a clear-cut relationship between a person's level of educational attainment and salary or earnings. Wolfle (1973) has summarized much of this evidence. A major problem with such research, of course, is that highly educated people may make more money in part because they are more able to begin with. This problem has led many researchers to introduce complex controls for student ability. Among the most sophisticated are Beaton's (1975) and Wachtel's (1975) analyses of the NBER-Thorndike longitudinal data. Beaton estimated that each additional IQ point is worth approximately $100 and each year of education about $800 in salary. Wachtel, who employed long-term longitudinal data collected by Rogers (1969), concluded unequivocally that ability is less important in determining earnings than years of additional education. One problem with both the NBER-Thorndike and Rogers data is that the measures of ability were obtained long before the subjects entered college. Because measures of ability change over time, such changes may have affected the person's decision to enter college and, ultimately, the chances of earning a degree. In short, the data used by Beaton and Wachtel would tend to underestimate the effects of ability on earnings and overestimate the effects of years of education.

Does the *type* of institution have any impact on income? Most studies of this issue have used a single measure of college prestige or "quality" based on the estimated academic ability of entering students.* An early study of quality (Morgan and Sira-geldin, 1968) using a cross-sectional design showed a pronounced relationship between quality and earnings. Because the researchers introduced no control for ability, their results surely inflate the importance of quality. Perhaps the best study on this question is Solmon's (1975) analysis of the NBER-Thorndike data. Depending on the measure of quality used, Solmon showed that up to 2 percent of a person's earnings fifteen to eighteen years after college may be attributed to the quality of the institution. Again, the lag between the initial ability testing and college entry may have inflated this estimate.

A number of other longitudinal studies have documented the relationship between college quality and earnings. Taubman and Wales (1975a), for example, showed that the quality of the college significantly improves earnings for both dropouts and those who complete a degree. Johnson and Stafford (1974) showed a relationship between the salaries of academic economists and the quality of their *graduate* institutions (they controlled for sex and experience but not for ability). One of the few studies that failed to show a relationship between earnings and institutional quality is Sewell and Hauser's (1975) elaborate analysis of long-term longitudinal data from high school students in Wisconsin. They found significant impacts of institutional types within the state but no overall impact of institutional quality. Although this negative result may be a consequence of the limited variation in quality of institutions attended by students in a single state, the Sewell and Hauser analysis involved control of many more variables than most other studies of this type.

Solmon (1975) found that quality is related to income over the long term but not the short term, a result that not only confirms the nonsignificant association of college quality to initial salaries reported in Chapter Five but also provides the most

*A detailed review of literature on the relationship between education and earnings has been prepared by Bowman (1976); for a review of literature on the relationship between college quality and earnings, see Psacharopoulos (1975).

persuasive evidence for the "channeling" effect of college quality. Can it be that graduates of the more prestigious institutions take jobs that pay no more than those obtained by graduates of the less elite institutions but that have *prospects* for greater earnings? Larger and more prestigious corporations, banks, and law firms may recruit graduates of more prestigious institutions but may find it unnecessary to pay more to hire them. The graduates, in turn, may be willing to accept relatively low pay in a prestigious firm because of long-term income prospects. Higher education data support this line of reasoning: In his early ratings of the quality of graduate schools, Cartter (1966) found that salaries for assistant professors in elite graduate departments were no greater than those paid in lesser departments. However, at the associate professor level, there was a significant correlation between average salaries and quality, and at the full-professor level the association was even stronger. Because the most prestigious departments are unlikely to settle for less than the best new doctorates at the assistant professor level, the better graduates are probably willing to accept the same pay at a more prestigious institution because of long-range prospects for salary and career development.

A variable that *does* seem to have short-term consequences for salary is student ability. Both the short-term data in Chapter Five and practically every long-term study reviewed here has shown a substantial relationship between student ability, as measured by either tests, school grades, or both, and short- and long-term earnings. Weisbrod and Karpoff (1968) have shown that college grades are strongly related to earnings *within* different levels of college quality. Campbell (1965) showed that the highest 10 percent of students, as measured by high school and college grades, was making $10,000 more per year than the lowest 10 percent at the time of follow-up. Although the effects of grades or ability on earnings are mediated in part by education and occupational attainment (Spaeth and Greeley, 1970)—students of higher ability attain higher levels of education, attend higher-quality institutions, and work in higher-level occupations—ability maintains a significant independent relationship to earnings even after these other factors are controlled. Indeed, college grades have a stronger impact on earnings in the initial postcollege job than any other single factor (see Chapter Five). Once again, these findings negate the conclusion (Hoyt, 1966) that high school and college grades are of little consequence in later life.

Satisfaction

Does satisfaction with a college persist into the post-college years? Are college-educated people more satisfied with their jobs and personal lives than those who do not go to college? Although satisfaction has not been as thoroughly researched as earnings, a few studies provide some clues about the long-range impacts of college. Cross-sectional studies have shown that college-educated persons tend to be more satisfied with their jobs and lives in general than persons without college degrees (Withey, 1971). However, longitudinal studies, which control for initial ability and other background characteristics of students, do not produce such clear-cut results. Beaton (1975), in his analysis of the NBER-Thorndike data, concluded that job satisfaction depends primarily on salary and that education per se has little direct effect. Similarly, Campbell (1965) found inconsistent relationships between early ability and educational attainment and later satisfaction with marriage and life in general. Part of these discrepancies may be attributed to the ways in which college-educated and noncollege persons respond to polls. Gurin, Veroff, and Feld (1960), for example, found that college-educated people reported greater satisfaction with their marriages and their jobs than noncollege people, but in response to a second set of questions they were more likely to report problems in their marriages and jobs. Perhaps college-educated people are more responsive to interviewers and therefore are more likely to admit to problems, as well as to high degrees of satisfaction.

Chapter Six indicates that student satisfaction depends in part on the type of institution attended. How permanent are these differences by types of institutions? Pace's survey (1974) of alumni twenty years after college provides some evidence:

Although his institutional typology did not conform precisely with the type of institutions described in Chapter Six, there are enough similarities to make some comparisons. When asked if they derived "very much" or "quite a bit" of benefit from their college experience, alumni of liberal arts colleges were most likely to say they had benefited in friendships and social development. Alumni of general universities and technological institutions were least likely to indicate that they had derived such benefits from their undergraduate experience. Alumni of selective and denominational liberal arts colleges were most likely to report such benefits. This latter finding is consistent with the result (Chapter Six) that students report greater satisfaction at small, selective, denominational institutions. The closest thing to a general-satisfaction question in the Pace alumni survey was a query asking alumni if they would "definitely" or "probably" go to the same college if they were starting over again. That this item closely parallels the general-satisfaction question in Chapter Six is suggested by Pace's results with undergraduates: The greatest degree of satisfaction generally occurs in the most selective institutions. Pace's alumni, however, did not show the same pattern: The percentage of alumni that indicated that they would go to the same college again does not vary substantially by type of institution. While this finding suggests that differences by type of institution in degree of student satisfaction may dissipate with time, another interpretation is possible: Because Pace's alumni included only graduates, the least satisfied students (a larger proportion of the total student body at the less selective institutions) may account for the lower degree of satisfaction at less selective institutions. An alumni survey in which all dropouts are excluded would tend to inflate the level of satisfaction at nonselective more than at selective institutions. Again, only longitudinal surveys, which would include follow-ups on dropouts and nondropouts alike, can provide the long-term data to test this assumption.

Summary

Although much has been learned about short-term effects of college on a variety of student outcomes, less is known about the permanence of these effects over long time periods. The greatest limitation on knowledge is lack of available longitudinal data. Another problem with long-term studies is their applicability to the future. The longer the period of time covered by any longitudinal study, the more hazardous it becomes to generalize the findings to present or future events. This problem is exacerbated in a situation where the society and the higher educational system are changing rapidly.

A number of large-scale studies, both cross-sectional and longitudinal, show clearly that a college education is associated with a relatively high-level job, making more money, and having more general knowledge. There is also some tendency for college-educated people to be more liberal politically, to have smaller families, and to be more satisfied with their jobs, marriages, and lives in general. The best longitudinal studies suggest that the relationship between a college education and making more money does not disappear when such factors as family background and ability are considered.

Perhaps the best-documented short- and long-term relationship concerns the effects of ability (ability tests and/or college grades): The short-term studies reported in Chapter Five and the long-term studies reviewed here show that the relationship between ability and both occupational level and income persist, regardless of how many other factors are included in the longitudinal analysis.

Information on the permanence of impacts of different *types* of colleges and college experiences is limited, primarily because such studies have focused on one outcome (income) and used one measure of college characteristics (selectivity or quality). Although there is some long-term longitudinal evidence to support a causal relationship between college quality and earnings, the results are somewhat ambiguous, because the controls for student ability were obtained some time before the persons actually entered college. Consequently *changes* in ability between initial testing and college entry may be confounded with the measures of college quality.

Long-term longitudinal studies show that differences in students' political attitudes, beliefs, interests, and career aspirations persist over relatively long periods of time. What is not clear from these studies is whether *changes that may be specifically attributed to the college experience* persist over time. This ambiguity can only be resolved with well-controlled longitudinal studies covering long periods.

VIII

Summary
of Effects

Students change in many ways after they enter college. These changes can be effected by a number of factors, including the student's characteristics at the time of college entry, the type of college attended, and the extent of the student's involvement in the college environment. From the major empirical findings of this study, it is possible to draw certain policy implications for students, teachers, administrators, and policymakers. In this chapter, these findings are summarized under seven major headings: student change during college, differences in change, impact of student involvement, impact of academic achievement, impact of major fields, impact of different types of colleges, and patterns of student development.

211

Student Change During College

The longitudinal data, derived from studies that collectively involved some 200,000 students (at different periods) show clearly that students change in many ways after they enter college. They develop a more positive self-image as reflected in greater interpersonal and intellectual competence, and they develop more liberal political views and attitudes toward social issues. At the same time, they show less religiousness and altruism and show reduced interest in athletics, business, music, and status. Some of these attitudinal and personality changes are accompanied by parallel changes in behavior. Most dramatic is the decline in religious behavior and the accompanying increase in hedonistic behavior. Freshmen appear to be less studious and to interact less with instructors than they did in high school, but studiousness and interaction with faculty increase with time in college.

Are these changes directly attributable to the effects of college, or does maturation play a part? A change is considered to be dependent on the impact of college if residents show larger changes than commuters, if students with high interpersonal involvement on campus show larger changes than uninvolved students, and if persons who stay for four years show larger changes than persons who drop out after a short time. Maturational effects are assumed to be operating when these differences do not occur and when older students show smaller changes than younger students. Using these criteria as a guideline, a number of changes appear to be attributable to the college experience. Increased interpersonal self-esteem seems most dependent on college attendance. Increased intellectual self-esteem and liberalism and decreased business interest also appear to be primarily attributable to the effects of college. Decreased religiousness and increased hedonism seem to result from a mixture of college and maturational effects, whereas decreased need for status and reduced interest in music and athletics appear to be entirely maturational. Indeed, college attendance appears, if anything, to impede the decline in status needs occurring among young people during this period of life.

Another factor influencing changes in students during the college years is *changes in the larger society*. Some of the "liberalizing" effects of colleges observed in earlier longitudinal studies appear to be in part a result of societal changes occurring during the same period. Longitudinal analyses covering the late 1960s and the early 1970s show, for example, large increases in student support for women's equality and student autonomy. Independent evidence from successive classes entering college during this period suggests that these changes in support for student autonomy are almost totally attributable to societal changes and that increased support for women's equality represents a mixture of societal and college influences.

Although college attendance is associated with an increase in both academic knowledge and competency across a variety of fields, students' college grades and rate of extracurricular achievement decline from those in high school. Reduced grades in college are attributable in part to the increased competition and higher academic standards of colleges compared with high schools. Reduced chances of achieving in extracurricular fields (music, leadership, theater, writing, athletics, and so forth) occur in part because of increased competition and in part because of the larger size of colleges compared with high schools. The greater the number of students, the less chance any given student has to participate in such activities as athletics or the school paper.

Although many students change career plans after they enter college, the amount of change varies across fields, and the "traffic" between fields is not random. The biggest dropout rates occur among students who initially plan careers in engineering, nursing, medicine, science, and school teaching. Careers that gain substantially in popularity are business, college teaching, law, and homemaking. Although the dropout rate from school teaching is large, that career captures a number of dropouts from other fields.

Students who have well-formulated career plans at college entry are only moderately successful in completing these plans. The greatest degree of success (about two thirds) occurs among students pursuing nursing and school teaching; the lowest success rates (about one third) occur among students planning to become doctors, lawyers, or social workers.

Students seem reasonably satisfied with various aspects of their undergraduate experience, although a significant minority (between 10 percent and 30 percent) reports moderate or extreme dissatisfaction with particular features of the college. The greatest degree of satisfaction is with student friendships, social life, and the college's academic reputation. Students tend to be least satisfied with the variety of courses offered, outlets for creative activities, and advice and guidance from faculty and staff.

Differences in Change

Not all students change in the same way after they enter college. For certain traits, men change more than women; for others, the reverse is true. The brightest students sometimes change more than the less well-prepared students. Differential change is evident in several student characteristics: sex, race, ability, and age.

Before turning to these four traits, it is necessary to point out that changes over time in the relative scores of two groups such as men and women involve certain conceptual and methodological problems. For example, if men score higher than women in freshman business interests, the only way this mean difference can persist over time is for men to show smaller average declines than women *with the same scores*. If men and women with the same scores change by the same average amount, the initial group differences will diminish. (See the Appendix of this book for an explanation of this paradox.) Freshman group differences may persist over time either because of measurement errors in the freshman score (see the Appendix) or because of environmental factors: If men initially develop stronger business interests because of stimulation and encouragement from family, teachers, peers, and the media (where businesspersons are typically portrayed as men), they may tend to retain these relatively strong interests over time better than women with a comparable degree of initial interest, because the same environmental effects continue to operate. One would expect that the common experience of attending college, where both men and women take similar courses and are exposed to the same professors, would tend to reduce some sex differences over time but such is not always the case.

Sex. Men and women differ as freshmen in numerous characteristics, and many of these differences persist during the four years following matriculation. Thus, men enter college with substantially stronger business interests, greater hedonism, and somewhat higher interpersonal and intellectual self-esteem, and these differences persist over time. Women enter college with stronger religious, altruistic, and artistic interests, and these differences also persist during the undergraduate years. Differences between men and women in athletic interests and musical interests decline slightly with time, but the most conspicuous convergence of the sexes occurs with political liberalism. Although both groups increase substantially in liberalism, men increase more, such that the relative positions of the sexes are reversed: Women begin college slightly more liberal than men, but men are slightly more liberal four years later. This reversal may be attributed in part to the men's greater involvement in campus political activities (Astin and others, 1975).

Differences between men and women on several other characteristics become greater with time. Although both groups decline in status needs, these declines are greater for women, so that the gap widens with time. Similarly, the large difference in aspirations for high-level degrees (Ph.D., M.D., LL.B., or J.D.) also widens slightly with time.

Sex is related to the development of competency and achievement during college, even after other entering characteristics are controlled. Although women earn higher grades than men in college, they are less likely to persist and to enroll in graduate or professional school. Women are more likely to acquire general cultural knowledge and skills in foreign language, music, typing, and homemaking. Men are more likely to achieve in athletics, to publish original writing, to acquire technical or scientific skills, to improve their knowledge of sports, and to improve their skill in swimming and general physical fitness.

Men are much more likely than women to show verbal aggressiveness. Men get involved in athletics during college, but women are slightly more likely to get involved in academics. Women are much more likely to get married during college, even after marriage plans at college entry are taken into account. Getting married appears to be one explanation for women's slightly reduced chances of completing college.

Sex is also related to career development. Men are more likely to implement initial plans to become a college teacher, doctor, or lawyer, whereas women are more likely to implement plans to become an elementary or secondary school teacher. Among students who go to work in business or school teaching immediately after college, men make approximately $1,000 per year more than women of comparable background and ability. That sex discrimination may be involved here suggests that this finding merits more intensive investigation.

Sex shows only minor relationships to student satisfaction. Women tend to be more satisfied with friendships with other students and with faculty-student relations, whereas men tend to be somewhat more satisfied with the quality of classroom instruction.

In summary, it seems clear that colleges do not serve to reduce many of the stereotypic differences between the sexes. With the exception of liberalism, where men and women converge during the college years, most sex differences are not eliminated or even reduced by the undergraduate experience. Even though men and women are presumably exposed to common liberal arts curriculum and other educational programs during the undergraduate years, it would seem that these programs serve more to preserve, rather than to reduce, stereotypic differences between men and women in behavior, personality, aspirations, and achievement.

Ability. Students of differing ability (as measured by college admissions tests) differ in characteristics at college entry, and these differences either persist or expand with time. High-ability students are more politically liberal, substantially less religious, and have much higher aspirations than middle- or low-ability students at the time of college entry; these differences become even greater during college. The highly able student's stronger musical and artistic interests, weaker business interests, and substantially higher intellectual self-esteem persist during the four college years. The only characteristic where the differences tend to equalize is interpersonal self-esteem, where the highly able student's slight advantage at college entry diminishes somewhat during the college years.

As expected, highly able students are much more likely than their less able peers to get involved academically, to participate in honors programs, to get high grades, to complete college, to graduate with honors, and to go to graduate or professional school. They are also more likely to achieve in science or creative writing and to implement careers in medicine, law, nursing, engineering, and science. In addition, high-ability students who take jobs in nursing or engineering immediately following college earn higher starting salaries than low-ability students.

Clearly, American higher education is designed primarily for highly able students. Such students generally go to more prestigious institutions, live away from home, get more involved, achieve at higher levels in both academic and nonacademic areas, and are better able to complete their career plans. Long-term studies show that ability continues to have an impact on occupational status and earnings over long periods of time, although much of this effect occurs because high-ability students generally attain higher levels of formal education than do low-ability students.

Race. Black students become more politically liberal and are more likely than white students to abandon traditional religious affiliations during college. Black men, more than white men, increase in interpersonal self-esteem, and black women, more than white women, show smaller declines in business interests. Black students are more likely than white students to strengthen their altruistic tendencies and their beliefs in preferential treatment for disadvantaged students and are less likely to support the notion that large families should be discouraged. Athletic interests decline somewhat more among blacks than among whites. Blacks are more likely than whites to get involved in demonstrations and to participate in student government, but they are less likely to get married. Blacks increase their general cultural knowledge, sports knowledge, and physical fitness somewhat more than whites during the freshman year, although whites increase their musical competence and skill in swimming more than blacks. Blacks are less likely to become involved academically and to graduate with honors. Although the absolute persistence rate for blacks is lower than that for whites, the persistence rate for black women is actually higher than that for white women of comparable preparation and ability. Also, although blacks and whites enroll in graduate and professional school at the same rate, the enrollment of blacks is substantially higher than that of whites once ability and other background factors are considered. Blacks are more likely than whites to implement plans for a medical career and less likely to implement plans for a career in nursing. Among students taking jobs in either business or school teaching immediately after college, blacks average better than $1,000 per year more in salaries than whites of comparable background and training. However, blacks tend to be somewhat less satisfied than whites with their college experience.

Age. Younger students are somewhat more likely than older students to abandon traditional religious beliefs and to increase their hedonistic tendencies after they enter college. Younger students are also more likely to get involved in athletics and in student government, whereas older students are more likely to interact with faculty, to get involved academically, and to participate in honors programs. Older students get better grades and are more likely to graduate with honors than younger students of comparable background and ability. While older students are less likely than younger students to implement plans to become lawyers, those in nursing obtain substantially higher starting salaries than their younger counterparts once they leave college. Age shows no relationship to satisfaction.

Other Student Predictors. Several other student characteristics of potential interest are associated with changed outcomes. Students with high interpersonal self-esteem are more likely to increase their educational aspirations and to become involved on an interpersonal level with other students and faculty after entering college. Students with high intellectual self-esteem are likely to become involved in honors programs and get high grades, but they are somewhat *less* likely than students with low intellectual self-esteem to become involved academically, that is, to study long hours or devote considerable energy to academic pursuits. Freshmen high in hedonism show larger declines in religiousness, become less involved academically, get poorer grades, and are more likely to drop out than nonhedonistic students. Students with high educational aspirations at college entry show a reverse pattern: They are more likely to participate in honors programs, to achieve in academic and extracurricular activities, and to graduate. They are also more likely to become involved in student government, to participate in demonstrations, and to increase their support for student autonomy.

Students from different social backgrounds show unique patterns of change after they enter college. Those from relatively wealthy families are more likely to participate in honors programs, have better chances of graduating, and earn substantially higher salaries if they work in engineering or business immediately after college. Students with highly educated parents are more likely than students with less-educated parents to increase in hedonism during college, to participate in honors programs, to be verbally aggressive, and to demonstrate; they are less likely to get married. Students are more likely to continue with plans to enter business, engineering, or medicine if their fathers are in these same fields. Finally, students from Jewish families show greater-than-average decreases in religiousness and increases in liberalism, but their business interests and status needs decrease less than those of non-Jews. Jews are more likely to be verbally aggressive and to participate in demonstrations, but less likely to get involved in student government. Jews are less likely to marry while in college and more likely to go to graduate or professional school.

Impact of Student Involvement

The fact that most measures of student involvement are associated with greater-than-average changes in entering student characteristics supports the hypothesis that many changes after college entry may be attributed in part to the college experience rather than to maturation. For certain outcomes, student involvement is more strongly associated with change than either entering freshman characteristics or institutional characteristics. There is, to be sure, some confounding of involvement with other factors. Students who live in college dormitories rather than at home, for example, tend to come from more affluent families and are more likely to attend four-year rather than two-year colleges. Nevertheless, involvement measures are strongly associated with many outcomes even after the effects of student and institutional characteristics are considered. Major findings for nine forms of involvement are summarized: place of residence, honors programs, undergraduate research participation, social fraternities and sororities, academic involvement, student-faculty interaction, athletic involvement, involvement in student government, and verbal aggressiveness.

Place of Residence. Leaving home to attend college affects student development in various ways. Since few freshmen live in private rooms, these effects compare dormitory living with living at home. Residents show slightly greater increases than commuters in artistic interests, liberalism, and interpersonal self-esteem and show slightly larger declines in musical interest. Effects are substantially larger, however, on behavior: Residents show much larger declines in religiousness and much larger increases in hedonism. Residents are also more likely to interact with faculty, to become involved in student government, and to join social fraternities or sororities.

Perhaps the most significant impacts of living on campus versus commuting are on achievement and career development. Living on campus substantially increases the student's chances of persisting in college and of aspiring to graduate or professional degrees. Residents are also more likely to achieve in extracurricular areas, in particular leadership and athletics.

Among men, living on campus increases undergraduate grade-point average. Residents are more likely than commuters to implement career plans in business, but those who commute to college earn somewhat higher salaries in nursing and school teaching. Residents express much more satisfaction than commuters with their undergraduate experience, particularly in the areas of student friendships, faculty-student relations, institutional reputation, and social life.

Honors Programs. Participation in honors programs is associated with much-larger-than-average increases in interpersonal self-esteem, intellectual self-esteem, and artistic interests. Participation also positively affects undergraduate grades, persistence, and aspirations for graduate or professional degrees. Honors participation is positively associated with student satisfaction in three areas—quality of the science program, closeness to faculty, and quality of instruction—and negatively associated with satisfaction with friendships and the institution's academic reputation. These findings suggest that honors participation enhances faculty-student relationships but also that it may isolate students somewhat from each other and raise the student's subjective norms concerning institutional reputations.

The findings on the impact of honors programs and other forms of involvement are somewhat ambiguous, because participation is not generally a condition of college entry but something that occurs after matriculation. Some of the behavioral changes associated with a particular involvement measure may have occurred *prior* to rather than as a consequence of involvement. (This ambiguity does not apply to residents, since only the freshman place of residence was used in these analyses.) In spite of this ambiguity, the magnitude of the relationships between involvement measures and certain student outcomes is such that it provides some support for a causal interpretation of the impact of involvement on student development. More definitive tests of causal relations require either controlled experimentation or at least longitudinal studies where pretests are obtained immediately before the involvement experience.

Undergraduate Research Participation. Participation in undergraduate research activities produces results similar to those associated with honors participation. Students who become involved in research activities show substantially larger increases in interpersonal and intellectual self-esteem, artistic interests, altruism, and political liberalism. They show smaller-than-expected declines in status needs. Research involvement most strongly affects undergraduate grades, persistence, aspirations for advanced degrees, and achievement in science and creative writing. Students involved in research are also more satisfied with the quality of instruction and the science program, closeness to faculty, and emphasis on social life.

Social Fraternities and Sororities. Membership in social fraternities or sororities substantially affects the student's intellectual self-esteem, business interests, status needs, and hedonism (in particular, drinking). Among women, membership is associated with smaller-than-average changes in both liberalism and traditional religious beliefs. Fraternity or sorority membership has a substantial positive effect on persistence, overall satisfaction with college, and satisfaction with instruction and social life.

Academic Involvement. Academic involvement produces one of the most unusual patterns of effects on student outcomes. In understanding this pattern, it is important to keep in mind the definition of the factor: Academically involved students are those who spend a good deal of time at and say they work hard at their studies. Students with low involvement study less, say they are not interested in their courses and are bored in class, and do not care much about their grades. Being heavily involved academically tends to retard the changes in personality and behavior that normally result from college attendance. Thus, academically involved students show smaller-than-average increases in liberalism, hedonism, artistic interests, and religious apostasy, and smaller-than-average decreases in business interests. The only personality change accentuated by academic involvement is status needs, which are strengthened. Being academically involved is strongly associated with satisfaction with all aspects of the institution except student friendships.

The pattern of results with academic involvement reinforces the hypothesis that students who become heavily involved with their studies in college tend to become isolated from their peers and, consequently, less susceptible to the peer-group influences that seem to be critical for developing political liberalism, hedonism, and religious apostasy. (It could also be argued, of course, that the causation may work in reverse: Students who feel isolated from their peers may take to studying hard. Possibly the causation works both ways.) However, perhaps because of the many institutional rewards for good academic performance, being heavily involved academically is associated with greater student satisfaction with almost all aspects of the undergraduate institution.

Student-Faculty Interaction. Interacting frequently with faculty during the undergraduate years has a positive impact on status needs, altruism, and musical and artistic interests. Stronger status needs are also associated with being familiar with the faculty in one's major field. It is of some interest that interacting with faculty is not associated with increased political liberalism, considering that faculty tend to be strongly politically liberal (Ladd and Lipset, 1975). Possibly the positive impact of college attendance on political liberalism is mediated more through a peer-group effect than an effect of faculty on student beliefs.

Student-faculty interaction has a stronger relationship to student satisfaction with the college experience than any other involvement variable or, indeed, any other student or institutional characteristic. Students who interact frequently with faculty are more satisfied with all aspects of their institutional experience, including student friendships, variety of courses, intellectual environment, and even administration of the institution. Finding ways to encourage greater personal contact between faculty and students might increase students' satisfaction with their college experiences.

Athletic Involvement. Involvement in athletic activities during the undergraduate years shows a pattern of effects on student development that closely parallels the pattern associated with academic involvement. Increases in political liberalism, religious apostasy, and artistic interests, and decreases in business interests are less among students who become involved in athletic activities. Unlike academic involvement, athletic involvement does not affect either status needs or overall hedonism. Athletic involvement does, however, have a positive effect on drinking and a negative effect on smoking during the undergraduate years. Athletic involvement is associated with greater student satisfaction in four areas: the institution's academic reputation, intellectual environment, student friendships, and institutional administration. These latter effects may reflect the special status given many athletes by students and administrators.

These results suggest that athletic involvement, like academic involvement, tends to isolate students from the peer-group effects on behavior that normally accompany college attendance. For the studious person, this isolation results from time and effort devoted to studying. For the athlete, the isolation may result from long practice hours, travel to athletic competitions, and, in some cases, special living quarters.

Involvement in Student Government. Involvement in student government is associated with greater-than-average increases in political liberalism, hedonism, and artistic interests. Involvement also has a positive effect on status needs and on satisfaction with student friendships. It has a negative impact on satisfaction with the intellectual climate. It shows no relationship to overall satisfaction.

This pattern of relationships supports the notion that changes in attitudes and behavior that normally accompany college attendance are attributable to peer-group effects. That is, students who become heavily involved in student government interact more frequently with peers than students who do not become so involved. Such interaction appears to enhance the changes resulting from the college experience.

Verbal Aggressiveness. Like involvement in student government, verbal aggressiveness is associated with greater-than-average increases in political liberalism, artistic interests, and hedonism, and smaller-than-expected decreases in status needs. Verbal aggressiveness, however, is also associated with greater-than-expected religious apostasy during the undergraduate years and with *dissatisfaction* in four areas: academic reputation, intellectual environment, student-faculty relations, and administration. Apparently, students who become verbally aggressive during the undergraduate years also become more critical of their undergraduate institutions.

In summary, it should be pointed out that most forms of interpersonal involvement—in research, in student government, interaction with faculty, and verbal aggressiveness—seem to retard the general lowering of interests (art, music, athletics, altruism, and status) that occurs after students enter college. The only exception here is business interests, which decline even more among students who become interpersonally involved.

Impact of Academic Achievement

Students who get high grades as undergraduates show substantially greater increases in intellectual self-esteem during the undergraduate years than students who get poor grades. They show smaller declines in business interests than other students and much smaller increases in hedonism. Good grades are related to substantially larger increases in interpersonal self-esteem among women and to increased status needs among men. Among low-ability students, good grades are also related to increased interpersonal self-esteem and religious apostasy.

As expected, good grades strongly relate to persistence in college and also to aspirations for graduate and professional training. Students with high grades are much more likely to implement career plans in almost all fields: medicine, law, science, school teaching, engineering, and business. Grades are most strongly related to successful pursuit of careers requiring graduate or professional training: math, law, and scientific research. For students who go to work immediately after college in business, school teaching, or engineering, undergraduate grades have a substantial effect on starting salaries. A difference of one letter grade equals approximately $900 in starting salary. Long-term longitudinal studies suggest that the effects of grades on occupational status and earnings persist over long periods of time.

Impact of Major Fields

Studying the impact of the student's major field presents certain analytical problems, given that more than half the students change majors in college. Nevertheless, even when the student's freshman major is used, certain significant relationships appear. Students show substantially larger increases in intellectual self-esteem, for example, if they enter college with plans to major in mathematics, physical sciences, engineering, or premedicine. Engineering majors, however, show other patterns that reverse the usual effects of college: smaller-than-average increases in interpersonal self-esteem, political liberalism, and artistic interest, and smaller-than-average declines in business interests. Students majoring in social sciences show the reverse pattern: greater-than-average increases in liberalism, artistic interest, altruism, and religious apostasy, and larger-than-average decreases in business interests. These patterns may reflect peer-group effects from the predominant values and attitudes of persons majoring in engineering and social sciences. With engineering, the results may also reflect the relative isolation from students in other fields that many engineering majors experience, particularly those in separate technological schools. Majoring in premedicine tends to increase students' apostasy, intellectual self-esteem, and altruism, but it also has a positive effect on business interests.

Students' undergraduate grades are also affected by their fields: The most stringent grading occurs in engineering, mathematics, and physical sciences, while the most lenient occurs in the humanities. Majors also affect aspirations for advanced degrees: Students in the humanities and the natural sciences are most likely to pursue plans for advanced degrees, whereas students in engineering are least likely to persist in their plans for an advanced degree.

A student's initial choice of a major can also have an impact on attaining career objectives. In general, majoring in a field closely related to one's career plans enhances the prospects for attaining those initial plans. This is particularly true in business (business majors), school teaching (education majors), and engineering (engineering majors). Women are more likely to conclude their college years with plans to be a homemaker if their initial major is business and less likely if it is in the social sciences.

Major fields also affect starting salaries for schoolteachers and engineers. New engineers make more money if they start college majoring in engineering; schoolteachers make more money if their initial field is education and less money is it is in the humanities.

Impact of Different Types of Colleges

Chapters Two through Seven have shown that different types of colleges have significant impacts on student outcomes. These findings, organized separately by different college types, are summarized and interpreted under eight general headings: selectivity, size, control, single-sex colleges, two-year colleges, religious colleges, predominantly black colleges, and geographic region.

Selectivity. Attending a selective institution* tends to accelerate some of the attitudinal and personality changes attributable to the college experience. Thus, students show greater-than-average declines in religiousness and larger increases in self-criticism and political liberalism. The liberalizing impact of selectivity is greatest at the highly selective private colleges. Increased liberalism is further reflected by the positive effect of selectivity on the student's support for student autonomy and power, preferential treatment for the disadvantaged, and women's rights. Selectivity has a negative effect on the concept that the chief benefit of going to college is monetary. Since the faculties of selective institutions tend to be highly liberal, it could be argued that these faculties at selective colleges and uni-

---

*Institutional selectivity, defined as the average academic ability of the entering freshman, and two closely related measures—prestige (selectivity weighted by institutional size) and affluence (student expenditures) —usually shows a similar effect. Unless otherwise noted, it can be assumed that selectivity shows effects equivalent to or stronger than the other two measures.

versities foster a greater liberalism among their students. However, because faculty-student contact and familiarity with faculty in the student's major field are not related to increased liberalism, the impact may be mediated more through peer-group effects than through faculty influence. That student bodies at selective institutions tend to be more liberal than those at nonselective institutions supports this interpretation.

Contrary to educational folklore, attending a highly selective institution does not have a negative impact on the intellectual self-esteem of bright students. Selectivity does, however, have a positive impact on the student's tendency to be self-critical. Perhaps the highly competitive atmosphere of the selective institution, where both faculty and peers tend to be bright and highly critical, makes the student more open to self-criticism.

Attending a selective institution increases the student's chances of demonstrating, drinking, and joining a social fraternity or sorority; chances of smoking, engaging in religious activity, and getting married are reduced. (The sole exception to this trend—the selective Roman Catholic college—is discussed later.) Students at prestigious institutions are more likely to be verbally aggressive and to be familiar with faculty in their major fields, but they are less likely to become involved in campus government.

One of the strongest effects of college selectivity is on the student's undergraduate grade-point average, which is substantially reduced by attending a highly selective institution. Selectivity also reduces the student's chances of participating in honors programs and of being academically involved. Selective institutions, in spite of their highly competitive environments, apparently do not stress long study hours and regular classroom attendance.

In spite of their negative impact on the student's grades, selective institutions do not reduce the student's chances of completing a baccalaureate degree and going to graduate or professional school. Indeed, highly selective private colleges slightly increase the student's aspirations for advanced graduate or professional schools, as well as their chances of actually enrolling in graduate school after college.

Attending a selective institution also strengthens the student's athletic interest and increases the likelihood of athletic achievement, such as playing on a varsity team. Selective colleges and universities, compared with less selective institutions of comparable size, may have more extensive athletic facilities and more teams in minor sports, such as lacrosse, rugby, skiing, crew, squash, sailing, and so forth. Thus, the typical student at the selective college would have more opportunities for participation in varsity sports.

The student's chances of entering medical school are enhanced by attending a selective private university, although selectivity is not related to success in implementing a medical career within the four-year colleges. The student's chances of implementing career plans in college teaching, business, engineering, and nursing are increased at a selective institution. At first the substantial positive effect of selectivity on a nursing career is difficult to understand, because few highly selective institutions have nursing programs. Closer consideration suggests that the effect is attributable primarily to colleges of very *low* selectivity: Students entering such institutions have substantially reduced chances of carrying out plans to become a nurse compared with students pursuing nursing careers in moderately selective colleges.

Selectivity has no consistent effect on starting salaries, but long-term longitudinal studies suggest a substantial positive effect over longer periods of time. Graduates of selective institutions may be able to obtain jobs with good *long-range* earnings potential, whereas graduates of less selective institutions may simply look for the highest-paying initial job.

Why students should be less likely to enter law school after graduation if they attend the more selective institutions is not immediately clear. One reason may be related to the great range in selectivity among law schools. Prelaw students at highly selective institutions may aspire only to the most prestigious law schools and, because of limited openings, switch to some other career such as business at graduation when they are not accepted. Prelaw students at the less selective colleges, however, may not develop such high aspirations and may thus be willing to attend any law school that admits them.

Selective institutions and, in particular, prestigious universities make strong academic demands on students. One of the most striking patterns of effects of a selective institution is in student satisfaction. Students at selective institutions are likely to be more satisfied with their undergraduate experience than are students at less selective institutions, in an overall sense as well as in specific areas: academic reputation, intellectual climate, quality of instruction, variety of the curriculum, quality of the science program, and even the college administration. The only areas where college selectivity does not positively influence student satisfaction are friendships with other students and close relations with faculty. This greater overall satisfaction seems partly attributable to the superior faculty and facilities at such institutions.

Size. Almost all student involvement in campus life is decreased by attending a large rather than a small institution. Students at large institutions are less likely to interact with faculty, to get involved in campus government, to participate in athletics, to become involved in honors programs, and to be verbally aggressive in their classrooms. The only exception is student involvement in demonstrations, which is increased at large institutions. This latter finding is consistent with the positive effect of size on liberalism and on support for student autonomy. Large institutions also reduce the student's chances of achieving in areas of leadership, athletics, journalism, and theater. The only achievement facilitated at large institutions is graduation with honors, which is more likely at selective public or private universities. Large institutions facilitate plans to pursue a career in business. Size also has a positive effect on starting salaries for schoolteachers.

Attending a university rather than a college has a negative effect on altruism and on the student's belief that organized sports should be emphasized. In all likelihood, this latter finding reflects some student resentment at the emphasis given athletics in large universities and at the special privileges accorded many athletes.

Students show a mixed pattern of satisfaction at large versus small institutions. The greatest satisfaction is with social

life, and they are also more satisfied than students at sm;
institutions with the quality of the science programs (at un....
sities), the institution's academic reputation, and the variety in
the curriculum. This latter finding may reflect the wide range of
courses offered at large institutions. Students are *much* less satisfied, however, with their relationships with faculty at large
institutions and with classroom instruction.

Control. Although the categories "public" and "private"
each comprise heterogeneous collections of institutions, the
public-private dichotomy attains increasing policy significance
as many private institutions are threatened by financial in-
solvency. Thus it is useful to review the overall effects of public
versus private institutions on student development. Some of
these overall effects are actually attributable to other institutional characteristics that differentiate some private from some
public institutions. Private institutions, for example, include
most single-sex colleges and tend to be smaller than most public
institutions. Two-year colleges, on the other hand, account for
more than half of the freshmen enrolling at public institutions,
compared to less than 15 percent of freshmen entering private
institutions (Astin, King, and Richardson, 1976).

Practically all the effects associated with college attendance are more pronounced among students at private institutions. Thus, increases in artistic interests, intellectual and
interpersonal self-esteem, political liberalism, and religious apostasy are greater among students at private institutions. Declines
in business interests and in the belief that the chief benefit of
college is monetary are also greater among students at private
institutions. The only change reversing the pattern is hedonism,
which is slightly greater among students at public than at private institutions.

Attending a private institution greatly increases the student's chances of interacting with faculty, participating in campus government, becoming familiar with instructors in the
major field, and being verbally aggressive in classes. Students at
private colleges are also more satisfied with classroom instruction, faculty-student contacts, closeness to faculty, and the
institution's reputation. Students at public colleges are some-

what more satisfied with the administration, variety of the curriculum, and emphasis on social life. Most of these effects on satisfaction are attributable to the smaller size of private colleges.

Attending a private college substantially increases the student's chance of pursuing a career in science. Smaller positive effects of attending a private college also occur on career plans in business, engineering, law, and social work.

Single-Sex Colleges. Some of the most dramatic effects were associated with attending men's or women's colleges. These single-sex colleges have a number of effects in common, other effects that are unique to one or the other type, and several contrasting effects. Both types of single-sex colleges facilitate student involvement in several areas: academic, interaction with faculty, and verbal aggressiveness. The latter is stronger at women's than at men's colleges. Men's and women's colleges also have a positive effect on intellectual self-esteem. Students at single-sex colleges are much more satisfied than students at coeducational colleges with virtually all aspects of college life: student-faculty relations, quality of instruction, curricular variety, student friendships, and quality of science program. The only area where students are less satisfied is social life. This negative effect is much stronger for men than for women. Possibly women at women's colleges are less likely to complain about a lack of social life because they have more organized social activities on the campus. Men, who may be more mobile than women, often go to women's colleges for social activities.

Men's and women's colleges have contrasting effects in two areas: athletics and academic achievement. Men attending men's colleges rather than coeducational colleges are more likely to participate and achieve in athletics, to participate in honors programs, and to obtain good grades. Women at women's colleges, by contrast, are less likely to participate in honors programs, to get good grades, and to become involved in athletics. These differences no doubt reflect the men's preoccupation with athletic competition and the women's superior level of academic performance. Thus, men do better academically if they have to compete only with men, whereas women do worse if they have to compete only with women.

Women's colleges have a number of unique effects. First, they facilitate artistic interests and political liberalism. More important, women are more likely to attain positions of leadership, to become involved in student government, to develop high aspirations, and to persist to graduation if they attend a women's college. They are more likely to implement plans to become schoolteachers but less likely to implement career plans in nursing or business. Apparently, women are much more likely to be verbally aggresssive and to seek positions of leadership if they are not in the presence of men: Men seem to deter women's assertiveness during the undergraduate years. Whether these effects will persist beyond the college years, once women leave the unique environment of the women's college, is a problem for future research.

Attending a college for men increases the men's chances of graduating with honors. It also tends to retard the decline in business interests and religious beliefs. Men's colleges also increase the student's chances of implementing career plans in business and in college teaching. However, the largest effect is on pursuit of a law career—defined as entry to law school after graduation. This effect may be due in part to the large number of peers pursuing legal careers at many colleges for men. Students pursuing business careers end up with larger beginning salaries if they start their education in a men's college. This finding suggests that recruiters for better-paying jobs in the business field may favor men's colleges. It also suggests that men's colleges have better connections with the business world than coeducational colleges.

Two-Year Colleges. Attending a two-year institution impedes changes that are normally a consequence of college attendance. Thus, increases in hedonism, interpersonal self-esteem, and support for student power are far less among two-year college students than among those at four-year colleges or universities. Two-year college students are also more likely to cling to traditional views of the role of women and to the idea that the chief benefit of college is monetary.

Although the *private* two-year institutions account for a small proportion of all two-year college students, these institutions, many of which are Roman Catholic, have some unique effects on women. Declines in religiousness and increases in hedonism, for example, are much smaller among women attending private two-year colleges than among women at other types of institutions. These negative effects on hedonism suggest that women at private two-year colleges, many of which are residential, are closely supervised and do not undergo the behavioral changes normally associated with college attendance.

Students at two-year colleges are less likely to get involved in student government, to participate in athletics, to be verbally aggressive in the classroom, and to be on familiar terms with faculty in their major fields. They are also less likely to attain positions of leadership. This lower degree of student involvement is the result, in part, of the relative lack of a campus life that characterizes many commuter colleges. The lowered contact with faculty in one's major may reflect the deemphasis on major fields that characterize many community colleges.

Perhaps the most significant impact of attending a community college is on the student's persistence and implementation of career plans. Even after controlling for the student's social background, ability, and motivation at college entrance, the chances of persisting to the baccalaureate degree are substantially reduced. Although this effect is greater among women than among men, it occurs in both public and private two-year colleges. Controlling for the fact that most community college students are commuters reduces the magnitude of the effect on persistence, but it does not eliminate it entirely. Perhaps the most significant consequence of the negative impact of these institutions on persistence is that the student's chances of implementing career plans are reduced in almost all fields: business, engineering, school teaching, nursing, and social work. (For possible remedies for the attrition problem at community colleges, see MacMillan and Kester, 1973.)

Assessing student satisfaction four years after college entry presents certain methodological difficulties with the community college, because most students have either dropped out or transferred to a four-year institution. Students at community colleges tend to be more satisfied than average with the curriculum, probably because of the diverse offerings. It is somewhat puzzling that students at community colleges are also more satisfied than students at other institutions with the quality of the science program. Given the small proportion of science majors at such colleges, it may be that their expectations or standards are modest. It is also somewhat surprising that students at community colleges are relatively satisfied with the social life. One explanation may be that many community college students already know their fellow students when they enter college, because most students are living at home and probably attended the same high schools.

Religious Colleges. Although both Roman Catholic and Protestant colleges show some common effects, they also differ in several important respects. Selective institutions within these two groups sometimes differ from nonselective institutions in their effect on student development. With these results, it is important to remember that Protestant institutions represent an extremely heterogeneous group comprising colleges controlled by fundamentalist sects as well as institutions with only a loose affiliation with more liberal denominations.

Both Roman Catholic and Protestant institutions have a positive effect on the student's altruistic tendencies, a finding consistent with a Christian religious belief. Declines in traditional beliefs are also less among students at these types of institutions, but this effect is much more dramatic in the Roman Catholic institutions. This differential effect may be attributed to at least three factors: peer-group effects (students at Catholic institutions are overwhelmingly Catholic, whereas students at many Protestant institutions come from diverse religious backgrounds); Roman Catholic institutions' imposition of more direct behavioral controls over students' religious behavior (required chapel attendance or prayers in classrooms); and faculty influence (faculties of Catholic institutions may include many clergy).

Religious apostasy is reduced in the nonselective Protestant colleges and increased at the selective colleges. Selective Protestant colleges have a *positive* impact on musical interests and hedonism, and they increase the student's chances of persisting to graduation, enrolling in graduate school, and becoming a college professor. Attending a nonselective Protestant college increases the student's grade-point average, but it decreases aspirations for advanced graduate and professional degrees. The negative impact of college selectivity on a law career is replicated within the Protestant colleges: Attending nonselective institutions substantially increases the student's chances of enrolling in law school, whereas attending a selective Protestant college reduces these chances somewhat.

Students in both Protestant and Roman Catholic colleges tend to be highly satisfied with closeness to faculty and the quality of student-faculty relationships. These effects, however, are entirely attributable to the small size of these colleges. Students in Catholic colleges are somewhat dissatisfied with the variety of courses and the science programs.

Selective and nonselective Catholic colleges also produce certain contrasting effects: Women attending selective Catholic colleges are more likely to achieve in leadership and creative writing than women in nonselective Catholic colleges, but they also show smaller increases in liberalism and hedonism. This latter differential may be explained in part by the recent tendency of many nonselective Catholic colleges to attract more students by becoming coeducational and deemphasizing parietal rules. The more selective institutions can maintain their single-sex status and relatively strict behavioral control because they are less threatened by declining enrollments (Anderson, 1977). While students get somewhat higher grades in nonselective Catholic colleges, their aspirations for advanced graduate and professional degrees are reduced. The nonselective Catholic colleges increase the student's likelihood of pursuing a career in nursing and homemaking.

Predominantly Black Colleges. In reviewing the effects of attending predominantly black colleges, it must be stressed that these are really the *relative* effects on black students of attending predominantly black versus predominantly white institutions. Virtually all students attending black colleges participating in the CIRP are black. For black students, many changes associated with college attendance are reduced in black compared with white colleges. Thus, there is less tendency toward religious apostasy, political liberalism, artistic interests, athletic interests, self-criticism, and interpersonal self-esteem among black students at black colleges. Apparently, black students are substantially influenced by their white peers when they attend predominantly white institutions. The only exception to this trend is hedonism, which increases somewhat more among black students at black than at white colleges.

Attending a black college substantially increases the black student's chances of implementing career plans in a variety of fields: college teaching, nursing, medicine, and science. Black students majoring in engineering earn somewhat higher salaries on graduation if they attend white colleges.

Students at black colleges are more satisfied with the quality of science programs and social life, but black students are more satisfied with student-faculty relations at white colleges.

Geographic Region. The region of the country in which an institution is located has a number of effects on students, even after other characteristics, such as control, size, and selectivity, are considered. Many regional contrasts involve the Northeast (New England and the mid-Atlantic states) and the West (California, the Pacific Northwest, and Southwest). Higher education in these two regions differs in important ways. Colleges in the Northeast, for example, are much older, generally smaller, and more frequently privately controlled than colleges in the West. The northeastern emphasis on tradition and private higher education is probably reflected in a number of impacts: reduced chances of marrying while in college, greater persistence rates, and greater likelihood of graduation with honors. Although these regional effects were obtained after controlling for characteristics of the student's institution, the preponderance of public institutions and, in particular, community colleges in the western states may create an atmosphere in which dropping out of college, transferring, or taking a leave of absence is much more acceptable simply because it occurs more often.* Also, since many more students attending colleges in

---

*Although this line of reasoning may sound tautological ("going to college in the West stimulates students to drop out because dropout rates are high in the West"), it is not. Just because the rates are high in a particular region, a *given student's* chances of dropping out may be no different

the West are commuters, dropping out is tempting because it involves less disruption in the daily living pattern.

Although the *absolute rate* of student satisfaction with institutions is greater in the Northeast than in other regions, a northeastern location has a negative effect on satisfaction once other institutional characteristics—primarily selectivity and public versus private control—are considered. Again, this effect appears to result from the characteristics of higher education in the region. Colleges in the Northeast are closely clustered and more diverse than colleges in other regions, particularly in the West. Thus, students attending northeastern colleges may be more aware of the institutional pecking order. While many bright students in the western states attend public institutions—primarily the Universities of California, Oregon, and Washington—bright students in the Northeast are more likely to attend private institutions. This awareness of pecking order and diversity may cause students in the East to develop greater consciousness of institutional prestige and more stringent subjective "norms" about reputation and quality. This interpretation is reinforced by the finding that northeastern students are *most* dissatisfied with their institution's academic reputation, intellectual climate, and academic demands.

Geographic region also has several effects on career development. Possibly because of their negative impact on persistence, attending institutions in the West reduces the student's chances of implementing career plans in almost all fields except law. A positive effect of western institutions on enrolling in law school may reflect the heavy concentration of less selective proprietary law schools in California. Other regional effects on starting salaries suggest the presence of local labor market factors. Students pursuing careers in nursing, for example, receive higher salaries in the Northeast and lower salaries in the Midwest. Salaries for engineers show the reverse pattern.

Institutions in the southern states show effects that gen-

---

in that region, once personal characteristics and institutional characteristics are taken into account. But even after these characteristics are controlled, a western location has a negative impact on persistence.

erally confirm the stereotype of the South as conservative. Students show smaller-than-expected declines in religiousness and smaller increases in liberalism and support for student autonomy. Students attending southern institutions also show smaller-than-expected increases in hedonism and smaller declines in support for a traditional role for women. The only exception to this trend toward conservatism occurs in preferential treatment for disadvantaged students: Attending southern institutions strengthens students' support for preferential treatment. Although it is difficult to account for this finding, one possibility may be that support for preferential treatment was on the decline in *other* regions at the time of the follow-up (1971) because of backlash among some whites concerning preferential treatment programs already in use by many colleges in those regions; preferential treatment programs may have been slower to evolve in the South.

Students attending southern institutions tend to become more involved in campus government and interact more frequently with faculty. Although they tend to get somewhat lower grades, they are slightly more likely to persist and more likely to get married than students in other regions. Students at southern institutions are somewhat more dissatisfied with their institution's academic reputation and intellectual climate than students in midwestern or western institutions.

Patterns of Student Development

The varied findings from this study make clear that students do not follow a uniform pattern of development during their undergraduate years. An overview of the specific empirical findings shows several distinctly different patterns. Perhaps the clearest way to distinguish different developmental patterns is through the concept of involvement. Typically, *highly involved students* come from educated and relatively affluent families and obtain good grades in high school and high scores on college admissions tests. They have high aspirations for advanced degrees. Such students usually attend relatively selective institutions and live on campus as freshmen. Once on campus, the highly involved student can pursue several different subpatterns of involvement, each associated with a slightly different set of outcomes.

The student who shows maximum interpersonal involvement, the first subpattern, frequently majors in the humanities or the social sciences and becomes active in student government or other student organizations. These students interact frequently with fellow students and with faculty and tend to be verbally aggressive. During times of campus unrest, such students become politically active and may lead student demonstrations. This subpattern of high interpersonal involvement is associated with larger personality and behavioral changes than any other pattern. Such students become much more liberal politically, more hedonistic, and less religious than other students. Their interest in business declines substantially. They develop stronger musical and artistic interests, altruistic tendencies, and status needs. Those who interact frequently with faculty tend to be highly satisfied with their undergraduate experiences, whereas those who opt primarily for political involvement tend to be somewhat dissatisfied.

A second subpattern for the highly involved student is academic involvement. Devoting much time and effort to academic pursuits leads to substantial satisfaction with the undergraduate experience, but it tends to reduce the personality and behavioral changes associated with college attendance by isolating students somewhat from their peers. This isolation tends to increase for students majoring in engineering. The most pronounced of these effects is on hedonism, which is substantially reduced by academic involvement.

The third subpattern is athletic involvement. Participating in varsity athletics, like academic involvement, tends to isolate the student from the main peer group, resulting in somewhat smaller personality and behavioral changes. Athletically involved students show smaller increases in liberalism and smaller decreases in business interests than interpersonally involved students, but they end up somewhat more satisfied with their undergraduate experience. The effects of athletic involvement on hedonistic tendencies are mixed. Drinking increases, but smoking decreases.

All three patterns of high involvement—interpersonal, academic, and athletic—lead to increased chances of completing college, implementing career objectives, and satisfaction with the undergraduate experience.

At the other end of the involvement continuum is the uninvolved student. Typically, these students come from less-educated families and have relatively poor academic preparation. Because of financial constraints and selective admissions policies in most public systems, such students are often forced to enroll in public community colleges. These students frequently have only modest educational aspirations and commute from home to college rather than living on campus. They often hold a job off campus. They do not participate in extracurricular activities, are seldom on campus except to attend classes, and interact infrequently with faculty and fellow students. This lack of involvement is exacerbated by living at home and by continuing associations with high school friends. Uninvolved students have relatively poor chances of persisting and of implementing career plans. These chances can be substantially increased, however, if these students become highly involved in their academic work.

While these different patterns of student development are stereotypic—few students follow any given path exactly as portrayed—the patterns serve to dramatize the great differences in student behavior and development that characterize what has come to be called "the college experience." They also raise questions about some recent trends and policies in higher education—the subject of the next and final chapter.

IX

Implications
for Policy
and Practice

American higher education has been studied intensively
by educational researchers during the past twenty years, but
this research has had little effect on educational policy. This gap
between research and policy results in part from the esoteric
nature of much research, and in part from the fact that policy is
guided more often by economic or social concerns than by educational considerations. This chapter reviews major policy
trends in higher education in light of the current study's principal findings.

Implications for Policy and Practice

Paradoxes in Policy

Major changes in American higher education dur
cent decades have been guided by policy decisions at bo
governmental and institutional levels. For example, the expansion of higher education during the 1950s and 1960s had two main policy objectives: (1) to provide access for segments of the population not previously served by the system and (2) to produce more highly trained professionals for certain fields deemed important to national interests. The increased costs of maintaining an expanded system, coupled with severe economic problems, resulted in still another policy change during the early 1970s—to cut costs and to make institutional operations more efficient economically.

Considering the major findings of this study, many of these policies seem almost paradoxical. Indeed, one can question at least seven policies introduced since World War II: the expansion of the public sector, the trend toward larger institutions, the near disappearance of single-sex colleges, the proliferation of public community colleges, the deemphasis on the residential experience, the development of open admissions, and, most recently, the popular tendency to deprecate college grades.

Expansion of the Public Sector. The extraordinary expansion of American higher education since 1945 has occurred almost entirely in the public sector. The few rare exceptions involve the conversion of formerly private institutions—the Universities of Pittsburgh and Buffalo, for example—into publicly controlled institutions. Until recently, this massive expansion has been carried out with little regard for its effects on private higher education. Consequently, private colleges have increasingly had to compete for students with low-cost public colleges. Since most revenue for operating private institutions comes from tuition, those private institutions that have found it increasingly difficult to attract students have been threatened with severe financial problems. Some institutions have actually closed. Since the expansion in the public sector has occurred primarily in institutions with nonstringent admissions policies, the private institutions most threatened have also been those that have traditionally attracted students of moderate and low ability. As it happens, these institutions are also coping with the severest financial pressure (Astin and Lee, 1971).

What are the implications of these trends for American higher education, given the findings of this study? Will students benefit from a system in which the public sector expands while the private sector remains stable or declines? Data from the present study suggest a very different policy, if favorable impact on students is a desired goal for the higher educational system. Private institutions seem to foster greater student change than public institutions in almost all areas. In addition, students become much more involved both academically and nonacademically in private colleges and are more likely to implement career plans. Finally, students at private institutions are more satisfied with the quality of their instruction and with their relationships with faculty. The only areas where public institutions provide greater satisfaction are the variety of courses offered and the emphasis on social life. In short, it appears that the net result of the massive expansion of the public system and the relative demise of private higher education is that the total benefits to college students have been diluted.

Trend Toward Larger Institutions. That the average size of American higher educational institutions has increased is, of course, partly a result of the expansion of the public sector. Several factors are involved in the tendency for public institutions to become large. The most obvious is the need to serve a highly diverse constituency, a need that many policies assume can be filled only by offering a wide variety of courses and programs in the same institution. A more subtle influence is the general national tendency toward bigness and the assumption that bigger is somehow better. Many college administrators have gained national reputations primarily because of the substantial expansion of institutions under their guidance. A related incentive to expanding institutions is that, as academic departments grow, the pressure to develop graduate or professional programs and to expand research activities also increases. Still another incentive is the belief in "economies of scale." This argument usually assumes that facilities such as libraries and gymnasiums can be more efficiently used with larger student bodies. These economies of scale are mainly illusory. Large institutions actually spend somewhat *more* per student for educational purposes than small institutions, the major reasons being the push to graduate and professional education, the complex administrative structure, and the increased research activity that usually results from expansion (Astin, 1975a).

What do the findings of the present study say about the relative virtue of large and small institutions? When it comes to personality changes in students, there is little to choose between the two types: Large institutions tend to increase student liberalism, business interests, hedonism, and religious apostasy. They also increase support for student autonomy and increase the student's chances of participating in demonstrations while in college. Small institutions foster a greater degree of altruism and intellectual self-esteem.

When it comes to student achievement and involvement, the results clearly favor smaller institutions: Students are more likely to participate in honors programs, to become involved with academic pursuits, to interact with faculty, to get involved in athletics, and to be verbally aggressive in small institutions. At the same time, they are more likely to achieve in areas of leadership, athletics, and journalism. Students in smaller institutions are more satisfied with their faculty-student relations and with classroom instruction, whereas students in larger institutions are more satisfied with the variety of courses, the quality of the science program, and the emphasis on social life. In short, there are certain benefits uniquely associated with attendance at a small institution: The proliferation of large institutions during the past twenty years has reduced the student's chances of becoming involved in campus life and of being on close terms with faculty. One aspect of this policy dilemma is whether large institutions can simulate smallness through cluster colleges or similar arrangements. Here is an important topic for future research.

Disappearance of Single-Sex Colleges. During the past ten years, colleges for men and colleges for women have increasingly become coeducational. Although various explanations have been provided for this trend, the most likely reasons are economic: Private institutions feel they can best maintain their enrollment and, hence, financial viability, by admitting students of both sexes. This trend toward coeducation has affected elite and nonelite colleges alike. The nonelite colleges became coeducational because they felt it would enhance their chances for survival. Although the formerly single-sex elite colleges did not face extinction from failure to attract students, many felt that expanding their clientele in this manner would permit them to maintain usually stringent admissions standards. Whatever the reasons, only a handful of those institutions that were single-sex in the early 1960s have been able to resist the temptation to become coeducational through the late 1970s.

Single-sex colleges show a pattern of effects on *both* sexes that is almost uniformly positive. Students of both sexes become more academically involved, interact with faculty frequently, show large increases in intellectual self-esteem, and are more satisfied with practically all aspects of the college experience (the sole exception is social life) compared with their counterparts in coeducational institutions. Men's colleges substantially increase the likelihood that men will carry out career plans in law, business, and college teaching; they also have a substantial positive effect on starting salaries in business. Women's colleges increase the chances that women will obtain positions of leadership, complete the baccalaureate degree, and aspire to higher degrees.

Why single-sex colleges should show such a pattern of effects is not entirely clear. One possibility is that students are able to invest more energy in academic pursuits and in interaction with faculty because they have fewer opportunities to dissipate energy in courtship activities. In all likelihood, heterosexual activity is more circumscribed—confined to weekends, for example—in single-sex colleges. The greater interaction with faculty and greater satisfaction with the collegiate experience, despite the constraints on social life, could result from the greater sense of identification and communal feeling when both students *and* faculty are predominantly of the same sex.

Proliferation of Public Community Colleges. Since 1960 a

large proportion of the growth in higher education has been due to the expansion of public community colleges. Not only has the number of such institutions increased dramatically since that time, but their enrollments have also expanded. These institutions are designed to serve numerous constituencies: adults, part-time students, students not interested in academic degrees, as well as the traditional eighteen-year-old coming directly from high school to pursue a baccalaureate degree.

While these institutions provide important services to adults, part-time students, and those pursuing technical courses that are not offered by four-year institutions, the results of this and other studies suggest that they may not really serve the interests of students coming directly from high school to pursue careers requiring baccalaureate degrees. These students' chances of persisting to the baccalaureate are simply less at a two-year college than at a four-year college, public or private. These reduced chances of persisting also lessen the student's chances of implementing career plans in fields requiring baccalaureate training. Lack of residential facilities and the low student involvement in campus life partly explain low persistence rates, but even when these factors are considered, students have less chance of persisting at a community college than they do at some other kind of institution. This lowered persistence may be related to the problem of transferring: The paperwork and physical move required to transfer from a two- to a four-year institution involve a certain amount of attrition, no matter how smooth the articulation mechanism. It may also be that the low degree of involvement and other aspects of the experience of attending a community college sometimes deter students from continuing on beyond the first two undergraduate years. Whatever the explanation, for the eighteen-year-old going directly to college from high school, the public community college does not represent an "equal educational opportunity" compared with other types of institutions. This pattern of results suggests that Burton Clark's (1960) prophecy that the public community colleges are designed to play a "cooling-out function" for overly ambitious but less-well-prepared students has become a reality.

Why has expansion of American higher education been so heavily concentrated in the community colleges? There are at least two explanations: Educators in more prestigious institutions have probably supported community college growth because it represented a way of expanding educational opportunities that did not threaten their own selectivity and eliteness. Legislators have supported the expansion on the ground that community colleges represent a much less expensive postsecondary education. This "economical" form of higher education, however, may be somewhat illusory. Even if one ignores the substantial capital costs of starting a new community college, the *operating expenditures* per student of many community colleges may actually be higher than those of some private colleges and only slightly lower than those of public four-year institutions (Astin, 1975a). Indeed, if one calculates the cost *per degree recipient,* community colleges may in certain instances be more expensive than four-year institutions. Whatever the explanation, clearly the benefits derived by students from the enormous expansion of public community colleges are generally less than those derived from other types of institutions.

It is generally assumed that the expansion of community colleges has brought "expanded opportunities" for students who have been denied access to postsecondary education. Policymakers have generally ignored the possible effects of community colleges on access among highly able students. Recent evidence (Peng, 1977) suggests that high school students in the top 25 percent of their classes are *less likely* today to attend four-year colleges than they were fifteen years ago. This is a remarkable finding, given the fact that the *absolute number* of students in this group going to college has declined slightly. For men, the proportion in the top-ability quartile that goes to four-year institutions has declined by 16 percent, and the corresponding proportion attending two-year colleges has increased by 10 percent since the early 1960s. For women, the decline in the proportion attending four-year institutions has been 9 percent and the corresponding increase in two-year institutions 12 percent. One explanation for this shift is that the low cost and convenient access to community colleges have tempted many stu-

dents who otherwise would have attended four-year instiⁿ
to opt for two-year colleges instead.

Deemphasis on the Residential Experience. A number of
public and private institutions embarked on major expansions
of their residential facilities during the late 1950s and early
1960s. Federal and state support for construction spurred much
of this expansion. This trend was almost entirely reversed in the
late 1960s and early 1970s, however, by at least two factors.
First was the student movement of the 1960s, which prompted
many students to opt for living in private rooms rather than
dormitories to escape parietal rules, a tendency encouraged
when many institutions abandoned residence requirements.
Second was the moratorium on federal and, in many cases, state
support for dormitory construction. The flight of students from
dormitories reversed in the mid 1970s. Many dormitories now
have waiting lists. This reversal has been stimulated by economic factors as well as by the demise of parietal rules. Some
students may find it cheaper to live in dormitories than in private rooms. Except for a few colleges that have maintained a
strong fundamentalist religious emphasis, residents in the 1970s
are free of most behavioral constraints that characterized dormitory living in the 1950s and early 1960s.

Results of this and other empirical studies (Chickering,
1974a) suggest that, from an educational viewpoint, cessation
of dormitory construction and expansion of places for commuters was a poor idea. In almost every respect, residents benefit more than commuters from their undergraduate experience.
Residents not only show greater changes in personality and attitudes but also become more involved in campus life. Most important is the increased chance of persistence, which in turn
maximizes the chance of implementing career plans. Residents
are much more satisfied with their undergraduate experience
than are commuters.

Although it is beyond the scope of the present study, it
would be valuable to calculate the "costs and benefits" of dormitories measured by degree completion and implementation of
career plans. Assuming that residential facilities, once constructed, can pay for themselves, is it possible that by amortiz-

ing construction costs over sufficient years, building more residential facilities would result in a net *lowering* of the costs of producing baccalaureate degrees? Again, this possibility represents a challenge for future research.

Open Admissions. The term *open admissions* generally refers to a policy that allows students to be admitted to colleges without regard to academic preparation. Open admissions, in other words, represents an alternative to traditional selective admissions policies where only those students with the highest high school grades and college admissions test scores are admitted. Open admissions has become a policy instrument of many public systems, most notably of the City University of New York, which adopted a modified open-admissions policy in fall 1970 but, because of financial constraints, reversed the policy in 1976. Open admissions is a policy designed specifically to increase higher educational opportunities for those formerly excluded from higher education.

In most public systems of higher education, open admissions has really not been open, in the sense that not all institutions within the system have adopted these policies. Even at the City University of New York, the number of less-well-prepared students that the four-year (more elite) institutions were expected to accept was limited. Two-year institutions absorbed most of those students who would have been excluded from the city system altogether. In other states (for example, California), the term *open admissions* refers to the open-door policies of community colleges, and only the highest achieving students are admitted to the university. A few large state universities have implemented a system of open admissions that is not hierarchical: Any graduate of a public high school in the state is admitted to the state university (Tennessee is one example of such a system). For the most part, however, the burden of open admissions has been absorbed primarily by the community colleges and other less selective institutions.

Results of the present study indicate that most academic institutions are not designed to meet the needs of the less-well-prepared student. Students with high test scores and high grades generally go to better colleges, they more often live on campus, they get more involved in campus activities, they acquire a broader range of knowledge and skills, they stay longer, they are more likely to persist to graduation and to attain their career objectives, and they are more satisfied with their under-graduate experience. That traditional admissions criteria still predict this wide range of outcomes suggests that institutions have greatly expanded the number of seats available to less-well-prepared students but have not developed programs that adequately meet their needs. Ideally, one would like to see the correlation between ability and such factors as attainment of career objectives and student satisfaction disappear. Such a change would indicate that the colleges are meeting the needs of traditional students and less-well-prepared students equally.

The problems confronting the less-well-prepared student would seem to be exacerbated by a hierarchical public system in which open admissions is limited only to the lowest tier in the system—the community college. These students' relatively poor chances of completing a degree program are further reduced by the lack of residential facilities and few opportunities for in-volvement that characterize most community colleges. In a sense, hierarchical public systems match the weakest students with the most limited educational opportunities. High-ability students, on the other hand, have access to all segments of the system and usually opt for the most selective institutions. Under these conditions, it is not surprising that many freshman differences between high- and low-ability students expand with time: "Them that has, gets."

Denigration of the Grade-Point Average. In recent years it has become increasingly popular to argue that grades obtained in college should be deemphasized because they have little or no relevance to success in later life. This bit of educational folklore received considerable support from several empirical studies (Hoyt, 1966) showing that the relative success of professionals in certain fields, such as medicine, has very little correlation with graduate and undergraduate grades. These negative findings may have resulted because the studies were retrospective rather than prospective; consequently, all the would-be members of the profession who have fallen by the wayside since college entry are excluded from the analysis.

The current study shows clearly that a student's under-

graduate grades are important determinants of many significant
outcomes. Indeed, college grades have stronger relationships to
several important outcomes than any other institutional or student characteristic studied. College grades are strongly related,
for example, to increases in interpersonal self-esteem among
women and substantially related to increased intellectual self-
esteem among both sexes and among students of all ability
levels. Students with good grades are, of course, much more
likely to persist than students with poor grades, including students with low but passing grades. They are also more likely to
aspire to higher degrees. Good grades in college substantially increase the student's chances of realizing career objectives in virtually every field: medicine, law, school teaching, engineering,
science, and business. This effect on attainment of career objectives is not simply mediated by the effects of grades on dropping out. Thus, with the exception of business careers, grades
are still substantially related to implementation of career objectives even when college dropouts are excluded from the analysis. Grades are also substantially related to starting salaries for
students in business, teaching, and engineering. For students followed up in 1974, a difference of one letter grade (A versus B,
for example) was worth between $500 and $900 in initial starting salary.

Long-term longitudinal studies suggest that college grades
have substantial long-range impact on the student's earnings and
occupational status. These long-term outcomes are mediated by
the effects of grades on educational attainment (students with
better grades go farther in postsecondary education) and on the
quality of the undergraduate and graduate institution attended (students with better grades go to more selective institutions).

Clearly, the current popular tendency to denigrate the
undergraduate grade-point average is a mistake. Grades continue
to have significant short- and long-term impacts on the student's
development. As a system of assessing student performance,
grades leave much to be desired (see Chapter Four and Astin,
1974). But until better alternatives are found, grades remain an
important factor in the student's development.

Implications for Governmental Policy

Although it would be unrealistic to expect legislators and executives in federal and state governments to reverse long-standing policies on the basis of empirical findings from a study such as this one, there are a number of less radical alternatives that these policymakers may wish to consider. These alternatives concern at least five general issues: the relationship between public and private institutions, institutional size, construction of facilities, the role of community colleges, and research.

Relationship Between Public and Private Institutions. Since this study has shown clearly that private institutions represent a valuable educational asset, public policies that pose a potential threat to the viability of private colleges should be re-examined. The most obvious threat concerns the competition for students between neighboring public and private institutions. Expansion of low cost public institutions—particularly those with relatively open admissions policies—has made it increasingly difficult for private institutions to recruit students. These problems have been especially acute for those private institutions that have traditionally attracted the less able, low income student (Astin and Lee, 1971). Since student tuition represents the main source of income for private colleges, declining enrollments threaten any private institution's very survival. Some states, Illinois being a notable example, have attempted to neutralize this competition by instituting scholarship programs that favor the private sector by providing the largest stipends for students who choose private institutions. Such programs would appear to be a more effective approach than direct institutional aid, since they are directed at the source of the problem—the student's motivation to attend a private institution. Other approaches to supporting private higher education are, of course, possible. The point is that any state or municipality with a sizable system of private institutions has a real stake in preserving and strengthening that system and in minimizing competition between its public and private institutions.

Institutional Size. Policy questions connected with institutional size are of two types: How to counteract the impersonal atmosphere and lack of student involvement that frequently results from bigness, and how to reduce institutional
incentives for growth. Legislators in state and local governments
are in a good position to discourage expansion, but current policies seem designed instead to encourage it. Perhaps the major
incentive comes from the way public institutions are funded.
Most public institutions derive their public funds directly from
enrollments, where a projected increase or decrease from one
year to the next brings a *proportionate* (per student) increase or
decrease in public funds. Thus, whereas a 10 percent enrollment
increase may bring close to a 10 percent increase in revenue, the
associated increase in costs will generally be far less. In other
words, the net effect of increasing enrollments is to generate
what amounts to discretionary funds—something most administrators will work hard to get. The problem is that administrators
faced with the possibility of declining enrollments usually
realize that the process does not work in reverse: A 10 percent
enrollment decline may be accompanied by a 10 percent decline
in revenue, but *not* by a 10 percent reduction in costs. The obvious solution here for legislators and policy makers is to change
from a per student funding basis to a system of marginal cost
funding. Once an institution's desired size has been reached, the
relationship between enrollment changes and funding changes
can be controlled to reflect actual rather than per student
changes in costs. In this way, the incentives both to expand and
to avoid contraction would be removed.

Facilities Construction. Since living in a campus residence
rather than commuting from home enhances the impact of college across a wide range of affective and behavioral outcomes,
legislators and policy makers—particularly at the federal level—
might reexamine the current moratorium on support for construction of residential facilities. While such a decision necessarily involves political considerations and possible tradeoffs
with other sources of support for education, the potential benefits are substantial. In particular, the fact that the residential
experience significantly reduces student attrition offers the possibility that some of the resources currently used for other pur-

poses—student loans, for example—could be more profitably diverted to support dormitory construction.

The Role of the Community College. For the eighteen-year-old pursuing a bachelor's degree, the typical community college offers only limited opportunities for involvement and decreased chances of completing the degree. These findings suggest that states or municipalities that wish to expand opportunities for such students should consider alternatives to building additional community colleges or expanding existing ones. Although community colleges are generally less expensive to construct and operate than four-year colleges, their "economy" may be somewhat illusory, particularly when measured in terms of the cost of producing each baccalaureate recipient.

Research. Although state governments provide the bulk of the funding for public postsecondary education in the United States, the federal government is in a unique position to influence policy through educational research. In addition to the resources of research agencies such as the National Institute of Education, the National Science Foundation, and the National Institute of Mental Health, substantial funds for evaluation research are available from the U.S. Office of Education, the National Center for Educational Statistics, and the Fund for the Improvement of Postsecondary Education. If such agencies are interested in affecting policy through research, the current study highlights a number of policy issues that appear to be amenable to systematic analysis: among them, the impact of public institutions on private higher education, methods for counteracting the negative effects of institutional size, the costs and benefits of residential facilities in terms of behavioral outcomes, alternative strategies for increasing student involvement, and the impact of grading policies on student motivation and achievement. These agencies can also fund demonstration projects, with accompanying evaluation research, for examining such problems.

Implications for Institutions

Faculty and administrators are in a position to utilize findings from this study in several areas of institutional policy

practice: general administration, grading practices, resi-
hall administration, and the special problem of combating
tion.

General Administration. As a general operating concept,
the administration of a college or university should strive to encourage students to get more *involved*—to invest more of their
time and physical and psychic energy in the educational process. There are many ways to facilitate involvement, and a good
starting point would be a thorough examination of the institution's information system. What kind of information concerning
student involvement (or lack of involvement) is currently available to key institutional personnel? Do classroom instructors
and faculty advisors regularly have access to data on students'
academic involvement and academic progress? Do student personnel administrators periodically receive information on students' extracurricular participation and residence hall life? Do
appropriate data get disseminated in a comprehensible form and
in time to take appropriate remedial action? Does the administration take the initiative in surveying faculty and staff needs
for information on student progress and development? Is the
administration responsive to requests for better information?
Since there are probably few, if any, institutional administra-
tions that can respond affirmatively to all of these questions,
evaluation and improvement of the institution's information
system appear to offer a useful means to encourage greater student involvement.

Several recommendations for administrative policy are
applicable only to special types of institutions. These include
single-sex colleges, two-year colleges, and large institutions. Administrators of single-sex colleges are continuously confronted
with the proposal to convert to coeducation. Although the economic consequences of such a change are appealing, the educational consequences are likely to be largely negative: students
will be less likely to get involved academically, less likely to
interact with faculty, and more likely to end up dissatisfied
with their undergraduate experience. If economic considerations make the change to coeducation irresistible, administrators of single-sex colleges should at least be prepared for a num-

ber of possibly undesirable changes in student attitudes and behavior. (These changes are summarized in more detail in Chapter Eight.)

Two-year colleges, particularly those public community colleges that serve commuters, are faced with a serious challenge: Lacking residential facilities, how can these institutions be administered so as to maximize student involvement and institutional impact? Is it possible to *simulate* the residential experience, at least for those eighteen-year-olds coming directly out of high school in pursuit of a bachelor's degree? A possible beginning would be for community colleges to distinguish clearly among different categories of students. Many so-called nontraditional students—adults, part-time students, and veterans, for example—do not require the same degree of involvement as the recent high school graduate attending college on a full-time basis. Clearly, policies for enhancing involvement will be less costly to implement and more likely to be effective if they are directed specifically at such students, rather than at students in general. The appropriateness of any policy will, of course, depend on the resources and needs of the particular college, but the options are, nevertheless, numerous: weekend or week-long residential "retreats," more cultural events on campus, improvements in parking facilities, required hours for faculty, conferences between students and advisers, organized study groups, improvements in campus recreational facilities, expansion of on-campus employment opportunities, organized tours of potential transfer institutions, and expanding the number and size of student clubs and organizations.

Large institutions face a problem very much like the one facing two-year colleges—how to live with bigness and how to counteract its usually negative consequences. Some large institutions, including a few state universities, have attempted to create a greater sense of community and to provide more opportunities for student involvement through the use of "cluster" arrangements—small and relatively autonomous colleges created within the larger institution. One problem with such arrangements is that the loyalties of faculty are frequently divided between the college and the discipline or department, which is usually university wide. These divisions are especially severe in universities that are heavily oriented toward research, since a strong research emphasis tends to reinforce the faculty's disciplinary orientation. Whether cluster arrangements can ever work with a faculty not primarily devoted to undergraduate teaching is doubtful. One approach is to foster the development of smaller student groupings that do not threaten the strong departmental orientation of faculty concerned with research. Most universities, of course, already have fraternal organizations, but these frequently do not accommodate the majority of students. Residential facilities could be organized around subject-matter or even cultural interests, and students could be assigned to residences or residence areas on the basis of common interests or orientations. Faculty could also be encouraged to take part in the activities of those residential groupings that fit their own disciplinary or cultural orientations. If nothing else, large institutions could experiment with such arrangements on a limited scale to determine their effectiveness in counteracting the alienation and lack of faculty-student interaction that frequently accompany bigness.

Grading Practices. This study has shown clearly that grades, despite claims to the contrary, continue to be an important determinant of student progress. Grades have both short- and long-range effects of considerable significance. They appear to affect not only academic and career progress, but also motivation. Many faculty and students oppose what they see as an overemphasis on grading, but attempts to deemphasize grades— the pass-fail option, for example—have proved to be generally unpopular. The problem here for any given institution is that grades represent a kind of currency to be used later on in pursuing graduate training and employment. If this currency is adulterated or otherwise altered, it tends to lose value. Unless most institutions simultaneously change their grading systems, it remains very difficult for any institution to do it unilaterally. Under these conditions, it is much easier to change the manner of awarding grades, rather than the grading system itself.

Results of the current study suggest that the major limitation of traditional grading systems is the negative effect of low grades on motivation, persistence, and career progress. Can ins tutions find ways to minimize the number of low grades given (or to reduce their negative impact) without compromising academic standards? One approach to this problem is to move from a relative grading system—such as grading "on the curve"—to an absolute system where all students could, in theory, get good grades. A few colleges have experimented with this approach by substituting a series of qualifying or proficiency examinations for traditional classroom examinations. Students take the examinations whenever they feel prepared, and those who fail any given examination are permitted to retake it. An obvious advantage of this alternative is that it allows for *individual differences* in students' initial levels of preparation and rates of growth. It also has the advantage of separating the evaluation process (grading) from the teaching-learning process.

Residence Hall Administration. Although the current study has demonstrated that the residential experience can have significant educational benefits, many institutions have never fully exploited the potential of the residence hall as an adjunct to the educational program. Considering that dormitory residents are a kind of captive audience, administration of residence halls offers an excellent opportunity to enhance significantly the student's total educational experience. One means of developing innovative programming plans for residence halls is periodically to involve small groups of resident counselors, faculty, and students in brainstorming sessions. Another approach is to conduct "time and motion" studies of student behavior in residence halls.

Combating Attrition. In the past few years, it has become fashionable in some academic circles to talk of "stopping out" and of the supposedly therapeutic value for certain students of attending college and then dropping out. There is little question that, for some students, leaving college before they complete a program of study may be highly beneficial to their personal development. But recent data (Astin, 1975b) suggest that such students represent a small minority and that students usually leave college for negative reasons: boredom, finances, poor grades, and so forth. Positive reasons, such as a good job offer, are given by less than 10 percent of the dropouts (Astin, 1975b). Perhaps the term *stopout* represents a rationalization for educators: It is easier to believe that students are taking time to "find themselves" than it is to confront the limitations of institutional programs and policies.

Some of the most negative consequences of dropping out, as revealed in the present study, are self-evident. Students are denied entry to many challenging and well-paying occupations that require baccalaureate or graduate training, such as medicine, law, teaching, engineering, social work, and many science fields. Even among those dropouts who eventually complete college, occupational entry and subsequent progress are delayed. From a national perspective, dropping out represents a loss of talent and a waste of limited educational resources. From the perspective of the student, results of the present study highlight a number of other more subtle consequences of dropping out. Students who fail to finish college are much less likely to show the usual development changes associated with attendance: increased interpersonal and intellectual self-esteem, greater tolerance and open-mindedness, and increased intellectual skill and competence. Another consequence is that students show smaller increases in hedonism.

A national study of dropouts (Astin, 1975b) proposes a number of practical suggestions to reduce attrition. For the most part, these recommendations argue for finding ways to increase student *involvement*: living on campus rather than commuting, working on campus, participating in extracurricular activities, and improving academic performance through counseling, honors programs, research, and other special academic programs (see also Blake, 1971; Siebel, 1973). The present study suggests that such efforts to increase student involvement will not only enhance the student's ability to persist but will also intensify the impact of the undergraduate experience on the student's personality, behavior, career progress, and satisfaction.

Research and Policy: A Postscript

Virtually every educational policy that seems to conflict with the findings of educational research has been instituted for economic rather than educational reasons: Expand public systems because they are cheap and let the private colleges fend for themselves because they are expensive. Let institutions get larger and larger to provide "economics of scale." Confine "expanded access" and open admissions to community colleges because they are cheaper to operate than four-year colleges. Stop constructing dormitories because they cost too much. Abandon single-sex colleges because they are not financially viable. If nothing else, these arguments underscore the fact that policy makers are not likely to be influenced by research on student development, no matter what the findings show.

The educational researcher is thus left with three alternatives: (1) try to change the policy makers' value system (a monumental task probably doomed to failure), (2) return to the ivory tower and forget educational policy, or (3) play the policy makers' game. This last possibility is especially appealing, because it raises the possibility of obtaining more grant funds and of becoming part of the "policy scene"—with all the associated feelings of power and self-aggrandizement. Playing the policy makers' game can take at least two forms. The first and most common form involves "telling them what they want to hear." A great deal of what passes for policy research really stems from the policy makers' desire to accumulate "evidence" that supports a preconceived position. Findings that provide such support are embraced uncritically because they provide a "scientific basis" for the position, and contrary findings are either ignored or discredited. The complexities and imperfections of empirical research in the social or behavioral sciences make it easy, if one is so inclined, to discount almost any unpalatable finding on purely technical grounds.

Playing the policy makers' game can take a somewhat less cynical form. Rather than simply telling them what they want to hear, researchers can accept the policy makers' value system as a general starting point for the research. To be successful, this approach requires the researchers to understand (1) that policy makers in higher education pay little attention to research on student development because their interest in educational outcomes is usually minimal; and (2) that most policy questions are concerned in one way or another with money: how to save it, how to invest it, how to allocate it. The centrality of money in policy making is perhaps the main reason the executive branch of the federal government has a Council of Economic Advisers but no council of social or educational advisers.

How does the policy researcher play the money game, without merely "telling them what they want to hear"? One approach is to find ways to translate educational findings into savings. For example, rather than arguing that we need more residential facilities in order to maximize the benefits of college and to minimize student attrition, researchers need to show that particular policies lead to reduced costs. Perhaps their data will not allow them to do this, but perhaps it will. For example, it might be possible to show that certain policy changes would actually lead to real savings in terms of *cost per degree produced.* Take the two-year college as an example. This "economical" form of higher education may not really be that economical. Even if one ignores the substantial capital costs of starting a new community college, the operating expenditures per student of many community colleges may actually be higher than those of some private colleges and only slightly lower than those of public four-year institutions (Astin, 1975a). Indeed, if one calculates the *cost per degree recipient,* community colleges may in certain instances be more expensive than four-year institutions.

Or take the matter of dormitories. It would be a useful exercise to calculate the costs and benefits of dormitories as measured by rates of degree completion and implementation of career plans. Assuming that residential facilities, once constructed, can pay for themselves, is it possible that by amortizing construction costs over sufficient years, building more residential facilities would result in a net *lowering* of the costs of producing baccalaureate degrees? Again, this possibility represents a challenge for frustrated policy researchers who would rather not retreat to the ivory tower.

The really difficult problem, of course, comes when educational research fails to show that cheaper is better. In much of education, one probably gets what one pays for: A watered-down educational experience will, more often than not, produce watered-down results. As long as policy makers persist in viewing resource allocation as an end in itself rather than as a means for achieving educational ends, the gap between educational policy and educational research is likely to remain.

Appendix

A Note on Measurement Error

One problem in using multivariate analyses to control entering student characteristics is that measurement errors (unreliability) in these pretest (input) characteristics attenuate the observed correlations between these characteristics and both (1) posttest (output) measures and (2) environmental measures. If these observed correlations are used in multiple partial regression analyses to adjust for initial differences in characteristics of students entering different college environments, such adjustments will *undercorrect* for initial differences. If the observed correlations among the pretest, posttest, and environmental measures are all positive and significant, this underadjustment can produce spurious college "effects" (Astin, 1970a). The likelihood of finding spurious effects is greatest when the environmental measure correlates more with the pretest measures than with the posttest measures and when the environment-posttest correlation shrinks but does not disappear when the pretest is controlled. The ideal solution to this problem is to inflate the regression coefficient associated with the pretest measure for unreliability (Tucker, Damarin, and Messick, 1966). A similar procedure in the multivariate case is to adjust the regression *composite* for unreliability. However, such a correction procedure requires a knowledge of the reliability of each pretest measure—information that unfortunately is lacking in this and most other survey research projects. As an alternative, each significant college effect from the initial analyses was examined to determine if (1) the pretest, posttest, and environmental characteristics were all significantly and positively intercorrelated; (2) the environmental measure correlated as high or higher with the pretest as with the posttest; and (3) controlling for pretest differences reduced but did not eliminate the environment-posttest correlation. If all three conditions were satisfied, the partial correlation between environment and posttest was recalculated and the regression composite adjusted for attenuation by using an arbitrary reliability estimate of .9. This relatively high estimate was used because the regression composites were based on an average of twenty input measures. (The few partial correlations that were reduced to nonsignificance by these procedures are treated as nonsignificant relationships in the text.)

Another issue involving measurement error concerns changes over time in mean differences between such groups as men and women (Chapter Eight).

If pretest and posttest scores on a given characteristic such as business interests are imperfectly correlated (as is true of all characteristics), persons with initially high scores will tend to show declines over time and persons with initially low scores will tend to show increases. This is the well-known "regression to the mean" phenomenon. Measurement error is one cause of regression effects: Large positive errors will tend to produce high scores, and these scores will tend to fall on posttest. Large negative errors tend to produce low scores, and these will tend to rise on posttest. Thus, if the mean freshman business interests for men is higher than the mean for women, regression effects will tend to cause the means to come together with time, since the men (higher scores) will tend to show declines and the women (lower scores) will tend to show increases. There are, to be sure, some women with high scores and some men with low scores, but they are fewer in number than their opposite-sex counterparts. However, for many traits these initial mean differences remained apart over time: The fact that the variable "sex" entered the regression equation for predicting follow-up business interests means that women with a given freshman score tend to show larger decreases than men with the same score. Thus, business interests for men and women tended to remain apart over time because the effect of regression to the mean was counteracted by differential change for men and women with identical scores.

The significance of this phenomenon for the study of change is two-fold: First, the only way for two groups that differ initially on some characteristic to remain apart over time is for members of those groups with identical initial scores to show differential change. Second, just because the members of the two groups show differential change does not necessarily cause the groups to move apart with time. Indeed, regression to the mean could still result in a net coming together; the *magnitude* of the differential change is the determining consideration. Thus, even though women with given pretest scores on business interests tend to show larger declines than men with identical scores, mean differences in business interests between men and women remain about the same from pretest to follow-up. In other words, regression to the mean is almost compensated for by differential change.

Paradoxically, measurement errors in the pretest score can also account for differential change in men and women with the same scores. If a woman has a relatively high score, that score is more likely to contain a positive measurement error than an identical score for a man, because the woman's score deviates more from *her* group's mean than the man's score from his. Conversely, a low score is more likely to contain a negative measurement error if it is a man's rather than a woman's score. These measurement errors show up on the posttest because the few men with initially low scores tend to decrease less than the (larger number of) women with the same low scores, and because the few women with initially high scores tend to decrease more than the (larger number of) men with equally high scores. A second source of influence on differential change—environmental factors—is discussed in Chapter Eight.

Table A. Summary of Stepwise Regression With 84 Student
Outcome Measures

Student Outcome Measures	Number of Predictors Entering Regression	Multiple Correlation After Entering	
		Freshman Variables	Environmental Variables
Self-Concept			
Liberalism versus conservatism	31	.44	.45
Interpersonal self-esteem	15	.59	.59
Intellectual self-esteem	18	.70	.72
Self-criticism	11	.33	.33
Values			
Altruism	13	.39	.39
Artistic interests	24	.57	.58
Athletic interests	19	.71	.71
Business interests	16	.55	.55
Musical interests		.64	.64
Status needs	16	.39	.39
Religious Affiliation			
Protestant	32	.72	.72
Roman Catholic	26	.77	.77
Jewish	9	.84	.84
None	20	.43	.43
Attitudes			
Student autonomy	32	.50	.52
Women's place in home	29	.46	.48
Discourage large families	24	.41	.41
Deemphasize college sports	23	.43	.44
Benefit of college is monetary	28	.39	.42
Preferential for disadvantaged	21	.31	.34
Behavior			
Religiousness	33	.64	.65
Hedonism	24	.53	.53
Drinking	33	.47	.49
Smoking	22	.56	.56
Marriage	9	.33	.34
Demonstrating	29	.43	.44
Academic involvement	33	.33	.34
Honors programs	25	.29	.31
Student-faculty interaction	28	.26	.35
Familiarity with major faculty	31	.21	.32
Verbal aggressiveness	35	.31	.34
Student government	36	.31	.35
Athletic involvement	38	.61	.63
Joined fraternity or sorority	36	.33	.36

(continued on next page)

Table A *(Continued)*

Student Outcome Measures	Number of Predictors Entering Regression	Multiple Correlation After Entering	
		Freshman Variables	Environmental Variables
Academic Achievement			
College grades	32	.55	.56
Graduation with honors	24	.37	.38
Educational Attainment			
Persistence	30	.41	.42
Enroll in graduate school	25	.37	.38
Degree aspirations	28	.54	.54
Extracurricular Achievement			
Student-faculty committee	24	.26	.28
Elected to student office	33	.27	.31
Journalism	18	.25	.27
Science	23	.22	.29
Creative writing	27	.24	.29
Theater	15	.26	.27
Athletics	25	.41	.43
Competencies			
Foreign language	18	.55	.56
Computer programming	19	.40	.44
Slide rule	13	.66	.66
Typing	13	.69	.69
Parliamentary knowledge	18	.52	.52
Homemaking	16	.82	.82
Music	11	.76	.76
Swimming	16	.67	.67
Sports knowledge	22	.72	.72
General culture	27	.60	.61
Physical fitness	9	.72	.72
Implementing Career Plans			
Businessperson	14	.33	.40
College teacher	15	.12-.38	.14-.38
Engineer	14	.35	.40
Homemaker	11	.18-.24	.19-.26
Lawyer	10	.47	.58
Nurse	21	.35	.46
Physician	12	.50	.56
School teacher	26	.27	.31
Scientific researcher	8	.41	.41
Social worker	4	.43	.43
Salary in			
Business	17	.35	.42
Engineering	12	.36	.40
Nursing	6	.37	.39
School teaching	20	.35	.37

Table A *(Continued)*

Student Outcome Measures	Number of Predictors Entering Regression	Multiple Correlation After Entering	
		Freshman Variables	Environmental Variables
Satisfaction			
Overall	48	.24	.48
Academic reputation	47	.21	.37
Intellectual environment	43	.19	.39
Student-faculty	42	.17	.50
Classroom instruction	45	.16	.46
Student friendships	41	.20	.35
Course variety	41	.21	.35
Administration	46	.25	.36
Perceptions of Environment			
Academic demands	33	.21	.31
Closeness of faculty	27	.16	.28
Emphasis on social life	25	.13	.25
Quality of science programs	35	.23	.30
Practicality	26	.21	.25

Table B. Summary of Stepwise Regressions on Selected Student
Outcomes by Sex

| Student Outcome Measure | Number of Predictors Entering Regression | | Multiple Correlation After Entering | | | |
| | | | Freshman Variables | | Environmental Variables | |
	Men	Women	Men	Women	Men	Women
Self-Concept						
Liberalism versus conservatism	28	19	.43	.46	.43	.48
Interpersonal self-esteem	14	9	.59	.59	.59	.59
Intellectual self-esteem	23	9	.69	.67	.71	.69
Self-criticism	4	14	.31	.35	.31	.35
Values						
Altruism	11	7	.38	.37	.39	.37
Artistic interests	13	10	.54	.57	.54	.57
Athletic interests	14	7	.69	.65	.70	.65
Business interests	12	14	.50	.44	.50	.44
Status needs	12	11	.31	.37	.32	.38
Religious Affiliation						
None	13	15	.41	.46	.41	.46
Behavior						
Religiousness	24	27	.62	.64	.63	.66
Hedonism	17	20	.53	.48	.53	.49
Academic Achievement						
College grades	24	23	.53	.53	.54	.54
Educational Attainment						
Persistence	18	23	.43	.40	.44	.41
Ph.D. aspirations	24	15	.52	.39	.53	.40
Satisfaction						
Overall	17	14	.25	.20	.28	.21

Table C. Summary of Stepwise Regressions on Selected Student Outcomes by Ability

| | Number of Predictors | | | Multiple Correlation After Entering | | | | | |
| | | | | Freshman Variables | | | Environmental Variables | | |
Student Outcome Measure	Low Ability	Medium Ability	High Ability	Low	Medium	High	Low	Medium	High
Self-Concept									
Liberalism versus conservatism	11	25	23	.35	.39	.45	.37	.39	.47
Interpersonal self-esteem	7	13	10	.53	.59	.62	.54	.59	.62
Intellectual self-esteem	8	17	17	.64	.60	.65	.66	.63	.67
Self-criticism	6	10	5	.34	.32	.36	.36	.32	.36
Values									
Altruism	5	11	8	.40	.39	.39	.40	.39	.39
Artistic interests	14	20	10	.52	.58	.58	.55	.58	.58
Athletic interests	7	10	12	.71	.70	.72	.71	.70	.72
Business interests	5	12	13	.51	.55	.54	.52	.55	.54
Status needs	12	12	9	.43	.39	.36	.45	.40	.37
Religious Affiliation									
None	9	17	16	.42	.42	.38	.42	.42	.39
Behavior									
Religiousness	10	28	24	.65	.62	.59	.66	.64	.62
Hedonism	9	21	11	.55	.53	.48	.56	.54	.49
Academic Achievement									
College grades	7	25	24	.44	.51	.52	.45	.52	.55
Educational Attainment									
Persistence	12	20	20	.41	.32	.31	.45	.37	.40
Ph.D. aspirations	15	20	19	.42	.49	.54	.44	.49	.55
Satisfaction									
Overall	8	11	20	.27	.21	.22	.27	.21	.26

References

Allport, G. W., Vernon, P. E., and Lindzey, G. *Study of Values: Manual.* (3rd ed.). Boston: Houghton Mifflin, 1960.

Anderson, R. E. "The Integration of Financial and Educational Considerations for Policy Analysis." Paper presented at annual conference of the Association of the Study of Higher Education, Chicago, March 1977.

Argyle, M. *Religious Behavior.* New York: Free Press, 1959.

Arsenian, S. "Change in Evaluative Attitudes During Twenty-Five Years." *Journal of Applied Psychology,* 1970, *54,* 302-304.

Astin, A. W. "Influences on the Student's Motivation to Seek Advanced Training: Another Look." *Journal of Educational Psychology,* 1962, *53,* 303-309.

Astin, A. W. "Differential College Effects on the Motivation of Talented Students to Obtain the Ph.D. Degree." *Journal of Educational Psychology,* 1963a, *54,* 63-71.

Astin, A. W. "Further Validation of the Environmental Assessment Technique." *Journal of Educational Psychology,* 1963b, *54,* 217-226.

Astin, A. W. "Undergraduate Institutions and the Production of Scientists." *Science,* 1963c, *141,* 334-338.

Astin, A. W. "Personal and Environmental Factors Associated with College Drop-Outs Among High Aptitude Students." *Journal of Educational Psychology,* 1964, *55,* 219-227.

Astin, A. W. *The College Environment.* Washington, D.C.: American Council on Education, 1968a.

Astin, A. W. "Undergraduate Achievement and Institutional Excellence." *Science,* 1968b, *161,* 661-668.

Astin, A. W. "The Methodology of Research on College Impact (I)." *Sociology of Education,* 1970a, *43,* 223-254.

Astin, A. W. "The Methodology of Research on College Impact (II)." *Sociology of Education,* 1970b, *43,* 437-450.

Astin, A. W. *Predicting Academic Performance in College.* New York: Free Press, 1971.

Astin, A. W. "Impact of Dormitory Living on Students." *Educational Record,* 1973, *54,* 204-210.

Astin, A. W. "Measuring the Outcomes of Higher Education." In H. Bowen (Ed.), *New Directions for Institutional Research: Evaluating Institutions for Accountability,* no. 1. San Francisco: Jossey-Bass, 1974.

Astin, A. W. *The Myth of Equal Access in Public Higher Education.* Atlanta: Southern Education Foundation, 1975a.

Astin, A. W. *Preventing Students from Dropping Out.* San Francisco: Jossey-Bass, 1975b.

Astin, A. W., and Henson, J. W. "New Measures of College Selectivity." *Research in Higher Education,* in press.

Astin, A. W., King, M. R., and Richardson, G. T. *The American Freshman: National Norms for Fall 1975.* Los Angeles: Graduate School of Education, University of California, 1975.

Astin, A. W., King, M. R., and Richardson, G. T. *The American Freshman: National Norms for Fall 1976.* Los Angeles: Graduate School of Education, University of California, 1976.

Astin, A. W., and Lee, C. B. T. *The Invisible Colleges.* New York: McGraw-Hill, 1971.

Astin, A. W., and Molm, L. D. "Correcting for Nonresponse Bias in Follow-up Surveys." Unpublished manuscript, Graduate School of Education, University of California, Los Angeles, 90024, 1972.

Astin, A. W., and Panos, R. J. *The Educational and Vocational Development of College Students*. Washington, D.C.: American Council on Education, 1969.

Astin, A. W., Panos, R. J., and Creager, J. A. *National Norms for Entering College Freshmen—Fall 1966*. Washington, D.C.: American Council on Education, 1967.

Astin, A. W., and others. *National Norms for Entering Freshmen—Fall 1969*. Washington, D.C.: American Council on Education, 1969.

Astin, A. W., and others. *The Power of Protest: A National Study of Student and Faculty Disruptions with Implications for the Future*. San Francisco: Jossey-Bass, 1975.

Astin, H. S., El-Khawas, E., and Bisconti, A. *Beyond the College Years*. Washington, D.C.: Center for Human Services, 1973.

Baird, L. L. "The Effects of College Residence Groups on Students' Self-Concepts, Goals and Achievements." *Personnel and Guidance Journal*, 1969, *47*, 1015-1021.

Bayer, A. E. "Marriage Plans and Educational Aspirations." *American Journal of Sociology*, September 1969, *75*, 239-244.

Bayer, A. E. "College Impact on Marriage." *Journal of Marriage and the Family*, 1972, *34*, 600-609.

Bayer, A. E., Royer, J. T., and Webb, R. M. *Four Years After College Entry*. Washington, D.C.: American Council on Education, 1973.

Beaton, A. E. "The Influence of Education and Ability on Salary and Attitudes." In F. T. Juster (Ed.), *Education, Income, and Human Behavior*. New York: McGraw-Hill, 1975.

Bender, I. E. "Changes in Religious Interest: A Retest After Fifteen Years." *Journal of Abnormal and Social Psychology*, 1958, *57*, 41-46.

Berdie, R. F. "A University Is a Many-Faceted Thing." *Personnel and Guidance Journal*, 1967, *45*, 768-775.

Bisconti, A. S., and Astin, A. W. *The Dynamics of Protest*. Los

Angeles: Laboratory for Research on Higher Education, Graduate School of Education, University of California, 1973.

Blai, B., Jr. "Roommate-Impact upon Academic Performance." ERIC Document number ED 052 228, 1971.

Blake, E., Jr. "A Case Study in Producing Equal Educational Results: The Thirteen-College Curriculum Program." In F. F. Harcleroad and J. H. Cornell (Eds.), *Monograph Six: Assessment of Colleges and Universities.* Iowa City: American College Testing Program, 1971.

Bowman, M. J. "Through Education to Earnings?" *Proceedings of the National Survey of Educational Statistics,* 1976, *3,* 221-292.

Bugelski, R., and Lester, O. P. "Changes in Attitudes in a Group of College Students During Their College Course and After Graduation." *Journal of Social Psychology,* 1940, *12,* 319-332.

Burchard, W. W. "Some Social Class Correlates of Changing Religious Beliefs in College." Paper presented to American Catholic Sociological Society, San Francisco, August 1969.

Campbell, D. P. *A Study of College Freshmen—Twenty-Five Years Later.* Minneapolis: Cooperative Research Program, University of Minnesota, 1965.

Cartter, A. M. *An Assessment of Quality in Higher Education.* Washington, D.C.: American Council on Education, 1966.

Cartter, A. M., and Brown, M. D. *Manpower Survey of 1967-1969 College Entrants.* Los Angeles: Graduate School of Education, University of California, 1976.

Chickering, A. W. *Education and Identity.* San Francisco: Jossey-Bass, 1969.

Chickering, A. W. *Commuting Versus Resident Students: Overcoming the Educational Inequities of Living Off Campus.* San Francisco: Jossey-Bass, 1974a.

Chickering, A. W. "The Impact of Various College Environments on Personality Development." *Journal of the American College Health Association,* 1974b, *23,* 82-93.

Chickering, A. W., and Kuper, E. "Educational Outcomes for

Commuters and Residents." *Educational Record,* 1971, *52,* 255-261.

Chickering, A. W., and McCormick, J. "Personality Development and the College Experience." *Research in Higher Education,* 1973, *1,* 43-70.

Christian, C. E. "Patterns of College Experience: An Empirical Typology of Students and College Interaction." Unpublished doctoral dissertation, University of California, Los Angeles, 1977.

Clark, B. R. *The Open-Door College: A Case Study.* New York: McGraw-Hill, 1960.

Constantinople, A. "An Eriksonian Measure of Personality Development in College Students." *Developmental Psychology,* 1969, *1,* 357-372.

Cooley, W. W., and Flanagan, J. C. (Eds.). *Project TALENT: One Year Follow-Up Studies.* U.S. Department of Health, Education and Welfare Cooperative Research Project No. 2333. Pittsburgh: School of Education, University of Pittsburgh, 1966.

Daniere, A., and Mechling, J. "Direct Marginal Productivity of College Education in Relation to College Aptitude of Students and Production Costs of Institutions." *Journal of Human Resources,* 1970, *5,* 51-70.

Davis, J. A. *Great Aspirations: The Graduate School Plans of America's College Seniors.* Chicago: Aldine, 1964.

Davis, J. A. *Undergraduate Career Decisions: Correlates of Occupational Choice.* Chicago: Aldine, 1965.

Dilley, J. W. "Smoking on Campus." *Journal of the American College Health Association,* 1971, *19,* 230-234.

Dvorak, E. J. "A Longitudinal Study of Nonmedical Drug Use Among University Students—A Brief Summary." Paper presented to American College Health Association, San Francisco, April 1971.

El-Khawas, E., and Bisconti, A. *Five and Ten Years After College Entry.* Washington, D.C.: American Council on Education, 1974.

Feldman, K. A., and Newcomb, T. M. *The Impact of College on*

Students. Vol. 1: *An Analysis of Four Decades of Research.* San Francisco: Jossey-Bass, 1969.

Fendrich, J. M. "Activists Ten Years Later: A Test of Generational Unit Continuity." *Journal of Social Issues,* 1974, *30,* 95-118.

Fenske, R. H., and Scott, C. S. "College Students' Goals, Plans, and Background Characteristics: A Synthesis of Three Empirical Studies." *Research in Higher Education,* 1973, *1,* 101-118.

Finney, H. C. "Political Dimensions of College Impact on Civil-Libertarianism and Integration of Political Perspective: A Longitudinal Analysis." *Sociology of Education,* 1974, *47,* 214-250.

Franks, D. D., Falk, R. F., and Hinton, J. "Differential Exposure to Courses in Two Majors and Differences in Students' Value Responses." *Sociology of Education,* 1973, *46,* 361-369.

Freedman, M. B., and Bereiter, C. "A Longitudinal Study of Personality Development in College Alumnae." *Merrill-Palmer Quarterly of Behavior and Development,* 1963, *9,* 295-301.

Freeman, R., and Hollomon, J. H. "The Declining Value of College Going." *Change,* 1975, *7,* 24-31, 62.

Gaff, J. G. "Making a Difference: The Impacts of Faculty." *Journal of Higher Education,* 1973, *44,* 605-622.

Gurin, G., Veroff, J., and Feld, S. *Americans View Their Mental Health.* New York: Basic Books, 1960.

Holland, J. L., and Astin, A. W. "The Prediction of the Academic, Artistic, Scientific, and Social Achievement of Undergraduates of Superior Scholastic Aptitude." *Journal of Educational Psychology,* 1962, *53,* 132-143.

Horner, M. "Sex Differences in Achievement Motivation and Performance in Competitive and Noncompetitive Situations." Unpublished doctoral dissertation, University of Michigan, Ann Arbor, 1968.

Hoyt, D. P. "College Grades and Adult Accomplishment: A Review of Research." *Educational Record.* 1966, *47,* 70-75.

Hyman, H. H., Wright, C. R., and Reed, J. S. *The Enduring Effects of Education.* Chicago: University of Chicago Press, 1975.

Jacob, P. E. *Changing Values in College: An Exploratory Study of the Impact of College Teaching.* New York: Harper & Row, 1957.

Johnson, G. E., and Stafford, F. P. "Lifetime Earnings in a Professional Labor Market: Academic Economists." *Journal of Political Economy,* 1974, *82,* 549-569.

Kamens, D. H. "The College 'Charter' and College Size: Effects on Occupational Choice and College Attrition." *Sociology of Education,* 1971, *44,* 270-296.

Katz, J., and Associates. *No Time for Youth: Growth and Constraint in College Students.* San Francisco: Jossey-Bass, 1968.

Ladd, E. C., and Lipset, S. M. "Republicans Are Few and Far Between on U.S. College Faculties." *Chronicle of Higher Education,* 1975, *11,* 15.

Learned, W. S., and Wood, B. D. *The Student and His Knowledge.* New York: Carnegie Foundation for the Advancement of Teaching, 1938.

Lenning, O. T., Munday, L. A., and Maxey, E. J. "Student Educational Growth During the First Two Years of College." *College and University,* 1969, *44,* 145-153.

Likert, R. "A Technique for the Measurement of Attitudes." *Archives of Psychology,* 1932, *140* (entire issue).

McConnell, T. R. "Do Colleges Affect Student Values?" *Change,* 1972, *4,* 9.

McGuire, W. J. "The Nature of Attitudes and Attitude Change." In G. Lindzey and E. Aronson, *Handbook of Social Psychology.* Vol. 3. (2nd ed.) Reading, Mass.: Addison-Wesley, 1969.

MacMillan, T. F., and Kester, D. M. "Promises to Keep: NORCAL Impact on Student Attrition." *Community and Junior College Journal,* 1973, *43* (5), 45-46.

Madison, P. "The Campus: Coming of Age at College." *Psychology Today,* 1971, *5,* 72.

Michael, R. T. "Education and Fertility." In F. T. Juster (Ed.), *Education, Income, and Human Behavior.* Carnegie Commission on Higher Education Report. New York: McGraw-Hill, 1975.

Morgan, J. N., and Sirageldin, I. A. "A Note on the Quality Dimension in Education." *Journal of Political Economy,* 1968, *76,* 1069-1077.

Nelson, E. A., and Johnson, N. C. "Attitude Changes on the College Student Questionnaires: A Study of Students Enrolled in Predominantly Black Colleges and Universities." Paper presented to American Educational Research Association, New York, February 1971.

Nelson, E. A., and Uhl, N. P. "The Impact of College upon Social Characteristics and Attitudes of Students Enrolled in Three Predominantly Black Colleges." Paper presented to American Educational Research Association, Chicago, April 1974.

Nelson, E. N. P. "Patterns of Religious Attitude Shifts from College to Fourteen Years Later." *Psychological Monographs: General and Applied,* 1956, *70* (424, entire issue).

Newcomb, T. M., and others. *Persistence and Change: Bennington College and Its Students After Twenty-Five Years.* New York: Wiley, 1967.

Nichols, R. C. "Personality Change and the College." *American Educational Research Journal,* 1967, *4,* 173-190.

Nosow, S., and Robertson, S. R. "Changing Socio-Political Attitudes of College Students, 1967-1971." *College Student Journal,* 1973, *7,* 7-14.

O'Toole, J. "The Reserve Army of the Underemployed: II—The Role of Education." *Change,* 1975, *7* (5), 26-33, 60-63.

Owens, W. A. "Age and Mental Abilities: A Longitudinal Study." *Genetic Psychological Monographs,* 1953, *48,* 3-54.

Pace, C. R. *They Went to College: A Study of 951 Former University Students.* Minneapolis: University of Minnesota Press, 1941.

Pace, C. R. *The Demise of Diversity: A Comparative Profile of Eight Types of Institutions.* New York: McGraw-Hill, 1974.

Pace, C. R., and Stern, G. G. "An Approach to the Measurement of Psychological Characteristics of College Environments." *Journal of Educational Psychology,* 1958, *49,* 269-277.

Peng, S. S. "Trends in the Entry to Higher Education." *Educational Researcher,* 1977, *6,* 15-19.

Pervin, L. A. "Reality and Nonreality in Student Expectations of College." *Journal of Psychology,* 1966, *64,* 41-48.

Psacharopoulos, G. *Earnings and Education in OECD Countries.* Paris: Organization for Economic Cooperation and Development, 1975.

Rock, D. A. "The Use of Taxonomic Procedures to Identify Both Overall College Effects and Those Effects Which Interact with Student Ability." Paper presented to American Educational Research Association, Chicago, April 1972.

Rock, D. A., Baird, L. L., and Linn, R. L. "Interaction Between College Effects and Students' Aptitudes." *American Educational Research Journal,* 1972, *9,* 149-161.

Rogers, D. C. "Private Rates of Return to Education in the United States: A Case Study." *Yale Economic Essays,* 1969, *9,* 88-134.

Rossmann, J. E., and others. *Open Admissions at CUNY: An Analysis of the First Year.* Englewood Cliffs, N.J.: Prentice-Hall, 1975.

Sanford, N. (Ed.). *The American College: A Psychological and Social Interpretation of Higher Learning.* New York: Wiley, 1962.

Schmidt, M. R. "Personality Change in College Women." *Journal of College Student Personnel,* 1970, *11,* 414-418.

Sewell, W. H., and Hauser, R. M. *Education, Occupation and Earnings: Achievement in the Early Career.* New York: Academic Press, 1975.

Sewell, W. H., and Shah, V. P. "Parents' Education and Children's Educational Aspirations and Achievements." *American Sociological Review,* 1968, *33,* 191-209.

Sharp, L. M. *Education and Employment: The Early Careers of College Graduates.* Baltimore, Md.: Johns Hopkins University Press, 1970.

Siebel, C. C. "Courses and a 'Plus'—An Innovative Program for Undergraduates: Fourth Year Evaluation." Paper presented to National Association of Women Deans and Counselors, Cleveland, April 1973.

Skager, R., Holland, J. L., and Braskamp, L. A. *Changes in Self-Ratings and Life Goals Among Students at Colleges with Different Characteristics.* Iowa City: American College Testing Program, 1966.

Solmon, L. C. "The Definition of College Quality and Its Impact on Earnings." *Explorations in Economic Research,* 1975, *2,* 537-587.

Solmon, L. C., Bisconti, A. S., and Ochsner, N. L. *College as a Training Ground for Jobs.* New York: Praeger, 1977.

Southworth, J. A., and Morningstar, M. E. "Persistence of Occupational Choice and Personality Congruence." *Journal of Counseling Psychology,* 1970, *17,* 409-412.

Spaeth, J. L., and Greeley, A. M. *Recent Alumni and Higher Education.* Carnegie Commission on Higher Education Report. New York: McGraw-Hill, 1970.

Starch, D. *The 35th Annual Media Study of Primary Audiences: Consumption of Media.* New York: Daniel Starch and Staff, 1969.

Stouffer, S. *Communism, Conformity and Civil Liberties.* Garden City, N.Y.: Doubleday, 1955.

Swanson, O. E. "A Follow-Up Study of College Trained Versus Noncollege Trained High School Graduates of High Ability." Unpublished doctoral dissertation, University of Minnesota, 1953.

Taubman, P., and Wales, T. "Education as an Investment and a Screening Device." In F. T. Juster (Ed.), *Education, Income, and Human Behavior.* Carnegie Commission on Higher Education Report. New York: McGraw-Hill, 1975a.

Taubman, P., and Wales, T. "Mental Ability and Higher Educational Attainment in the 20th Century." In F. T. Juster (Ed.), *Education, Income, and Human Behavior.* Carnegie Commission on Higher Education Report. New York: McGraw-Hill, 1975b.

Taylor, E. K., and Wolfe, A. C. "Political Behavior." In S. B. Withey (Ed.), *A Degree and What Else? Correlates and Consequences of a College Education.* Carnegie Commission on Higher Education Report. New York: McGraw-Hill, 1971.

Thistlethwaite, D. L. *Effects of College Upon Student Aspirations.* Nashville, Tenn.: Cooperative Research Project, Vanderbilt University, 1965.

Trent, J. W., and Medsker, L. L. *Beyond High School: A Study of 10,000 High School Graduates.* Berkeley, Calif.: Center for Research and Development in Higher Education, University of California, 1967. (Published subsequently by Jossey-Bass, San Francisco, 1968.)

Tucker, L. R., Damarin, F., and Messick, S. "A Base-Free Measure of Change." *Psychometrika,* 1966, *31,* 457-473.

Wachtel, P. "The Returns to Investment in Higher Education: Another View." In F. T. Juster (Ed.), *Education, Income, and Human Behavior.* New York: McGraw-Hill, 1975.

Weisbrod, B. A., and Karpoff, P. "Monetary Return to College Education, Student Ability, and College Quality." *Review of Economics and Statistics,* 1968, *50* (4), 491-497.

Williamson, E. G., and Bordin, E. S. "Evaluating Counseling by Means of a Control-Group Experiment." *School and Society,* 1940, *52,* 434-440.

Withey, S. B. *A Degree and What Else? Correlates and Consequences of a College Education.* Carnegie Commission on Higher Education Report. New York: McGraw-Hill, 1971.

Wolfle, D. "To What Extent Do Monetary Returns to Education Vary with Family Background, Mental Ability, and School Quality?" In L. C. Solmon and P. J. Taubman (Eds.), *Does College Matter?* New York: Academic Press, 1973.

Wood, L., and Wilson, R. C. "Teachers With Impact." *Research Reporter,* 1972, *7,* 1-4.

Index